FOUR MODERN PLAYS

FOUR MODERN PLAYS

FIRST SERIES

HENRIK IBSEN

Hedda Gabler

BERNARD SHAW

Pygmalion

EUGENE O'NEILL

The Emperor Jones

ARTHUR MILLER

Death of a Salesman

HOLT, RINEHART AND WINSTON   NEW YORK

23924–0117
Eighth Printing, April 1961

Typography by Stefan Salter

Printed in the United States of America, 1957

Library of Congress Catalog Card Number: 57–7742

CONTENTS

HENRIK IBSEN

Hedda Gabler

TRANSLATED FROM THE NORWEGIAN BY EDMUND GOSSE
AND WILLIAM ARCHER

CAST

GEORGE TESMAN

HEDDA TESMAN, *his wife*

MISS JULIANA TESMAN, *his aunt*

MRS. ELVSTED

JUDGE BRACK

EILERT LÖVBORG

BERTA, *servant at the Tesmans'*

SCENE: *The action is Tesman's villa, in the west end of Christiania*

ACT I

‍

SCENE: *A spacious, handsome, and tastefully furnished drawing room, decorated in dark colors. In the back, a wide doorway with curtains drawn back, leading into a smaller room decorated in the same style as the drawing room. In the right-hand wall of the front room, a folding door leading out to the hall. In the opposite wall, on the left, a glass door, also with curtains drawn back. Through the panes can be seen part of a veranda outside, and trees covered with autumn foliage. An oval table, with a cover on it, and surrounded by chairs, stands well forward. In front, by the wall on the right, a wide stove of dark porcelain, a high-backed armchair, a cushioned footrest, and two footstools. A settee, with a small round table in front of it, fills the upper right-hand corner. In front, on the left, a little way from the wall, a sofa. Farther back than the glass door, a piano. On either side of the doorway at the back a whatnot with terra-cotta and majolica ornaments. Against the back wall of the inner room a sofa, with a table, and one or two chairs. Over the sofa hangs the portrait of a handsome elderly man in a General's uniform. Over the table a hanging lamp, with an opal glass shade. A number of bouquets are arranged about the drawing room, in vases and glasses. Others lie upon the tables. The floors in both rooms are covered with thick carpets. Morning light. The sun shines in through the glass door.*

MISS JULIANA TESMAN, *with her bonnet on and carrying a parasol, comes in from the hall, followed by* BERTA, *who carries a bouquet wrapped in paper.* MISS TESMAN *is a comely and pleasant-looking lady of about sixty-five. She is nicely but simply dressed in a gray walking costume.* BERTA *is a middle-aged woman of plain and rather countrified appearance.*

MISS TESMAN [*Stops close to the door, listens, and says softly.*] Upon my word, I don't believe they are stirring yet!

BERTA [*Also softly.*] I told you so, Miss. Remember how late the steamboat got in last night. And then, when they got home!—good Lord, what a lot the young mistress had to unpack before she could get to bed.

MISS TESMAN Well, well—let them have their sleep out. But let us see that they get a good breath of the fresh morning air when they do appear. [*She goes to the glass door and throws it open.*]

BERTA [*Beside the table, at a loss what to do with the bouquet in her hand.*] I declare, there isn't a bit of room left. I think I'll put it down here, Miss. [*She places it on the piano.*]

MISS TESMAN So you've got a new mistress now, my dear Berta. Heaven knows it was a wrench to me to part with you.

BERTA [*On the point of weeping.*] And do you think it wasn't hard for me, too, Miss? After all the blessed years I've been with you and Miss Rina.

MISS TESMAN We must make the best of it, Berta. There was nothing else to be done. George can't do without you, you see—he absolutely can't. He has had you to look after him ever since he was a little boy.

BERTA Ah, but, Miss Julia, I can't help thinking of Miss Rina lying helpless at home there, poor thing. And with only that new girl, too! She'll never learn to take proper care of an invalid.

MISS TESMAN Oh, I shall manage to train her. And, of course, you know I shall take most of it upon myself. You needn't be uneasy about my poor sister, my dear Berta.

BERTA Well, but there's another thing, Miss. I'm so mortally afraid I shan't be able to suit the young mistress.

MISS TESMAN Oh, well—just at first there may be one or two things . . .

BERTA Most like she'll be terrible grand in her ways.

MISS TESMAN Well, you can't wonder at that—General Gabler's daughter! Think of the sort of life she was accustomed to in her father's time. Don't you remember how we used to see her riding down the road along with the General? In that long black habit—and with feathers in her hat?

BERTA Yes, indeed—I remember well enough!—But, good Lord, I should never have dreamt in those days that she and Master George would make a match of it.

MISS TESMAN Nor I. But by the by, Berta—while I think of it: in future you mustn't say Master George. You must say Dr. Tesman.

BERTA Yes, the young mistress spoke of that, too—last night—the moment they set foot in the house. Is it true then, Miss?

MISS TESMAN Yes, indeed it is. Only think, Berta—some foreign university has made him a doctor—while he has been abroad, you understand. I hadn't heard a word about it, until he told me himself upon the pier.

BERTA Well, well, he's clever enough for anything, he is. But I didn't think he'd have gone in for doctoring people, too.

MISS TESMAN No, no, it's not that sort of doctor he is. [*Nods significantly.*] But let me tell you, we may have to call him something still grander before long.

BERTA You don't say so! What can that be, Miss?

MISS TESMAN [*Smiling.*] H'm—wouldn't you like to know! [*With emotion.*] Ah, dear, dear—if my poor brother could only look up from his grave now, and see what his little boy has grown into! [*Looks around.*] But bless me, Berta—why have you done this? Taken the chintz covers off all the furniture?

BERTA The mistress told me to. She can't abide covers on the chairs, she says.

MISS TESMAN Are they going to make this their everyday sitting room then?

BERTA Yes, that's what I understood—from the mistress. Master George—the doctor—he said nothing.

[GEORGE TESMAN *comes from the right into the inner room, humming to himself, and carrying an unstrapped empty portmanteau. He is a middle-sized, young-looking man of thirty-three, rather stout, with a round, open, cheerful face, fair hair and beard. He wears spectacles, and is somewhat carelessly dressed in comfortable indoor clothes.*]

MISS TESMAN Good morning, good morning, George.

TESMAN [*In the doorway between the rooms.*] Aunt Julia! Dear Aunt Julia! [*Goes up to her and shakes hands warmly.*] Come all this way—so early! Eh?

MISS TESMAN Why, of course I had to come and see how you were getting on.

TESMAN In spite of your having had no proper night's rest?

MISS TESMAN Oh, that makes no difference to me.

TESMAN Well, I suppose you got home all right from the pier? Eh?

MISS TESMAN Yes, quite safely, thank goodness. Judge Brack was good enough to see me right to my door.

TESMAN We were so sorry we couldn't give you a seat in the carriage. But you saw what a pile of boxes Hedda had to bring with her.

MISS TESMAN Yes, she had certainly plenty of boxes.

BERTA [*To* TESMAN.] Shall I go in and see if there's anything I can do for the mistress?

TESMAN No thank you, Berta—you needn't. She said she would ring if she wanted anything.

BERTA. [*Going towards the right.*] Very well.

TESMAN But look here—take this portmanteau with you.

BERTA [*Taking it.*] I'll put it in the attic.

[*She goes out by the hall door.*]

TESMAN Fancy, Auntie—I had the whole of that portmanteau chock full of copies of documents. You wouldn't believe how much I have picked up from all the archives I have been examining—curious old details that no one has had any idea of . . .

MISS TESMAN Yes, you don't seem to have wasted your time on your wedding trip, George.

TESMAN No, that I haven't. But do take off your bonnet, Auntie. Look here! Let me untie the strings—eh?

MISS TESMAN [*While he does so.*] Well, well—this is just as if you were still at home with us.

TESMAN [*With the bonnet in his hand, looks at it from all sides.*] Why, what a gorgeous bonnet you've been investing in!

MISS TESMAN I bought it on Hedda's account.

TESMAN On Hedda's account? Eh?

MISS TESMAN   Yes, so that Hedda needn't be ashamed of me if we happened to go out together.

TESMAN [*Patting her cheek.*]   You always think of everything, Aunt Julia. [*Lays the bonnet on a chair beside the table.*] And now, look here—suppose we sit comfortably on the sofa and have a little chat, till Hedda comes. [*They seat themselves. She places her parasol in the corner of the sofa.*]

MISS TESMAN [*Takes both his hands and looks at him.*]   What a delight it is to have you again, as large as life, before my very eyes, George! My George—my poor brother's own boy!

TESMAN   And it's a delight for me, too, to see you again, Aunt Julia! You, who have been father and mother in one to me.

MISS TESMAN   Oh yes, I know you will always keep a place in your heart for your old aunts.

TESMAN   And what about Aunt Rina? No improvement—eh?

MISS TESMAN   Oh no—we can scarcely look for any improvement in her case, poor thing. There she lies, helpless, as she has lain for all these years. But heaven grant I may not lose her yet awhile. For if I did, I don't know what I should make of my life, George—especially now that I haven't you to look after any more.

TESMAN [*Patting her back.*]   There, there, there . . . !

MISS TESMAN [*Suddenly changing her tone.*]   And to think that here you are a married man, George! And that you should be the one to carry off Hedda Gabler—the beautiful Hedda Gabler! Only think of it—she, that was so beset with admirers!

TESMAN [*Hums a little and smiles complacently.*]   Yes, I fancy I have several good friends about town who would like to stand in my shoes—eh?

MISS TESMAN   And then this fine long wedding tour you have had! More than five—nearly six months . . .

TESMAN   Well, for me it has been a sort of tour of research as well. I have had to do so much grubbing among old records—and to read no end of books too, Auntie.

MISS TESMAN   Oh yes, I suppose so. [*More confidentially, and lowering her voice a little.*]   But listen now, George—have you nothing—nothing special to tell me?

TESMAN   As to our journey?

MISS TESMAN   Yes.

TESMAN   No, I don't know of anything except what I have told you in my letters. I had a doctor's degree conferred on me—but that I told you yesterday.

MISS TESMAN   Yes, yes, you did. But what I mean is—haven't you any—any—expectations . . . ?

TESMAN   Expectations?

MISS TESMAN   Why you know, George—I'm your old auntie!

TESMAN   Why, of course I have expectations.

MISS TESMAN   Ah!

TESMAN   I have every expectation of being a professor one of these days.

MISS TESMAN   Oh yes, a professor . . .

TESMAN   Indeed, I may say I am certain of it. But my dear Auntie—you know all about that already!

MISS TESMAN [Laughing to herself.]   Yes, of course I do. You are quite right there. [Changing the subject.]   But we were talking about your journey. It must have cost a great deal of money, George?

TESMAN   Well, you see—my handsome traveling scholarship went a good way.

MISS TESMAN   But I can't understand how you can have made it go far enough for two.

TESMAN   No, that's not so easy to understand—eh?

MISS TESMAN   And especially traveling with a lady—they tell me that makes it ever so much more expensive.

TESMAN   Yes, of course—it makes it a little more expensive. But Hedda had to have this trip, Auntie! She really had to. Nothing else would have done.

MISS TESMAN   No, no, I suppose not. A wedding tour seems to be quite indispensable nowadays. But tell me now—have you gone thoroughly over the house yet.

TESMAN   Yes, you may be sure I have. I have been afoot ever since daylight.

MISS TESMAN   And what do you think of it all?

TESMAN   I'm delighted! Quite delighted! Only I can't think what we are to do with the two empty rooms between this inner parlor and Hedda's bedroom.

MISS TESMAN [*Laughing.*] Oh my dear George, I daresay you may find some use for them—in the course of time.

TESMAN Why of course you are quite right, Aunt Julia! You mean as my library increases—eh?

MISS TESMAN Yes, quite so, my dear boy. It was your library I was thinking of.

TESMAN I am specially pleased on Hedda's account. Often and often, before we were engaged, she said that she would never care to live anywhere but in Secretary Falk's villa.

MISS TESMAN Yes, it was lucky that this very house should come into the market, just after you had started.

TESMAN Yes, Aunt Julia, the luck was on our side, wasn't it—eh?

MISS TESMAN But the expense, my dear George! You will find it very expensive, all this.

TESMAN [*Looks at her, a little cast down.*] Yes, I suppose I shall, Aunt!

MISS TESMAN Oh, frightfully!

TESMAN How much do you think? In round numbers?—Eh?

MISS TESMAN Oh, I can't even guess until all the accounts come in.

TESMAN Well, fortunately, Judge Brack has secured the most favorable terms for me—so he said in a letter to Hedda.

MISS TESMAN Yes, don't be uneasy, my dear boy. Besides, I have given security for the furniture and all the carpets.

TESMAN Security? You? My dear Aunt Julia—what sort of security could you give?

MISS TESMAN I have given a mortgage on our annuity.

TESMAN [*Jumps up.*] What! On your—and Aunt Rina's annuity!

MISS TESMAN Yes, I knew of no other plan, you see.

TESMAN [*Placing himself before her.*] Have you gone out of your senses, Auntie! Your annuity—it's all that you and Aunt Rina have to live upon.

MISS TESMAN Well, well—don't get so excited about it. It's

only a matter of form you know—Judge Brack assured me of that. It was he that was kind enough to arrange the whole affair for me. A mere matter of form, he said.

TESMAN   Yes, that may be all very well. But nevertheless . . .

MISS TESMAN   You will have your own salary to depend upon now. And, good heavens, even if we did have to pay up a little . . . ! To eke things out a bit at the start . . . ! Why, it would be nothing but a pleasure to us.

TESMAN   Oh Auntie—will you never be tired of making sacrifices for me!

MISS TESMAN   [*Rises and lays her hands on his shoulders.*] Have I any other happiness in this world except to smooth your way for you, my dear boy? You, who have had neither father nor mother to depend on. And now we have reached the goal, George! Things have looked black enough for us, sometimes; but, thank heaven, now you have nothing to fear.

TESMAN   Yes, it is really marvelous how everything has turned out for the best.

MISS TESMAN   And the people who opposed you—who wanted to bar the way for you—now you have them at your feet. They have fallen, George. Your most dangerous rival—his fall was the worst. And now he has to lie on the bed he has made for himself —poor misguided creature.

TESMAN   Have you heard anything of Eilert? Since I went away, I mean.

MISS TESMAN   Only that he is said to have published a new book.

TESMAN   What! Eilert Lövborg! Recently—eh?

MISS TESMAN   Yes, so they say. Heaven knows whether it can be worth anything! Ah, when your new book appears—that will be another story, George! What is it to be about?

TESMAN   It will deal with the domestic industries of Brabant during the Middle Ages.

MISS TESMAN   Fancy—to be able to write on such a subject as that!

TESMAN   However, it may be some time before the book is ready. I have all these collections to arrange first, you see.

MISS TESMAN Yes, collecting and arranging—no one can beat you at that. There you are my poor brother's own son.

TESMAN I am looking forward eagerly to setting to work at it; especially now that I have my own delightful home to work in.

MISS TESMAN And, most of all, now that you have got a wife of your heart, my dear George.

TESMAN [Embracing her.] Oh yes, yes, Aunt Julia. Hedda—she is the best part of it all! [Looks towards the doorway.] I believe I hear her coming—eh?

[HEDDA enters from the left through the inner room. She is a woman of nine-and-twenty. Her face and figure show refinement and distinction. Her complexion is pale and opaque. Her steel-gray eyes express a cold, unruffled repose. Her hair is of an agreeable medium brown, but not particularly abundant. She is dressed in a tasteful, somewhat loose-fitting morning gown.]

MISS TESMAN [Going to meet HEDDA.] Good morning, my dear Hedda! Good morning, and a hearty welcome!

HEDDA [Holds out her hand.] Good morning, dear Miss Tesman! So early a call! That is kind of you.

MISS TESMAN [With some embarrassment.] Well—has the bride slept well in her new home?

HEDDA Oh yes, thanks. Passably.

TESMAN [Laughing.] Passably! Come, that's good, Hedda! You were sleeping like a stone when I got up.

HEDDA Fortunately. Of course one has always to accustom one's self to new surroundings, Miss Tesman—little by little. [Looking towards the left.] Oh—there the servant has gone and opened the veranda door, and let in a whole flood of sunshine.

MISS TESMAN [Going towards the door.] Well, then we will shut it.

HEDDA No, no, not that! Tesman, please draw the curtains. That will give a softer light.

TESMAN [At the door.] All right—all right. There now, Hedda, now you have both shade and fresh air.

HEDDA Yes, fresh air we certainly must have, with all these stacks of flowers . . . But—won't you sit down, Miss Tesman?

MISS TESMAN No, thank you. Now that I have seen that

everything is all right here—thank heaven!—I must be getting home again. My sister is lying longing for me, poor thing.

TESMAN   Give her my very best love, Auntie; and say I shall look in and see her later in the day.

MISS TESMAN   Yes, yes, I'll be sure to tell her. But by the by, George—[*feeling in her dress pocket*]—I had almost forgotten— I have something for you here.

TESMAN   What is it, Auntie? Eh?

MISS TESMAN [*Produces a flat parcel wrapped in newspaper and hands it to him.*]   Look here, my dear boy.

TESMAN [*Opening the parcel.*]   Well, I declare! Have you really saved them for me, Aunt Julia! Hedda! Isn't this touching— eh?

HEDDA [*Beside the whatnot on the right.*]   Well, what is it?

TESMAN   My old morning shoes! My slippers.

HEDDA   Indeed. I remember you often spoke of them while we were abroad.

TESMAN   Yes, I missed them terribly. [*Goes up to her.*]   Now you shall see them, Hedda!

HEDDA [*Going towards the stove.*]   Thanks, I really don't care about it.

TESMAN [*Following her.*]   Only think—ill as she was, Aunt Rina embroidered these for me. Oh you can't think how many associations cling to them.

HEDDA [*At the table.*]   Scarcely for me.

MISS TESMAN   Of course not for Hedda, George.

TESMAN   Well, but now that she belongs to the family, I thought . . .

HEDDA [*Interrupting.*]   We shall never get on with this serv- ant, Tesman.

MISS TESMAN   Not get on with Berta?

TESMAN   Why, dear, what puts that in your head? Eh?

HEDDA [*Pointing.*]   Look there! She has left her old bonnet lying about on a chair.

TESMAN [*In consternation, drops the slippers on the floor.*] Why, Hedda . . .

HEDDA   Just fancy, if any one should come in and see it!

TESMAN But Hedda—that's Aunt Julia's bonnet.

HEDDA Is it!

MISS TESMAN [*Taking up the bonnet.*] Yes, indeed it's mine. And, what's more, it's not old, Madam Hedda.

HEDDA I really did not look closely at it, Miss Tesman.

MISS TESMAN [*Trying on the bonnet.*] Let me tell you it's the first time I have worn it—the very first time.

TESMAN And a very nice bonnet it is too—quite a beauty!

MISS TESMAN Oh, it's no such great thing, George. [*Looks around her.*] My parasol . . . ? Ah, here. [*Takes it.*] For this is mine too—[*mutters*]—not Berta's.

TESMAN A new bonnet and a new parasol! Only think, Hedda!

HEDDA Very handsome indeed.

TESMAN Yes, isn't it? Eh? But Auntie, take a good look at Hedda before you go! See how handsome she is!

MISS TESMAN Oh, my dear boy, there's nothing new in that. Hedda was always lovely. [*She nods and goes towards the right.*]

TESMAN [*Following.*] Yes, but have you noticed what splendid condition she is in? How she has filled out on the journey?

HEDDA [*Crossing the room.*] Oh, do be quiet . . . !

MISS TESMAN [*Who has stopped and turned.*] Filled out?

TESMAN Of course you don't notice it so much now that she has that dress on. But I, who can see . . .

HEDDA [*At the glass door, impatiently.*] Oh, you can't see anything.

TESMAN It must be the mountain air in the Tyrol . . .

HEDDA [*Curtly, interrupting.*] I am exactly as I was when I started.

TESMAN So you insist; but I'm quite certain you are not. Don't you agree with me, Auntie?

MISS TESMAN [*Who has been gazing at her with folded hands.*] Hedda is lovely—lovely—lovely. [*Goes up to her, takes her head between both hands, draws it downwards, and kisses her hair.*] God bless and preserve Hedda Tesman—for George's sake.

HEDDA [*Gently freeing herself.*] Oh—! Let me go.

MISS TESMAN [*In quiet emotion.*] I shall not let a day pass without coming to see you.

TESMAN   No you won't, will you, Auntie? Eh?

MISS TESMAN   Good-bye—good-bye!

[*She goes out by the hall door.* TESMAN *accompanies her. The door remains half open.* TESMAN *can be heard repeating his message to* AUNT RINA *and his thanks for the slippers. In the meantime,* HEDDA *walks about the room, raising her arms and clenching her hands as if in desperation. Then she flings back the curtains from the glass door, and stands there looking out. Presently* TESMAN *returns and closes the door behind him.*]

TESMAN [*Picks up the slippers from the floor.*]   What are you looking at, Hedda?

HEDDA [*Once more calm and mistress of herself.*]   I am only looking at the leaves. They are so yellow—so withered.

TESMAN [*Wraps up the slippers and lays them on the table.*] Well you see, we are well into September now.

HEDDA [*Again restless.*]   Yes, to think of it! Already in—in September.

TESMAN   Don't you think Aunt Julia's manner was strange, dear? Almost solemn? Can you imagine what was the matter with her? Eh?

HEDDA   I scarcely know her, you see. Is she not often like that?

TESMAN   No, not as she was today.

HEDDA [*Leaving the glass door.*]   Do you think she was annoyed about the bonnet?

TESMAN   Oh, scarcely at all. Perhaps a little, just at the moment . . .

HEDDA   But what an idea, to pitch her bonnet about in the drawing room! No one does that sort of thing.

TESMAN   Well you may be sure Aunt Julia won't do it again.

HEDDA   In any case, I shall manage to make my peace with her.

TESMAN   Yes, my dear, good Hedda, if you only would.

HEDDA   When you call this afternoon, you might invite her to spend the evening here.

TESMAN   Yes, that I will. And there's one thing more you could do that would delight her heart.

HEDDA   What is it?

TESMAN If you could only prevail on yourself to say *du*[1] to her. For my sake, Hedda? Eh?

HEDDA No, no, Tesman—you really mustn't ask that of me. I have told you so already. I shall try to call her "Aunt"; and you must be satisfied with that.

TESMAN Well, well. Only I think now that you belong to the family, you . . .

HEDDA H'm—I can't in the least see why . . . [*She goes up towards the middle doorway.*]

TESMAN [*After a pause.*] Is there anything the matter with you, Hedda? Eh?

HEDDA I'm only looking at my old piano. It doesn't go at all well with all the other things.

TESMAN The first time I draw my salary, we'll see about exchanging it.

HEDDA No, no—no exchanging. I don't want to part with it. Suppose we put it there in the inner room, and then get another here in its place. When it's convenient, I mean.

TESMAN [*A little taken aback.*] Yes—of course we could do that.

HEDDA [*Takes up the bouquet from the piano.*] These flowers were not here last night when we arrived.

TESMAN Aunt Julia must have brought them for you.

HEDDA [*Examining the bouquet.*] A visiting card. [*Takes it out and reads.*] "Shall return later in the day." Can you guess whose card it is?

TESMAN No. Whose? Eh?

HEDDA The name is "Mrs. Elvsted."

TESMAN Is it really? Sheriff Elvsted's wife? Miss Rysing that was.

HEDDA Exactly. The girl with the irritating hair, that she was always showing off. An old flame of yours I've been told.

TESMAN [*Laughing.*] Oh, that didn't last long; and it was before I knew you, Hedda. But fancy her being in town!

---

1. The familiar form of the pronoun, used only between persons who are on a footing of intimacy; hence its significance here and later.

HEDDA It's odd that she should call upon us. I have scarcely seen her since we left school.

TESMAN I haven't seen her either for—heaven knows how long. I wonder how she can endure to live in such an out-of-the-way hole—eh?

HEDDA [*After a moment's thought, says suddenly.*] Tell me, Tesman—isn't it somewhere near there that he—that—Eilert Lövborg is living?

TESMAN Yes, he is somewhere in that part of the country.

[BERTA *enters by the hall door.*]

BERTA That lady, ma'am, that brought some flowers a little while ago, is here again. [*Pointing.*] The flowers you have in your hand, ma'am.

HEDDA Ah, is she? Well, please show her in.

[BERTA *opens the door for* MRS. ELVSTED, *and goes out herself.* —MRS. ELVSTED *is a woman of fragile figure, with pretty, soft features. Her eyes are light blue, large, round, and somewhat prominent, with a startled, inquiring expression. Her hair is remarkably light, almost flaxen, and unusually abundant and wavy. She is a couple of years younger than* HEDDA. *She wears a dark visiting dress, tasteful, but not quite in the lastest fashion.*]

HEDDA [*Receives her warmly.*] How do you do, my dear Mrs. Elvsted? It's delightful to see you again.

MRS. ELVSTED [*Nervously, struggling for self-control.*] Yes, it's a very long time since we met.

TESMAN [*Gives her his hand.*] And we too—eh?

HEDDA Thanks for your lovely flowers . . .

MRS. ELVSTED Oh, not at all . . . I would have come straight here yesterday afternoon; but I heard that you were away . . .

TESMAN Have you just come to town? Eh?

MRS. ELVSTED I arrived yesterday, about midday. Oh, I was quite in despair when I heard that you were not at home.

HEDDA In despair! How so?

TESMAN Why, my dear Mrs. Rysing—I mean Mrs. Elvsted . . .

HEDDA I hope that you are not in any trouble?

MRS. ELVSTED   Yes, I am. And I don't know another living creature here that I can turn to.

HEDDA [*Laying the bouquet on the table.*]   Come—let us sit here on the sofa . . .

MRS. ELVSTED   Oh, I am too restless to sit down.

HEDDA   Oh no, you're not. Come here. [*She draws* MRS. ELVSTED *down upon the sofa and sits at her side.*]

TESMAN   Well? What is it, Mrs. Elvsted . . . ?

HEDDA   Has anything particular happened to you at home?

MRS. ELVSTED   Yes—and no. Oh—I am so anxious you should not misunderstand me . . .

HEDDA   Then your best plan is to tell us the whole story, Mrs. Elvsted.

TESMAN   I suppose that's what you have come for—eh?

MRS. ELVSTED   Yes, yes—of course it is. Well then, I must tell you, if you don't already know, that Eilert Lövborg is in town, too.

HEDDA   Lövborg . . . !

TESMAN   What! Has Eilert Lövborg come back? Fancy that, Hedda!

HEDDA   Well, well—I hear it.

MRS. ELVSTED   He has been here a week already. Just fancy— a whole week! In this terrible town, alone! With so many temptations on all sides.

HEDDA   But, my dear Mrs. Elvsted—how does he concern you so much?

MRS. ELVSTED [*Looks at her with a startled air, and says rapidly*] He was the children's tutor.

HEDDA   Your children's?

MRS. ELVSTED   My husband's. I have none.

HEDDA   Your stepchildren's, then?

MRS. ELVSTED   Yes.

TESMAN [*Somewhat hesitatingly.*]   Then was he—I don't know how to express it—was he—regular enough in his habits to be fit for the post? Eh?

MRS. ELVSTED   For the last two years his conduct has been irreproachable.

TESMAN   Has it indeed? Fancy that, Hedda!

HEDDA   I hear it.

MRS. ELVSTED   Perfectly irreproachable, I assure you! In every respect. But all the same—now that I know he is here—in this great town—and with a large sum of money in his hands—I can't help being in mortal fear for him.

TESMAN   Why did he not remain where he was? With you and your husband? Eh?

MRS. ELVSTED   After his book was published he was too restless and unsettled to remain with us.

TESMAN   Yes, by the by, Aunt Julia told me he had published a new book.

MRS. ELVSTED   Yes, a big book, dealing with the march of civilization—in broad outline, as it were. It came out about a fortnight ago. And since it has sold so well, and been so much read —and made such a sensation . . .

TESMAN   Has it indeed? It must be something he has had lying by since his better days.

MRS. ELVSTED   Long ago, you mean?

TESMAN   Yes.

MRS. ELVSTED   No, he has written it all since he has been with us—within the last year.

TESMAN   Isn't that good news, Hedda? Think of that.

MRS. ELVSTED   Ah yes, if only it would last!

HEDDA   Have you seen him here in town?

MRS. ELVSTED   No, not yet. I have had the greatest difficulty in finding out his address. But this morning I discovered it at last.

HEDDA [Looks searchingly at her.]   Do you know, it seems to me a little odd of your husband—h'm . . .

MRS. ELVSTED [Starting nervously.]   Of my husband! What?

HEDDA   That he should send you to town on such an errand— that he does not come himself and look after his friend.

MRS. ELVSTED   Oh no, no—my husband has no time. And besides, I—I had some shopping to do.

HEDDA [With a slight smile.]   Ah, that is a different matter.

MRS. ELVSTED [Rising quickly and uneasily.]   And now I beg and implore you, Mr. Tesman—receive Eilert Lövborg kindly if he comes to you! And that he is sure to do. You see you were such great friends in the old days. And then you are interested in the same studies—the same branch of science—so far as I can understand.

TESMAN   We used to be, at any rate.

MRS. ELVSTED   That is why I beg so earnestly that you—you too—will keep a sharp eye upon him. Oh, you will promise me that, Mr. Tesman— won't you?

TESMAN   With the greatest of pleasure, Mrs. Rysing . . .

HEDDA   Elvsted.

TESMAN   I assure you I shall do all I possibly can for Eilert. You may rely upon me.

MRS. ELVSTED   Oh, how very, very kind of you! [*Presses his hands.*] Thanks, thanks, thanks! [*Frightened.*] You see, my husband is so very fond of him!

HEDDA [*Rising.*]   You ought to write to him, Tesman. Perhaps he may not care to come to you of his own accord.

TESMAN   Well, perhaps it would be the right thing to do, Hedda? Eh?

HEDDA   And the sooner the better. Why not at once?

MRS. ELVSTED [*Imploringly.*]   Oh, if you only would!

TESMAN   I'll write this moment. Have you his address, Mrs.—Mrs. Elvsted?

MRS. ELVSTED   Yes. [*Takes a slip of paper from her pocket, and hands it to him.*]   Here it is.

TESMAN   Good, good. Then I'll go in . . . [*Looks about him.*] By the by—my slippers? Oh, here. [*Takes the packet, and is about to go.*]

HEDDA   Be sure you write him a cordial, friendly letter. And a good long one too.

TESMAN   Yes, I will.

MRS. ELVSTED   But please, please don't say a word to show that I have suggested it.

TESMAN   No, how could you think I would? Eh? [*He goes out to the right, through the inner room.*]

HEDDA [*Goes up to* MRS. ELVSTED, *smiles and says in a low voice.*]   There! We have killed two birds with one stone.

MRS. ELVSTED What do you mean?

HEDDA Could you not see that I wanted him to go?

MRS. ELVSTED Yes, to write the letter . . .

HEDDA And that I might speak to you alone.

MRS. ELVSTED [*Confused.*] About the same thing?

HEDDA Precisely.

MRS. ELVSTED [*Apprehensively.*] But there is nothing more, Mrs. Tesman! Absolutely nothing!

HEDDA Oh yes, but there is. There is a great deal more—I can see that. Sit here—and we'll have a cozy, confidential chat. [*She forces* MRS. ELVSTED *to sit in the easy-chair beside the stove, and seats herself on one of the footstools.*]

MRS. ELVSTED [*Anxiously, looking at her watch.*] But, my dear Mrs. Tesman—I was really on the point of going.

HEDDA Oh, you can't be in such a hurry. Well? Now tell me something about your life at home.

MRS. ELVSTED Oh, that is just what I care least to speak about.

HEDDA But to me, dear . . . ? Why, weren't we schoolfellows?

MRS. ELVSTED Yes, but you were in the class above me. Oh, how dreadfully afraid of you I was then!

HEDDA Afraid of me?

MRS. ELVSTED Yes, dreadfully. For when we met on the stairs you used always to pull my hair.

HEDDA Did I, really?

MRS. ELVSTED Yes, and once you said you would burn it off my head.

HEDDA Oh, that was all nonsense, of course.

MRS. ELVSTED Yes, but I was so silly in those days. And since then, too—we have drifted so far—far apart from each other. Our circles have been so entirely different.

HEDDA Well then, we must try to drift together again. Now listen! At school we said *du*[2] to each other; and we called each other by our Christian names . . .

MRS. ELVSTED No, I am sure you must be mistaken.

HEDDA No, not at all! I can remember quite distinctly. So now

---

2. See note, p. 15.

HEDDA   Well, my dear—I should say, when he sends you after him all the way to town . . . [*Smiling almost imperceptibly.*] And besides, you said so yourself, to Tesman.

MRS. ELVSTED   [*With a little nervous twitch.*]   Did I? Yes, I suppose I did. [*Vehemently, but not loudly.*]   No—I may just as well make a clean breast of it at once! For it must all come out in any case.

HEDDA   Why, my dear Thea . . . ?

MRS. ELVSTED   Well, to make a long story short: My husband did not know that I was coming.

HEDDA   What! Your husband didn't know it!

MRS. ELVSTED   No, of course not. For that matter, he was away from home himself—he was traveling. Oh, I could bear it no longer, Hedda! I couldn't indeed—so utterly alone as I should have been in future.

HEDDA   Well? And then?

MRS. ELVSTED   So I put together some of my things—what I needed most—as quietly as possible. And then I left the house.

HEDDA   Without a word?

MRS. ELVSTED   Yes—and took the train straight to town.

HEDDA   Why, my dear, good Thea—to think of you daring to do it!

MRS. ELVSTED   [*Rises and moves about the room.*]   What else could I possibly do?

HEDDA   But what do you think your husband will say when you go home again?

MRS. ELVSTED   [*At the table, looks at her.*]   Back to him?

HEDDA   Of course.

MRS. ELVSTED   I shall never go back to him again.

HEDDA   [*Rising and going towards her.*]   Then you have left your home—for good and all?

MRS. ELVSTED   Yes. There was nothing else to be done.

HEDDA   But then—to take flight so openly.

MRS. ELVSTED   Oh, it's impossible to keep things of that sort secret.

HEDDA   But what do you think people will say of you, Thea?

MRS. ELVSTED   They may say what they like, for aught I care.

[*Seats herself wearily and sadly on the sofa.*] I have done nothing but what I had to do.

HEDDA [*After a short silence.*] And what are your plans now? What do you think of doing?

MRS. ELVSTED I don't know yet. I only know this, that I must live here, where Eilert Lövborg is—if I am to live at all.

HEDDA [*Takes a chair from the table, seats herself beside her, and strokes her hands.*] My dear Thea—how did this—this friendship—between you and Eilert Lövborg come about?

MRS. ELVSTED Oh it grew up gradually. I gained a sort of influence over him.

HEDDA Indeed?

MRS. ELVSTED He gave up his old habits. Not because I asked him to, for I never dared do that. But of course he saw how repulsive they were to me; and so he dropped them.

HEDDA [*Concealing an involuntary smile of scorn.*] Then you have reclaimed him—as the saying goes—my little Thea.

MRS. ELVSTED So he says himself, at any rate. And he, on his side, has made a real human being of me—taught me to think, and to understand so many things.

HEDDA Did he give you lessons too, then?

MRS. ELVSTED No, not exactly lessons. But he talked to me—talked about such an infinity of things. And then came the lovely, happy time when I began to share in his work—when he allowed me to help him!

HEDDA Oh he did, did he?

MRS. ELVSTED Yes! He never wrote anything without my assistance.

HEDDA You were two good comrades, in fact?

MRS. ELVSTED [*Eagerly.*] Comrades! Yes, fancy, Hedda—that is the very word he used! Oh, I ought to feel perfectly happy; and yet I cannot; for I don't know how long it will last.

HEDDA Are you no surer of him than that?

MRS. ELVSTED [*Gloomily.*] A woman's shadow stands between Eilert Lövborg and me.

HEDDA [*Looks at her anxiously.*] Who can that be?

MRS. ELVSTED   I don't know. Some one he knew in his—in his past. Some one he has never been able wholly to forget.

HEDDA   What has he told you—about this?

MRS. ELVSTED   He has only once—quite vaguely—alluded to it.

HEDDA   Well! And what did he say?

MRS. ELVSTED   He said that when they parted, she threatened to shoot him with a pistol.

HEDDA [*With cold composure.*]   Oh, nonsense! No one does that sort of thing here.

MRS. ELVSTED   No. And that is why I think it must have been that red-haired singing woman whom he once . . .

HEDDA   Yes, very likely.

MRS. ELVSTED   For I remember they used to say of her that she carried loaded firearms.

HEDDA   Oh— then of course it must have been she.

MRS. ELVSTED [*Wringing her hands.*]   And now just fancy, Hedda—I hear that this singing woman—that she is in town again! Oh, I don't know what to do . . .

HEDDA [*Glancing towards the inner room.*]   Hush! Here comes Tesman. [*Rises and whispers.*] Thea—all this must remain between you and me.

MRS. ELVSTED [*Springing up.*]   Oh yes—yes! For heaven's sake . . . !

[GEORGE TESMAN, *with a letter in his hand, comes from the right through the inner room.*]

TESMAN   There now—the epistle is finished.

HEDDA   That's right. And now Mrs. Elvsted is just going. Wait a moment—I'll go with you to the garden gate.

TESMAN   Do you think Berta could post the letter, Hedda dear?

HEDDA [*Takes it.*]   I will tell her to.

[BERTA *enters from the hall.*]

BERTA   Judge Brack wishes to know if Mrs. Tesman will receive him.

HEDDA   Yes, ask Judge Brack to come in. And look here—put this letter in the post.

BERTA [*Taking the letter.*] Yes, ma'am.

[*She opens the door for* JUDGE BRACK *and goes out herself.* BRACK *is a man of forty-five; thickset, but well built and elastic in his movements. His face is roundish with an aristocratic profile. His hair is short, still almost black, and carefully dressed. His eyes are lively and sparkling. His eyebrows thick. His mustaches are also thick, with short-cut ends. He wears a well-cut walking suit, a little too youthful for his age. He uses an eyeglass, which he now and then lets drop.*]

JUDGE BRACK [*With his hat in his hand, bowing.*] May one venture to call so early in the day?

HEDDA Of course one may.

TESMAN [*Presses his hand.*] You are welcome at any time. [*Introducing him.*] Judge Brack—Miss Rysing . . .

HEDDA Oh . . . !

BRACK [*Bowing.*] Ah—delighted . . .

HEDDA [*Looks at him and laughs.*] It's nice to have a look at you by daylight, Judge!

BRACK Do you find me—altered?

HEDDA A little younger, I think.

BRACK Thank you so much.

TESMAN But what do you think of Hedda—eh? Doesn't she look flourishing? She has actually . . .

HEDDA Oh, do leave me alone. You haven't thanked Judge Brack for all the trouble he has taken . . .

BRACK Oh, nonsense—it was a pleasure to me . . .

HEDDA Yes, you are a friend indeed. But here stands Thea all impatience to be off—so *au revoir*, Judge. I shall be back again presently.

[*Mutual salutations.* MRS. ELVSTED *and* HEDDA *go out by the hall door.*]

BRACK Well, is your wife tolerably satisfied . . .

TESMAN Yes, we can't thank you sufficiently. Of course she talks of a little rearrangement here and there; and one or two things are still wanting. We shall have to buy some additional trifles.

BRACK Indeed!

TESMAN But we won't trouble you about these things. Hedda says she herself will look after what is wanting. Shan't we sit down? Eh?

BRACK Thanks, for a moment. [*Seats himself beside the table.*] There is something I wanted to speak to you about, my dear Tesman.

TESMAN Indeed? Ah, I understand! [*Seating himself.*] I suppose it's the serious part of the frolic that is coming now. Eh?

BRACK Oh, the money question is not so very pressing; though, for that matter, I wish we had gone a little more economically to work.

TESMAN But that would never have done, you know! Think of Hedda, my dear fellow! You, who know her so well . . . I couldn't possibly ask her to put up with a shabby style of living!

BRACK No, no—that is just the difficulty.

TESMAN And then—fortunately—it can't be long before I receive my appointment.[4]

BRACK Well, you see—such things are often apt to hang fire for a time.

TESMAN Have you heard anything definite? Eh?

BRACK Nothing exactly definite . . . [*Interrupting himself.*] But by the by—I have one piece of news for you.

TESMAN Well?

BRACK Your old friend, Eilert Lövborg, has returned to town.

TESMAN I know that already.

BRACK Indeed! How did you learn it?

TESMAN From that lady who went out with Hedda.

BRACK Really? What was her name? I didn't quite catch it.

TESMAN Mrs. Elvsted.

BRACK Aha—Sheriff Elvsted's wife? Of course—he has been living up in their regions.

TESMAN And fancy—I'm delighted to hear that he is quite a reformed character!

BRACK So they say.

TESMAN And then he has published a new book—eh?

BRACK Yes, indeed he has.

4. As professor.

TESMAN   And I hear it has made some sensation!

BRACK   Quite an unusual sensation.

TESMAN   Fancy—isn't that good news! A man of such extraordinary talents . . . I felt so grieved to think that he had gone irretrievably to ruin.

BRACK   That was what everybody thought.

TESMAN   But I cannot imagine what he will take to now! How in the world will he be able to make his living? Eh?

[*During the last words,* HEDDA *has entered by the hall door.*]

HEDDA   [*To* BRACK, *laughing with a touch of scorn.*]   Tesman is for ever worrying about how people are to make their living.

TESMAN   Well you see, dear—we were talking about poor Eilert Lövborg.

HEDDA   [*Glancing at him rapidly.*]   Oh, indeed? [*Seats herself in the armchair beside the stove and asks indifferently.*]   What is the matter with him?

TESMAN   Well—no doubt he has run through all his property long ago; and he can scarcely write a new book every year—eh? So I really can't see what is to become of him.

BRACK   Perhaps I can give you some information on that point.

TESMAN   Indeed!

BRACK   You must remember that his relations have a good deal of influence.

TESMAN   Oh, his relations, unfortunately, have entirely washed their hands of him.

BRACK   At one time they called him the hope of the family.

TESMAN   At one time, yes! But he has put an end to all that.

HEDDA   Who knows? [*With a slight smile.*]   I hear they have reclaimed him up at Sheriff Elvsted's . . .

BRACK   And then this book that he has published . . .

TESMAN   Well, well, I hope to goodness they may find something for him to do. I have just written to him. I asked him to come and see us this evening, Hedda dear.

BRACK   But my dear fellow, you are booked for my bachelors' party this evening. You promised on the pier last night.

HEDDA   Had you forgotten, Tesman?

TESMAN   Yes, I had utterly forgotten.

BRACK   But it doesn't matter, for you may be sure he won't come.

TESMAN   What makes you think that? Eh?

BRACK   [*With a little hesitation, rising and resting his hands on the back of his chair.*]   My dear Tesman—and you too, Mrs. Tesman—I think I ought not to keep you in the dark about something that—that . . .

TESMAN   That concerns Eilert . . . ?

BRACK   Both you and him.

TESMAN   Well, my dear Judge, out with it.

BRACK   You must be prepared to find your appointment deferred longer than you desired or expected.

TESMAN   [*Jumping up uneasily.*]   Is there some hitch about it? Eh?

BRACK   The nomination may perhaps be made conditional on the result of a competition . . .

TESMAN   Competition! Think of that, Hedda!

HEDDA   [*Leans further back in the chair.*]   Aha—aha!

TESMAN   But who can my competitor be? Surely not . . . ?

BRACK   Yes, precisely—Eilert Lövborg.

TESMAN   [*Clasping his hands.*]   No, no—it's quite inconceivable! Quite impossible! Eh?

BRACK   H'm—that is what it may come to, all the same.

TESMAN   Well but, Judge Brack—it would show the most incredible lack of consideration for me. [*Gesticulates with his arms.*] For—just think—I'm a married man! We have married on the strength of these prospects, Hedda and I; and run deep into debt; and borrowed money from Aunt Julia too. Good heavens, they had as good as promised me the appointment. Eh?

BRACK   Well, well, well—no doubt you will get it in the end; only after a contest.

HEDDA   [*Immovable in her armchair.*]   Fancy, Tesman, there will be a sort of sporting interest in that.

TESMAN   Why, my dearest Hedda, how can you be so indifferent about it?

HEDDA   [*As before.*]   I am not at all indifferent. I am most eager to see who wins.

BRACK   In any case, Mrs. Tesman, it is best that you should know how matters stand. I mean—before you set about the little purchases I hear you are threatening.

HEDDA   This can make no difference.

BRACK   Indeed! Then I have no more to say. Good-bye! [*To* TESMAN.]   I shall look in on my way back from my afternoon walk, and take you home with me.

TESMAN   Oh yes, yes—your news has quite upset me.

HEDDA   [*Reclining, holds out her hand.*]   Good-bye, Judge; and be sure you call in the afternoon.

BRACK   Many thanks. Good-bye, good-bye!

TESMAN   [*Accompanying him to the door.*]   Good-bye, my dear Judge! You must really excuse me . . .

[JUDGE BRACK *goes out by the hall door.*]

TESMAN   [*Crosses the room.*]   Oh Hedda—one should never rush into adventures. Eh?

HEDDA   [*Looks at him, smiling.*]   Do you do that?

TESMAN   Yes, dear—there is no denying—it was adventurous to go and marry and set up house upon mere expectations.

HEDDA   Perhaps you are right there.

TESMAN   Well—at all events, we have our delightful home, Hedda! Fancy, the home we both dreamed of—the home we were in love with, I may almost say. Eh?

HEDDA   [*Rising slowly and wearily.*]   It was part of our compact that we were to go into society—to keep open house.

TESMAN   Yes, if you only knew how I had been looking forward to it! Fancy—to see you as hostess—in a select circle! Eh? Well, well, well—for the present we shall have to get on without society, Hedda—only to invite Aunt Julia now and then. Oh, I intended you to lead such an utterly different life, dear . . . !

HEDDA   Of course I cannot have my man in livery just yet.

TESMAN   Oh no, unfortunately. It would be out of the question for us to keep a footman, you know.

HEDDA   And the saddle horse I was to have had . . .

TESMAN   [*Aghast.*]   The saddle horse!

HEDDA   . . . I suppose I must not think of that now.

TESMAN   Good heavens, no!—that's as clear as daylight.

HEDDA [*Goes up the room.*] Well, I shall have one thing at least to kill time with in the meanwhile.

TESMAN [*Beaming.*] Oh thank heaven for that! What is it, Hedda? Eh?

HEDDA [*In the middle doorway, looks at him with covert scorn.*] My pistols, George.

TESMAN [*In alarm.*] Your pistols!

HEDDA [*With cold eyes.*] General Gabler's pistols. [*She goes out through the inner room, to the left.*]

TESMAN [*Rushes up to the middle doorway and calls after her.*] No, for heaven's sake, Hedda darling—don't touch those dangerous things! For my sake, Hedda! Eh?

ACT II

SCENE: *The room at the* TESMANS' *as in the first act, except that the piano has been removed, and an elegant little writing table with bookshelves put in its place. A smaller table stands near the sofa on the left. Most of the bouquets have been taken away.* MRS. ELVSTED'S *bouquet is upon the large table in front. It is afternoon.* HEDDA, *dressed to receive callers, is alone in the room. She stands by the open glass door, loading a revolver. The fellow to it lies in an open pistol case on the writing table.*

HEDDA [*Looks down the garden, and calls.*] So you are here again, Judge!

BRACK [*Is heard calling from a distance.*] As you see, Mrs. Tesman!

HEDDA [*Raises the pistol and points.*] Now I'll shoot you, Judge Brack!

BRACK [*Calling unseen.*] No, no, no! Don't stand aiming at me!

HEDDA This is what comes of sneaking in by the back way. [*She fires.*]

BRACK [*Nearer.*] Are you out of your senses! . . .

HEDDA Dear me—did I happen to hit you?

BRACK [*Still outside.*] I wish you would let these pranks alone!

HEDDA Come in then, Judge.

[JUDGE BRACK, *dressed as though for a men's party, enters by the glass door. He carries a light overcoat over his arm.*]

BRACK What the deuce—haven't you tired of that sport, yet? What are you shooting at?

HEDDA Oh, I am only firing in the air.

BRACK [*Gently takes the pistol out of her hand.*] Allow me, Madam! [*Looks at it.*] Ah—I know this pistol well! [*Looks around.*] Where is the case? Ah, here it is. [*Lays the pistol in it, and shuts it.*] Now we won't play at that game any more today.

HEDDA Then what in heaven's name would you have me do with myself?

BRACK Have you had no visitors?

HEDDA [*Closing the glass door.*] Not one. I suppose all our set are still out of town.

BRACK And is Tesman not at home either?

HEDDA [*At the writing table, putting the pistol case in a drawer which she shuts.*] No. He rushed off to his aunts' directly after lunch; he didn't expect you so early.

BRACK H'm—how stupid of me not to have thought of that!

HEDDA [*Turning her head to look at him.*] Why stupid?

BRACK Because if I had thought of it I should have come a little—earlier.

HEDDA [*Crossing the room.*] Then you would have found no one to receive you; for I have been in my room changing my dress ever since lunch.

BRACK And is there no sort of little chink that we could hold a parley through?

HEDDA You have forgotten to arrange one.

BRACK That was another piece of stupidity.

HEDDA Well, we must just settle down here—and wait. Tesman is not likely to be back for some time yet.

BRACK Never mind; I shall not be impatient.

[HEDDA *seats herself in the corner of the sofa.* BRACK *lays his overcoat over the back of the nearest chair, and sits down, but keeps his hat in his hand. A short silence. They look at each other.*]

HEDDA   Well?

BRACK   [*In the same tone.*]   Well?

HEDDA   I spoke first.

BRACK   [*Bending a little forward.*]   Come, let us have a cozy little chat, Mrs. Hedda.

HEDDA   [*Leaning further back in the sofa.*]   Does it not seem like a whole eternity since our last talk? Of course I don't count those few words yesterday evening and this morning.

BRACK   You mean since our last confidential talk? Our last *tête-à-tête*?

HEDDA   Well, yes—since you put it so.

BRACK   Not a day has passed but I have wished that you were home again.

HEDDA   And I have done nothing but wish the same thing.

BRACK   You? Really, Mrs. Hedda? And I thought you had been enjoying your tour so much!

HEDDA   Oh, yes, you may be sure of that!

BRACK   But Tesman's letters spoke of nothing but happiness.

HEDDA   Oh, Tesman! You see, he thinks nothing so delightful as grubbing in libraries and making copies of old parchments, or whatever you call them.

BRACK   [*With a spice of malice.*]   Well, that is his vocation in life—or part of it at any rate.

HEDDA   Yes, of course; and no doubt when it's your vocation . . . But *I!* Oh, my dear Mr. Brack, how mortally bored I have been.

BRACK   [*Sympathetically.*]   Do you really say so? In downright earnest?

HEDDA   Yes, you can surely understand it . . . ! To go for six whole months without meeting a soul that knew anything of our circle, or could talk about the things we are interested in.

BRACK   Yes, yes—I, too, should feel that a deprivation.

HEDDA   And then, what I found most intolerable of all . . .

BRACK   Well?

HEDDA   . . . was being everlastingly in the company of—one and the same person . . .

BRACK   [*With a nod of assent.*]   Morning, noon, and night, yes—at all possible times and seasons.

HEDDA   I said "everlastingly."

BRACK   Just so. But I should have thought, with our excellent Tesman, one could . . .

HEDDA   Tesman is—a specialist, my dear Judge.

BRACK   Undeniably.

HEDDA   And specialists are not at all amusing to travel with. Not in the long run at any rate.

BRACK   Not even—the specialist one happens to love?

HEDDA   Faugh—don't use that sickening word!

BRACK   [*Taken aback.*]   What do you say, Mrs. Hedda?

HEDDA   [*Half laughingly, half irritated.*]   You should just try it! To hear of nothing but the history of civilization morning, noon, and night . . .

BRACK   Everlastingly.

HEDDA   Yes, yes, yes! And then all this about the domestic industry of the Middle Ages . . . ! That's the most disgusting part of it!

BRACK   [*Looks searchingly at her.*]   But tell me—in that case, how am I to understand your . . . ? H'm . . .

HEDDA   My accepting George Tesman, you mean?

BRACK   Well, let us put it so.

HEDDA   Good heavens, do you see anything so wonderful in that?

BRACK   Yes and no—Mrs. Hedda.

HEDDA   I had positively danced myself tired, my dear Judge. My day was done . . . [*With a slight shudder.*]   Oh, no—I won't say that; nor think it, either!

BRACK   You have assuredly no reason to.

HEDDA   Oh, reasons . . . [*Watching him closely.*]   And George Tesman—after all, you must admit that he is correctness itself.

BRACK His correctness and respectability are beyond all question.

HEDDA And I don't see anything absolutely ridiculous about him. Do you?

BRACK Ridiculous? N—no—I shouldn't exactly say so . . .

HEDDA Well—and his powers of research, at all events, are untiring. I see no reason why he should not one day come to the front, after all.

BRACK [*Looks at her hesitatingly.*] I thought that you, like every one else, expected him to attain the highest distinction.

HEDDA [*With an expression of fatigue.*] Yes, so I did—And then, since he was bent, at all hazards, on being allowed to provide for me—I really don't know why I should not have accepted his offer.

BRACK No—if you look at it in that light . . .

HEDDA It was more than my other adorers were prepared to do for me, my dear Judge.

BRACK [*Laughing.*] Well, I can't answer for all the rest; but as for myself, you know quite well that I have always entertained a—a certain respect for the marriage tie—for marriage as an institution, Mrs. Hedda.

HEDDA [*Jestingly.*] Oh, I assure you I have never cherished any hopes with respect to you.

BRACK All I require is a pleasant and intimate interior, where I can make myself useful in every way, and am free to come and go as—as a trusted friend . . .

HEDDA Of the master of the house, do you mean?

BRACK [*Bowing.*] Frankly—of the mistress first of all; but, of course, of the master, too, in the second place. Such a triangular friendship—if I may call it so—is really a great convenience for all parties, let me tell you.

HEDDA Yes, I have many a time longed for some one to make a third on our travels. Oh—those railway-carriage *tête-à-têtes* . . . !

BRACK Fortunately your wedding journey is over now.

HEDDA [*Shaking her head.*] Not by a long—long way. I have only arrived at a station on the line.

BRACK Well, then the passengers jump out and move about a little, Mrs. Hedda.

HEDDA I never jump out.

BRACK Really?

HEDDA No—because there is always some one standing by to . . .

BRACK [Laughing.] To look at your legs, do you mean?

HEDDA Precisely.

BRACK Well, but, dear me . . .

HEDDA [With a gesture of repulsion.] I won't have it. I would rather keep my seat where I happen to be—and continue the tête-à-tête.

BRACK But suppose a third person were to jump in and join the couple.

HEDDA Ah—that is quite another matter!

BRACK A trusted, sympathetic friend . . .

HEDDA . . . with a fund of conversation on all sorts of lively topics . . .

BRACK . . . and not the least bit of a specialist!

HEDDA [With an audible sigh.] Yes, that would be a relief, indeed.

BRACK [Hears the front door open, and glances in that direction.] The triangle is completed.

HEDDA [Half aloud.] And on goes the train.

[GEORGE TESMAN, in a gray walking suit, with a soft felt hat, enters from the hall. He has a number of unbound books under his arm and in his pockets.]

TESMAN [Goes up to the table beside the corner settee.] Ouf—what a load for a warm day—all these books. [Lays them on the table.] I'm positively perspiring, Hedda. Hallo—are you there already, my dear Judge? Eh? Berta didn't tell me.

BRACK [Rising.] I came in through the garden.

HEDDA What books have you got there?

TESMAN [Stands looking them through.] Some new books on my special subjects—quite indispensable to me.

HEDDA Your special subjects?

BRACK   Yes, books on his special subjects, Mrs. Tesman.

[BRACK *and* HEDDA *exchange a confidential smile.*]

HEDDA   Do you need still more books on your special subjects?

TESMAN   Yes, my dear Hedda, one can never have too many of them. Of course, one must keep up with all that is written and published.

HEDDA   Yes, I suppose one must.

TESMAN   [*Searching among his books.*]   And look here—I have got hold of Eilert Lövborg's new book, too. [*Offering it to her.*] Perhaps you would like to glance through it, Hedda? Eh?

HEDDA   No, thank you. Or rather—afterwards perhaps.

TESMAN   I looked into it a little on the way home.

BRACK   Well, what do you think of it—as a specialist?

TESMAN   I think it shows quite remarkable soundness of judgment. He never wrote like that before. [*Putting the books together.*]   Now I shall take all these into my study. I'm longing to cut the leaves . . . ! And then I must change my clothes. [*To* BRACK.]   I suppose we needn't start just yet? Eh?

BRACK   Oh, dear, no—there is not the slightest hurry.

TESMAN   Well, then, I will take my time. [*Is going with his books, but stops in the doorway and turns.*]   By the by, Hedda— Aunt Julia is not coming this evening.

HEDDA   Not coming? Is it that affair of the bonnet that keeps her away?

TESMAN   Oh, not at all. How could you think such a thing of Aunt Julia? Just fancy . . . ! The fact is, Aunt Rina is very ill.

HEDDA   She always is.

TESMAN   Yes, but today she is much worse than usual, poor dear.

HEDDA   Oh, then it's only natural that her sister should remain with her. I must bear my disappointment.

TESMAN   And you can't imagine, dear, how delighted Aunt Julia seemed to be—because you had come home looking so flourishing!

HEDDA   [*Half aloud, rising.*]   Oh, those everlasting aunts!

TESMAN   What?

HEDDA [*Going to the glass door.*]   Nothing.

TESMAN   Oh, all right. [*He goes through the inner room, out to the right.*]

BRACK   What bonnet were you talking about?

HEDDA   Oh, it was a little episode with Miss Tesman this morning. She had laid down her bonnet on the chair there—[*looks at him and smiles*]—and I pretended to think it was the servant's.

BRACK [*Shaking his head.*]   Now, my dear Mrs. Hedda, how could you do such a thing? To that excellent old lady, too!

HEDDA [*Nervously crossing the room.*]   Well, you see—these impulses come over me all of a sudden; and I cannot resist them. [*Throws herself down in the easy-chair by the stove.*]   Oh, I don't know how to explain it.

BRACK [*Behind the easy-chair.*]   You are not really happy—that is at the bottom of it.

HEDDA [*Looking straight before her.*]   I know of no reason why I should be—happy. Perhaps you can give me one?

BRACK   Well—amongst other things, because you have got exactly the home you had set your heart on.

HEDDA [*Looks up at him and laughs.*]   Do you, too, believe in that legend?

BRACK   Is there nothing in it, then?

HEDDA   Oh, yes, there is something in it.

BRACK   Well?

HEDDA   There is this in it, that I made use of Tesman to see me home from evening parties last summer . . .

BRACK   I, unfortunately, had to go quite a different way.

HEDDA   That's true. I know you were going a different way last summer.

BRACK [*Laughing.*]   Oh fie, Mrs. Hedda! Well, then—you and Tesman . . . ?

HEDDA   Well, we happened to pass here one evening; Tesman, poor fellow, was writhing in the agony of having to find conversation; so I took pity on the learned man . . .

BRACK [*Smiles doubtfully.*]   You took pity? H'm . . .

HEDDA   Yes, I really did. And so—to help him out of his torment—I happened to say, in pure thoughtlessness, that I should like to live in this villa.

BRACK   No more than that?

HEDDA   Not that evening.

BRACK   But afterwards?

HEDDA   Yes, my thoughtlessness had consequences, my dear Judge.

BRACK   Unfortunately that too often happens, Mrs. Hedda.

HEDDA   Thanks! So you see it was this enthusiasm for Secretary Falk's villa that first constituted a bond of sympathy between George Tesman and me. From that came our engagement and our marriage, and our wedding journey, and all the rest of it. Well, well, my dear Judge—as you make your bed so you must lie, I could almost say.

BRACK   This is exquisite! And you really cared not a rap about it all the time?

HEDDA   No, heaven knows I didn't.

BRACK   But now? Now that we have made it so homelike for you?

HEDDA   Ugh—the rooms all seem to smell of lavender and dried roseleaves. But perhaps it's Aunt Julia that has brought that scent with her.

BRACK   [Laughing.]   No, I think it must be a legacy from the late Mrs. Secretary Falk.

HEDDA   Yes, there is an odor of mortality about it. It reminds me of a bouquet—the day after the ball. [Clasps her hands behind her head, leans back in her chair and looks at him.]   Oh, my dear Judge—you cannot imagine how horribly I shall bore myself here.

BRACK   Why should not you, too, find some sort of vocation in life, Mrs. Hedda?

HEDDA   A vocation—that should attract me?

BRACK   If possible, of course.

HEDDA   Heaven knows what sort of a vocation that could be. I often wonder whether . . . [Breaking off.]   But that would never do, either.

BRACK   Who can tell? Let me hear what it is.

HEDDA   Whether I might not get Tesman to go into politics, I mean.

BRACK [*Laughing.*]   Tesman? No, really now, political life is not the thing for him—not at all in his line.

HEDDA   No, I daresay not. But if I could get him into it all the same?

BRACK   Why—what satisfaction could you find in that? If he is not fitted for that sort of thing, why should you want to drive him into it?

HEDDA   Because I am bored, I tell you! [*After a pause.*] So you think it quite out of the question that Tesman should ever get into the ministry?

BRACK   H'm—you see, my dear Mrs. Hedda—to get into the ministry, he would have to be a tolerably rich man.

HEDDA [*Rising impatiently.*]   Yes, there we have it! It is this genteel poverty I have managed to drop into . . . ! [*Crosses the room.*]   That is what makes life so pitiable! So utterly ludicrous! —For that's what it is.

BRACK   Now *I* should say the fault lay elsewhere.

HEDDA   Where, then?

BRACK   You have never gone through any really stimulating experience.

HEDDA   Anything serious, you mean?

BRACK   Yes, you may call it so. But now you may perhaps have one in store.

HEDDA [*Tossing her head.*]   Oh, you're thinking of the annoyances about this wretched professorship! But that must be Tesman's own affair. I assure you I shall not waste a thought upon it.

BRACK   No, no, I daresay not. But suppose now that what people call—in elegant language—a solemn responsibility were to come upon you? [*Smiling.*] A new responsibility, Mrs. Hedda?

HEDDA [*Angrily.*]   Be quiet! Nothing of that sort will ever happen!

BRACK [*Warily.*]   We will speak of this again a year hence— at the very outside.

HEDDA [*Curtly.*] I have no turn for anything of the sort, Judge Brack. No responsibilities for me!

BRACK Are you so unlike the generality of women as to have no turn for duties which . . . ?

HEDDA [*Beside the glass door.*] Oh, be quiet, I tell you! I often think there is only one thing in the world I have any turn for.

BRACK [*Drawing near to her.*] And what is that, if I may ask?

HEDDA [*Stands looking out.*] Boring myself to death. Now you know it. [*Turns, looks towards the inner room, and laughs.*] Yes, as I thought! Here comes the Professor.

BRACK [*Softly, in a tone of warning.*] Come, come, come, Mrs. Hedda!

[GEORGE TESMAN, *dressed for the party, with his gloves and hat in his hand, enters from the right through the inner room.*]

TESMAN Hedda, has no message come from Eilert Lövborg? Eh?

HEDDA No.

TESMAN Then you'll see he'll be here presently.

BRACK Do you really think he will come?

TESMAN Yes, I am almost sure of it. For what you were telling us this morning must have been a mere floating rumor.

BRACK You think so?

TESMAN At any rate, Aunt Julia said she did not believe for a moment that he would ever stand in my way again. Fancy that!

BRACK Well, then, that's all right.

TESMAN [*Placing his hat and gloves on a chair on the right.*] Yes, but you must really let me wait for him as long as possible.

BRACK We have plenty of time yet. None of my guests will arrive before seven or half-past.

TESMAN Then meanwhile we can keep Hedda company, and see what happens. Eh?

HEDDA [*Placing* BRACK's *hat and overcoat upon the corner settee.*] And at the worst Mr. Lövborg can remain here with me.

BRACK [*Offering to take his things.*] Oh, allow me, Mrs. Tesman! What do you mean by "at the worst"?

HEDDA   If he won't go with you and Tesman.

TESMAN [*Looks dubiously at her.*]   But, Hedda, dear—do you think it would quite do for him to remain with you? Eh? Remember, Aunt Julia can't come.

HEDDA   No, but Mrs. Elvsted is coming. We three can have a cup of tea together.

TESMAN   Oh, yes, that will be all right.

BRACK [*Smiling.*]   And that would perhaps be the safest plan for him.

HEDDA   Why so?

BRACK   Well, you know, Mrs. Tesman, how you used to jeer at my little bachelor parties. You declared they were adapted only for men of the strictest principles.

HEDDA   But no doubt Mr. Lövborg's principles are strict enough now. A converted sinner . . .

[BERTA *appears at the hall door.*]

BERTA   There's a gentleman asking if you are at home, ma'am . . .

HEDDA   Well, show him in.

TESMAN [*Softly.*]   I'm sure it is he! Fancy that!

[EILERT LÖVBORG *enters from the hall. He is slim and lean; of the same age as* TESMAN, *but looks older and somewhat worn-out. His hair and beard are of a blackish brown, his face long and pale, but with patches of color on the cheekbones. He is dressed in a well-cut black visiting suit, quite new. He has dark gloves and a silk hat. He stops near the door, and makes a rapid bow, seeming somewhat embarrassed.*]

TESMAN [*Goes up to him and shakes him warmly by the hand.*] Well, my dear Eilert—so at last we meet again!

EILERT LÖVBORG [*Speaks in a subdued voice.*]   Thanks for your letter, Tesman. [*Approaching* HEDDA.]   Will you, too, shake hands with me, Mrs. Tesman?

HEDDA [*Taking his hand.*]   I am glad to see you, Mr. Lövborg. [*With a motion of her hand.*]   I don't know whether you two gentlemen . . . ?

LÖVBORG [*Bowing slightly.*]   Judge Brack, I think.

BRACK [*Doing likewise.*]   Oh, yes—in the old days . . .

TESMAN [*To* LÖVBORG, *with his hands on his shoulders.*] And now you must make yourself entirely at home, Eilert! Mustn't he, Hedda?—For I hear you are going to settle in town again? Eh?

LÖVBORG   Yes, I am.

TESMAN   Quite right, quite right. Let me tell you, I have got hold of your new book; but I haven't had time to read it yet.

LÖVBORG   You may spare yourself the trouble.

TESMAN   Why so?

LÖVBORG   Because there is very little in it.

TESMAN   Just fancy—how can you say so?

BRACK   But it has been very much praised, I hear.

LÖVBORG   That was what I wanted; so I put nothing into the book but what every one would agree with.

BRACK   Very wise of you.

TESMAN   Well, but, my dear Eilert . . . !

LÖVBORG   For now I mean to win myself a position again—to make a fresh start.

TESMAN [*A little embarrassed.*]   Ah, that is what you wish to do? Eh?

LÖVBORG [*Smiling, lays down his hat, and draws a packet, wrapped in paper, from his coat pocket.*]   But when this one appears, George Tesman, you will have to read it. For this is the real book—the book I have put my true self into.

TESMAN   Indeed? And what is it?

LÖVBORG   It is the continuation.

TESMAN   The continuation? Of what?

LÖVBORG   Of the book.

TESMAN   Of the new book?

LÖVBORG   Of course.

TESMAN   Why, my dear Eilert—does it not come down to our own days?

LÖVBORG   Yes, it does; and this one deals with the future.

TESMAN   With the future! But, good heavens, we know nothing of the future!

LÖVBORG   No; but there is a thing or two to be said about it all the same. [*Opens the packet.*]   Look here . . .

TESMAN   Why, that's not your handwriting.

LÖVBORG   I dictated it. [*Turning over the pages.*]   It falls into two sections. The first deals with the civilizing forces of the future. And here is the second—[*running through the pages towards the end*]—forecasting the probable line of development.

TESMAN   How odd now! I should never have thought of writing anything of that sort.

HEDDA [*At the glass door, drumming on the pane.*]   H'm . . . I daresay not.

LÖVBORG [*Replacing the manuscript in its paper and laying the packet on the table.*]   I brought it, thinking I might read you a little of it this evening.

TESMAN   That was very good of you, Eilert. But this evening . . . ? [*Looking at* BRACK.]   I don't quite see how we can manage it . . .

LÖVBORG   Well, then, some other time. There is no hurry.

BRACK   I must tell you, Mr. Lövborg—there is a little gathering at my house this evening—mainly in honor of Tesman, you know . . .

LÖVBORG [*Looking for his hat.*]   Oh—then I won't detain you . . .

BRACK   No, but listen—will you not do me the favor of joining us?

LÖVBORG [*Curtly and decidedly.*]   No, I can't—thank you very much.

BRACK   Oh, nonsense—do! We shall be quite a select little circle. And I assure you we shall have a "lively time," as Mrs. Hed—as Mrs. Tesman says.

LÖVBORG   I have no doubt of it. But nevertheless . . .

BRACK   And then you might bring your manuscript with you, and read it to Tesman at my house. I could give you a room to yourselves.

TESMAN   Yes, think of that, Eilert—why shouldn't you? Eh?

HEDDA [*Interposing.*]   But, Tesman, if Mr. Lövborg would really rather not! I am sure Mr. Lövborg is much more inclined to remain here and have supper with me.

LÖVBORG [*Looking at her.*]   With you, Mrs. Tesman?

HEDDA   And with Mrs. Elvsted.

LÖVBORG Ah . . . [*Lightly.*] I saw her for a moment this morning.

HEDDA Did you? Well, she is coming this evening. So you see you are almost bound to remain, Mr. Lövborg, or she will have no one to see her home.

LÖVBORG That's true. Many thanks, Mrs. Tesman—in that case I will remain.

HEDDA Then I have one or two orders to give the servant . . .

[*She goes to the hall door and rings.* BERTA *enters.* HEDDA *talks to her in a whisper, and points towards the inner room.* BERTA *nods and goes out again.*]

TESMAN [*At the same time, to* LÖVBORG.] Tell me, Eilert— is it this new subject—the future—that you are going to lecture about?

LÖVBORG Yes.

TESMAN They told me at the bookseller's that you are going to deliver a course of lectures this autumn.

LÖVBORG That is my intention. I hope you won't take it ill, Tesman.

TESMAN Oh no, not in the least! But . . . ?

LÖVBORG I can quite understand that it must be disagreeable to you.

TESMAN [*Cast down.*] Oh, I can't expect you, out of consideration for me, to . . .

LÖVBORG But I shall wait till you have received your appointment.

TESMAN Will you wait? Yes, but—yes, but—are you not going to compete with me? Eh?

LÖVBORG No; it is only the moral victory I care for.

TESMAN Why, bless me—then Aunt Julia was right after all! Oh, yes—I knew it! Hedda! Just fancy—Eilert Lövborg is not going to stand in our way!

HEDDA [*Curtly.*] Our way? Pray leave me out of the question.

[*She goes up towards the inner room, where* BERTA *is placing a tray with decanters and glasses on the table.* HEDDA *nods approval, and comes forward again.* BERTA *goes out.*]

TESMAN [*At the same time.*]   And you, Judge Brack—what do you say to this? Eh?

BRACK   Well, I say that a moral victory—h'm—may be all very fine . . .

TESMAN   Yes, certainly. But all the same . . .

HEDDA [*Looking at* TESMAN *with a cold smile.*]   You stand there looking as if you were thunderstruck . . .

TESMAN   Yes—so I am—I almost think . . .

BRACK   Don't you see, Mrs. Tesman, a thunderstorm has just passed over?

HEDDA [*Pointing towards the inner room.*]   Will you not take a glass of cold punch, gentlemen?

BRACK [*Looking at his watch.*]   A stirrup cup? Yes, it wouldn't come amiss.

TESMAN   A capital idea, Hedda! Just the thing! Now that the weight has been taken off my mind . . .

HEDDA   Will you not join them, Mr. Lövborg?

LÖVBORG [*With a gesture of refusal.*]   No, thank you. Nothing for me.

BRACK   Why bless me—cold punch is surely not poison.

LÖVBORG   Perhaps not for every one.

HEDDA   I will keep Mr. Lövborg company in the meantime.

TESMAN   Yes, yes, Hedda dear, do.

[*He and* BRACK *go into the inner room, seat themselves, drink punch, smoke cigarettes, and carry on a lively conversation during what follows.* EILERT LÖVBORG *remains standing beside the stove.* HEDDA *goes to the writing table.*]

HEDDA [*Raising her voice a little.*]   Do you care to look at some photographs, Mr. Lövborg? You know Tesman and I made a tour in the Tyrol on our way home?

[*She takes up an album, and places it on the table beside the sofa, in the further corner of which she seats herself.* EILERT LÖVBORG *approaches, stops, and looks at her. Then he takes a chair and seats himself to her left, with his back towards the inner room.*]

HEDDA [*Opening the album.*]   Do you see this range of mountains, Mr. Lövborg? It's the Ortler group. Tesman has written the name underneath. Here it is: "The Ortler group near Meram."

LÖVBORG [*Who has never taken his eyes off her, says softly and slowly.*] Hedda—Gabler!

HEDDA [*Glancing hastily at him.*] Ah! Hush!

LÖVBORG [*Repeats softly.*] Hedda Gabler!

HEDDA [*Looking at the album.*] That was my name in the old days—when we two knew each other.

LÖVBORG And I must teach myself never to say Hedda Gabler again—never, as long as I live.

HEDDA [*Still turning over the pages.*] Yes, you must. And I think you ought to practice in time. The sooner the better, I should say.

LÖVBORG [*In a tone of indignation.*] Hedda Gabler married? And married to—George Tesman!

HEDDA Yes—so the world goes.

LÖVBORG Oh, Hedda, Hedda—how could you[5] throw yourself away!

HEDDA [*Looks sharply at him.*] What? I can't allow this!

LÖVBORG What do you mean?

[TESMAN *comes into the room and goes towards the sofa.*]

HEDDA [*Hears him coming and says in an indifferent tone.*] And this is a view from the Val d'Ampezzo, Mr. Lövborg. Just look at these peaks! [*Looks affectionately up at* TESMAN.] What's the name of these curious peaks, dear?

TESMAN Let me see. Oh, those are the Dolomites.

HEDDA Yes, that's it! Those are the Dolomites, Mr. Lövborg.

TESMAN Hedda, dear, I only wanted to ask whether I shouldn't bring you a little punch after all? For yourself, at any rate—eh?

HEDDA Yes, do, please; and perhaps a few biscuits.

TESMAN No cigarettes?

HEDDA No.

TESMAN Very well.

[*He goes into the inner room and out to the right.* BRACK *sits in the inner room, and keeps an eye from time to time on* HEDDA *and* LÖVBORG.]

---

5. Lövborg uses the familiar *du.*

LÖVBORG [*Softly, as before.*] Answer me, Hedda—how could you go and do this?

HEDDA [*Apparently absorbed in the album.*] If you continue to say *du* to me I won't talk to you.

LÖVBORG May I not say *du* even when we are alone?

HEDDA No. You may think it; but you mustn't say it.

LÖVBORG Ah, I understand. It is an offense against George Tesman, whom you[6] love.

HEDDA [*Glances at him and smiles.*] Love? What an idea!

LÖVBORG You don't love him then!

HEDDA But I won't hear of any sort of unfaithfulness! Remember that.

LÖVBORG Hedda—answer me one thing . . .

HEDDA Hush!

[TESMAN *enters with a small tray from the inner room.*]

TESMAN Here you are! Isn't this tempting?

[*He puts the tray on the table.*]

HEDDA Why do you bring it yourself?

TESMAN [*Filling the glasses.*] Because I think it's such fun to wait upon you, Hedda.

HEDDA But you have poured out two glasses. Mr. Lövborg said he wouldn't have any . . .

TESMAN No, but Mrs. Elvsted will soon be here, won't she?

HEDDA Yes, by the by—Mrs. Elvsted . . .

TESMAN Had you forgotten her? Eh?

HEDDA We were so absorbed in these photographs. [*Shows him a picture.*] Do you remember this little village?

TESMAN Oh, it's that one just below the Brenner Pass. It was there we passed the night . . .

HEDDA . . . and met that lively party of tourists.

TESMAN Yes, that was the place. Fancy—if we could only have had you with us, Eilert! Eh?

[*He returns to the inner room and sits beside* BRACK.]

LÖVBORG Answer me this one thing, Hedda . . .

HEDDA Well?

---

6. From here on Lövborg uses the formal *De.*

LÖVBORG Was there no love in your friendship for me, either? Not a spark—not a tinge of love in it?

HEDDA I wonder if there was? To me it seems as though we were two good comrades—two thoroughly intimate friends. [*Smilingly.*] You especially were frankness itself.

LÖVBORG It was you that made me so.

HEDDA As I look back upon it all, I think there was really something beautiful, something fascinating—something daring—in—in that secret intimacy—that comradeship which no living creature so much as dreamed of.

LÖVBORG Yes, yes, Hedda! Was there not?—When I used to come to your father's in the afternoon—and the General sat over at the window reading his papers—with his back towards us . . .

HEDDA And we two on the corner sofa . . .

LÖVBORG Always with the same illustrated paper before us . . .

HEDDA For want of an album, yes.

LÖVBORG Yes, Hedda, and when I made my confessions to you—told you about myself, things that at that time no one else knew! There I would sit and tell you of my escapades—my days and nights of devilment. Oh, Hedda—what was the power in you that forced me to confess these things?

HEDDA Do you think it was any power in me?

LÖVBORG How else can I explain it? And all those—those roundabout questions you used to put to me . . .

HEDDA Which you understood so particularly well . . .

LÖVBORG How could you sit and question me like that? Question me quite frankly . . .

HEDDA In roundabout terms, please observe.

LÖVBORG Yes, but frankly nevertheless. Cross-question me about—all that sort of thing?

HEDDA And how could you answer, Mr. Lövborg?

LÖVBORG Yes, that is just what I can't understand—in looking back upon it. But tell me now, Hedda—was there not love at the bottom of our friendship? On your side, did you not feel as though you might purge my stains away—if I made you my confessor? Was it not so?

HEDDA No, not quite.

LÖVBORG   Yes!

HEDDA   . . . that was not my most arrant cowardice—that evening.

LÖVBORG [*Looks at her a moment, understands and whispers passionately.*]   Oh, Hedda! Hedda Gabler! Now I begin to see a hidden reason beneath our comradeship! You[7] and I . . . ! After all, then, it was your craving for life . . .

HEDDA [*Softly, with a sharp glance.*]   Take care! Believe nothing of the sort!

[*Twilight has begun to fall. The hall door is opened from without by* BERTA.]

HEDDA [*Closes the album with a bang and calls smilingly.*] Ah, at last! My darling Thea—come along!

[MRS. ELVSTED *enters from the hall. She is in evening dress. The door is closed behind her.*]

HEDDA [*On the sofa, stretches out her arms towards her.*]   My sweet Thea—you can't think how I have been longing for you!

[MRS. ELVSTED, *in passing, exchanges slight salutations with the gentlemen in the inner room, then goes up to the table and gives* HEDDA *her hand.* EILERT LÖVBORG *has risen. He and* MRS. ELVSTED *greet each other with a silent nod.*]

MRS. ELVSTED   Ought I to go in and talk to your husband for a moment?

HEDDA   Oh, not at all. Leave those two alone. They will soon be going.

MRS. ELVSTED   Are they going out?

HEDDA   Yes, to a supper party.

MRS. ELVSTED [*Quickly, to* LÖVBORG.]   Not you?

LÖVBORG   No.

HEDDA   Mr. Lövborg remains with us.

MRS. ELVSTED [*Takes a chair and is about to seat herself at his side.*]   Oh, how nice it is here!

HEDDA   No, thank you, my little Thea! Not there! You'll be good enough to come over here to me. I will sit between you.

MRS. ELVSTED   Yes, just as you please.

---

7. *Du* once more. Hedda uses *De* consistently.

[*She goes round the table and seats herself on the sofa on* HEDDA'S *right.* LÖVBORG *reseats himself on his chair.*]

LÖVBORG [*After a short pause, to* HEDDA.]   Is not she lovely to look at?

HEDDA [*Lightly stroking her hair.*]   Only to look at?

LÖVBORG   Yes. For we two—she and I—we are two real comrades. We have absolute faith in each other; so we can sit and talk with perfect frankness . . .

HEDDA   Not roundabout, Mr. Lövborg?

LÖVBORG   Well . . .

MRS. ELVSTED [*Softly clinging close to* HEDDA.]   Oh, how happy I am, Hedda! For, only think, he says I have inspired him, too.

HEDDA [*Looks at her with a smile.*]   Ah! Does he say that, dear?

LÖVBORG   And then she is so brave, Mrs. Tesman!

MRS. ELVSTED   Good heavens—am I brave?

LÖVBORG   Exceedingly—where your comrade is concerned.

HEDDA   Ah, yes—courage! If one only had that!

LÖVBORG   What then? What do you mean?

HEDDA   Then life would perhaps be livable, after all. [*With a sudden change of tone.*]   But now, my dearest Thea, you really must have a glass of cold punch.

MRS. ELVSTED   No, thanks—I never take anything of that kind.

HEDDA   Well, then, you, Mr. Lövborg.

LÖVBORG   Nor I, thank you.

MRS. ELVSTED   No, he doesn't, either.

HEDDA [*Looks fixedly at him.*]   But if I say you shall?

LÖVBORG   It would be no use.

HEDDA [*Laughing.*]   Then I, poor creature, have no sort of power over you?

LÖVBORG   Not in that respect.

HEDDA   But seriously, I think you ought to—for your own sake.

MRS. ELVSTED   Why, Hedda . . . !

LÖVBORG   How so?

HEDDA   Or rather on account of other people.

LÖVBORG Indeed?

HEDDA Otherwise people might be apt to suspect that—in your heart of hearts—you did not feel quite secure—quite confident in yourself.

MRS. ELVSTED [*Softly.*] Oh, please, Hedda . . . !

LÖVBORG People may suspect what they like—for the present.

MRS. ELVSTED [*Joyfully.*] Yes, let them!

HEDDA I saw it plainly in Judge Brack's face a moment ago.

LÖVBORG What did you see?

HEDDA His contemptuous smile, when you dared not go with them into the inner room.

LÖVBORG Dared not? Of course I preferred to stop here and talk to you.

MRS. ELVSTED What could be more natural, Hedda?

HEDDA But the Judge could not guess that. And I saw, too, the way he smiled and glanced at Tesman when you dared not accept his invitation to this wretched little supper party of his.

LÖVBORG Dared not? Do you say I dared not?

HEDDA I don't say so. But that was how Judge Brack understood it.

LÖVBORG Well, let him.

HEDDA Then you are not going with them?

LÖVBORG I will stay here with you and Thea.

MRS. ELVSTED Yes, Hedda—how can you doubt that?

HEDDA [*Smiles and nods approvingly to* LÖVBORG.] Firm as a rock! Faithful to your principles, now and forever! Ah, that is how a man should be! [*Turns to* MRS. ELVSTED *and caresses her.*] Well, now, what did I tell you, when you came to us this morning in such a state of distraction . . .

LÖVBORG [*Surprised.*] Distraction!

MRS. ELVSTED [*Terrified.*] Hedda—oh, Hedda . . . !

HEDDA You can see for yourself! You haven't the slightest reason to be in such mortal terror . . . [*Interrupting herself.*] There! Now we can all three enjoy ourselves!

LÖVBORG [*Who has given a start.*] Ah—what is all this, Mrs. Tesman?

MRS. ELVSTED Oh, my God, Hedda! What are you saying? What are you doing?

HEDDA Don't get excited! That horrid Judge Brack is sitting watching you.

LÖVBORG So she was in mortal terror! On my account!

MRS. ELVSTED [Softly and piteously.] Oh, Hedda—now you have ruined everything!

LÖVBORG [Looks fixedly at her for a moment. His face is distorted.] So that was my comrade's frank confidence in me?

MRS. ELVSTED [Imploringly.] Oh, my dearest friend—only let me tell you . . .

LÖVBORG [Takes one of the glasses of punch, raises it to his lips, and says in a low, husky voice.] Your health, Thea!

[He empties the glass, puts it down, and takes the second.]

MRS. ELVSTED [Softly.] Oh, Hedda, Hedda—how could you do this?

HEDDA I do it? I? Are you crazy?

LÖVBORG Here's to your health, too, Mrs. Tesman. Thanks for the truth. Hurrah for the truth!

[He empties the glass and is about to refill it.]

HEDDA [Lays her hand on his arm.] Come, come—no more for the present. Remember you are going out to supper.

MRS. ELVSTED No, no, no!

HEDDA Hush! They are sitting watching you.

LÖVBORG [Putting down the glass.] Now, Thea—tell me the truth . . .

MRS. ELVSTED Yes.

LÖVBORG Did your husband know that you had come after me?

MRS. ELVSTED [Wringing her hands.] Oh, Hedda—do you hear what he is asking?

LÖVBORG Was it arranged between you and him that you were to come to town and look after me? Perhaps it was the Sheriff himself that urged you to come? Aha, my dear—no doubt he wanted my help in his office. Or was it at the card table that he missed me?

MRS. ELVSTED [Softly, in agony.] Oh, Lövborg, Lövborg . . . !

LÖVBORG [*Seizes a glass and is on the point of filling it.*] Here's a glass for the old Sheriff, too!

HEDDA [*Preventing him.*] No more just now. Remember, you have to read your manuscript to Tesman.

LÖVBORG [*Calmly, putting down the glass.*] It was stupid of me all this, Thea—to take it in this way, I mean. Don't be angry with me, my dear, dear comrade. You shall see—both you and the others—that if I was fallen once—now I have risen again! Thanks to you, Thea.

MRS. ELVSTED [*Radiant with joy.*] Oh, heaven be praised . . . !

[BRACK *has in the meantime looked at his watch. He and TES-MAN rise and come into the drawing room.*]

BRACK [*Takes his hat and overcoat.*] Well, Mrs. Tesman, our time has come.

HEDDA I suppose it has.

LÖVBORG [*Rising.*] Mine too, Judge Brack.

MRS. ELVSTED [*Softly and imploringly.*] Oh, Lövborg, don't do it!

HEDDA [*Pinching her arm.*] They can hear you!

MRS. ELVSTED [*With a suppressed shriek.*] Ow!

LÖVBORG [*To BRACK.*] You were good enough to invite me.

BRACK Well, are you coming after all?

LÖVBORG Yes, many thanks.

BRACK I'm delighted . . .

LÖVBORG [*To TESMAN, putting the parcel of MS. in his pocket.*] I should like to show you one or two things before I send it to the printers.

TESMAN Fancy—that will be delightful. But, Hedda dear, how is Mrs. Elvsted to get home? Eh?

HEDDA Oh, that can be managed somehow.

LÖVBORG [*Looking towards the ladies.*] Mrs. Elvsted? Of course, I'll come again and fetch her. [*Approaching.*] At ten or thereabouts, Mrs. Tesman? Will that do?

HEDDA Certainly. That will do capitally.

TESMAN Well, then, that's all right. But you must not expect me so early, Hedda.

HEDDA   Oh, you may stop as long—as long as ever you please.

MRS. ELVSTED [*Trying to conceal her anxiety.*]   Well, then, Mr. Lövborg—I shall remain here until you come.

LÖVBORG [*With his hat in his hand.*]   Pray do, Mrs. Elvsted.

BRACK   And now off goes the excursion train, gentlemen! I hope we shall have a lively time, as a certain fair lady puts it.

HEDDA   Ah, if only the fair lady could be present unseen . . . !

BRACK   Why unseen?

HEDDA   In order to hear a little of your liveliness at first hand, Judge Brack.

BRACK [*Laughing.*]   I should not advise the fair lady to try it.

TESMAN [*Also laughing.*]   Come, you're a nice one, Hedda! Fancy that!

BRACK   Well, good-bye, good-bye, ladies.

LÖVBORG [*Bowing.*]   About ten o'clock, then.

[BRACK, LÖVBORG, *and* TESMAN *go out by the hall door. At the same time,* BERTA *enters from the inner room with a lighted lamp, which she places on the drawing room table; she goes out by the way she came.*]

MRS. ELVSTED [*Who has risen and is wandering restlessly about the room.*]   Hedda—Hedda—what will come of all this?

HEDDA   At ten o'clock—he will be here. I can see him already—with vine leaves[8] in his hair—flushed and fearless . . .

MRS. ELVSTED   Oh, I hope he may.

HEDDA   And then, you see—then he will have regained control over himself. Then he will be a free man for all his days.

MRS. ELVSTED   Oh, God!—if he would only come as you see him now!

HEDDA   He will come as I see him—so, and not otherwise! [*Rises and approaches* THEA].   You may doubt him as long as you please; I believe in him. And now we will try . . .

MRS. ELVSTED   You have some hidden motive in this, Hedda!

HEDDA   Yes, I have. I want for once in my life to have power to mold a human destiny.

MRS. ELVSTED   Have you not the power?

8. Bacchus (Greek god of wine) wore vine leaves in his hair. For Hedda, the vine leaves symbolize triumphantly courageous unconventionality.

HEDDA I have not—and have never had it.

MRS. ELVSTED Not your husband's?

HEDDA Do you think that is worth the trouble? Oh, if you could only understand how poor I am. And fate has made you so rich! [*Clasps her passionately in her arms.*] I think I must burn your hair off, after all.

MRS. ELVSTED Let me go! Let me go! I am afraid of you, Hedda!

BERTA [*In the middle doorway.*] Tea is laid in the dining room, ma'am.

HEDDA Very well. We are coming.

MRS. ELVSTED No, no, no! I would rather go home alone! At once!

HEDDA Nonsense! First you shall have a cup of tea, you little stupid. And then—at ten o'clock—Eilert Lövborg will be here—with vine leaves in his hair.

[*She drags* MRS. ELVSTED *almost by force towards the middle doorway.*]

ACT III

SCENE: *The room at the* TESMANS'. *The curtains are drawn over the middle doorway, and also over the glass door. The lamp, half turned down, and with a shade over it, is burning on the table. In the stove, the door of which stands open, there has been a fire, which is now nearly burnt out.* MRS. ELVSTED, *wrapped in a large shawl, and with her feet upon a footrest, sits close to the stove, sunk back in the armchair.* HEDDA, *fully dressed, lies sleeping upon the sofa, with a sofa-blanket over her.*

MRS. ELVSTED [*After a pause, suddenly sits up in her chair, and listens eagerly. Then she sinks back again wearily, moaning to herself.*] Not yet! Oh, God—oh, God—not yet!

[BERTA *slips cautiously in by the hall door. She has a letter in her hand.*]

MRS. ELVSTED [*Turns and whispers eagerly.*] Well—has any one come?

BERTA [*Softly.*] Yes, a girl has just brought this letter.

MRS. ELVSTED [*Quickly, holding out her hand.*] A letter! Give it to me!

BERTA No, it's for Dr. Tesman, ma'am.

MRS. ELVSTED Oh, indeed.

BERTA It was Miss Tesman's servant that brought it. I'll lay it here on the table.

MRS. ELVSTED Yes, do.

BERTA [*Laying down the letter.*] I think I had better put out the lamp. It's smoking.

MRS. ELVSTED Yes, put it out. It must soon be daylight now.

BERTA [*Putting out the lamp.*] It is daylight already, ma'am.

MRS. ELVSTED Yes, broad day! And no one come back yet . . . !

BERTA Lord bless you, ma'am—I guessed how it would be.

MRS. ELVSTED You guessed?

BERTA Yes, when I saw that a certain person had come back to town—and that he went off with them. For we've heard enough about that gentleman before now.

MRS. ELVSTED Don't speak so loud. You will waken Mrs. Tesman.

BERTA [*Looks towards the sofa and sighs.*] No, no—let her sleep, poor thing. Shan't I put some wood on the fire?

MRS. ELVSTED Thanks, not for me.

BERTA Oh, very well.

[*She goes softly out by the hall door.*]

HEDDA [*Is awakened by the shutting of the door, and looks up.*] What's that . . . ?

MRS. ELVSTED It was only the servant . . .

HEDDA [*Looking about her.*] Oh, we're here . . . ! Yes, now I remember. [*Sits erect upon the sofa, stretches herself, and rubs her eyes.*] What o'clock is it, Thea?

MRS. ELVSTED [*Looks at her watch.*] It's past seven.

HEDDA When did Tesman come home?

MRS. ELVSTED He has not come.

HEDDA Not come home yet?

MRS. ELVSTED [*Rising.*] No one has come.

HEDDA Think of our watching and waiting here till four in the morning . . .

MRS. ELVSTED [*Wringing her hands.*] And how I watched and waited for him!

HEDDA [*Yawns, and says with her hand before her mouth.*] Well, well—we might have spared ourselves the trouble.

MRS. ELVSTED Did you get a little sleep?

HEDDA Oh, yes; I believe I have slept pretty well. Have you not?

MRS. ELVSTED Not for a moment. I couldn't, Hedda!—not to save my life.

HEDDA [*Rises and goes towards her.*] There, there, there! There's nothing to be so alarmed about. I understand quite well what has happened.

MRS. ELVSTED Well, what do you think? Won't you tell me?

HEDDA Why, of course, it has been a very late affair at Judge Brack's . . .

MRS. ELVSTED Yes, yes—that is clear enough. But all the same . . .

HEDDA And then, you see, Tesman hasn't cared to come home and ring us up in the middle of the night. [*Laughing.*] Perhaps he wasn't inclined to show himself either—immediately after a jollification.

MRS. ELVSTED But in that case—where can he have gone?

HEDDA Of course, he has gone to his aunts' and slept there. They have his old room ready for him.

MRS. ELVSTED No, he can't be with them; for a letter has just come for him from Miss Tesman. There it lies.

HEDDA Indeed? [*Looks at the address.*] Why, yes, it's addressed in Aunt Julia's own hand. Well, then, he has remained at Judge Brack's. And as for Eilert Lövborg—he is sitting, with vine leaves in his hair, reading his manuscript.

MRS. ELVSTED Oh, Hedda, you are just saying things you don't believe a bit.

HEDDA You really are a little blockhead, Thea.

MRS. ELVSTED Oh, yes, I suppose I am.

HEDDA And how mortally tired you look.

MRS. ELVSTED Yes, I am mortally tired.

HEDDA Well, then, you must do as I tell you. You must go into my room and lie down for a little while.

MRS. ELVSTED Oh, no, no—I shouldn't be able to sleep.

HEDDA I am sure you would.

MRS. ELVSTED Well, but your husband is certain to come soon now; and then I want to know at once . . .

HEDDA I shall take care to let you know when he comes.

MRS. ELVSTED Do you promise me, Hedda?

HEDDA Yes, rely upon me. Just you go in and have a sleep in the meantime.

MRS. ELVSTED Thanks; then I'll try to.

[*She goes off through the inner room.* HEDDA *goes up to the glass door and draws back the curtains. The broad daylight streams into the room. Then she takes a little hand glass from the writing table, looks at herself in it and arranges her hair. Next she goes to the hall door and presses the bell button.* BERTA *presently appears at the hall door.*]

BERTA Did you want anything, ma'am?

HEDDA Yes; you must put some more wood in the stove. I am shivering.

BERTA Bless me—I'll make up the fire at once. [*She rakes the embers together and lays a piece of wood upon them; then stops and listens.*] That was a ring at the front door, ma'am.

HEDDA Then go to the door. I will look after the fire.

BERTA It'll soon burn up.

[*She goes out by the hall door.* HEDDA *kneels on the footrest and lays some more pieces of wood in the stove. After a short pause,* GEORGE TESMAN *enters from the hall. He looks tired and rather serious. He steals on tiptoe towards the middle doorway and is about to slip through the curtains.*]

HEDDA [*At the stove, without looking up.*] Good morning.

TESMAN [*Turns.*] Hedda! [*Approaching her.*] Good heavens —are you up so early? Eh?

HEDDA   Yes, I am up very early this morning.

TESMAN   And I never doubted you were still sound asleep! Fancy that, Hedda!

HEDDA   Don't speak so loud. Mrs. Elvsted is resting in my room.

TESMAN   Has Mrs. Elvsted been here all night?

HEDDA   Yes, since no one came to fetch her.

TESMAN   Ah, to be sure.

HEDDA   [*Closes the door of the stove and rises.*]   Well, did you enjoy yourselves at Judge Brack's?

TESMAN   Have you been anxious about me? Eh?

HEDDA   No, I should never think of being anxious. But I asked if you had enjoyed yourself.

TESMAN   Oh, yes—for once in a way. Especially the beginning of the evening; for then Eilert read me part of his book. We arrived more than an hour too early—fancy that! And Brack had all sorts of arrangements to make—so Eilert read to me.

HEDDA   [*Seating herself by the table on the right.*]   Well? Tell me, then . . .

TESMAN   [*Sitting on a footstool near the stove.*]   Oh, Hedda, you can't conceive what a book that is going to be! I believe it is one of the most remarkable things that have ever been written. Fancy that!

HEDDA   Yes, yes; I don't care about that . . .

TESMAN   I must make a confession to you, Hedda. When he had finished reading—a horrid feeling came over me.

HEDDA   A horrid feeling?

TESMAN   I felt jealous of Eilert for having had it in him to write such a book. Only think, Hedda!

HEDDA   Yes, yes, I am thinking!

TESMAN   And then how pitiful to think that he—with all his gifts—should be irreclaimable, after all.

HEDDA   I suppose you mean that he has more courage than the rest?

TESMAN   No, not at all—I mean that he is incapable of taking his pleasures in moderation.

HEDDA   And what came of it all—in the end?

TESMAN   Well, to tell the truth, I think it might best be described as an orgy, Hedda.

HEDDA   Had he vine leaves in his hair?

TESMAN   Vine leaves? No, I saw nothing of the sort. But he made a long, rambling speech in honor of the woman who had inspired him in his work—that was the phrase he used.

HEDDA   Did he name her?

TESMAN   No, he didn't; but I can't help thinking he meant Mrs. Elvsted. You may be sure he did.

HEDDA   Well—where did you part from him?

TESMAN   On the way to town. We broke up—the last of us at any rate—all together; and Brack came with us to get a breath of fresh air. And then, you see, we agreed to take Eilert home; for he had had far more than was good for him.

HEDDA   I daresay.

TESMAN   But now comes the strange part of it, Hedda; or, I should rather say, the melancholy part of it. I declare I am almost ashamed—on Eilert's account—to tell you . . .

HEDDA   Oh, go on . . . !

TESMAN   Well, as we were getting near town, you see, I happened to drop a little behind the others. Only for a minute or two—fancy that!

HEDDA   Yes, yes, yes, but . . . ?

TESMAN   And then, as I hurried after them—what do you think I found by the wayside? Eh?

HEDDA   Oh, how should I know!

TESMAN   You mustn't speak of it to a soul, Hedda! Do you hear? Promise me, for Eilert's sake. [Draws a parcel, wrapped in paper, from his coat pocket.]   Fancy, dear—I found this.

HEDDA   Is not that the parcel he had with him yesterday?

TESMAN   Yes, it is the whole of his precious, irreplaceable manuscript! And he had gone and lost it, and knew nothing about it. Only fancy, Hedda! So deplorably . . .

HEDDA   But why did you not give him back the parcel at once?

TESMAN   I didn't dare to—in the state he was then in . . .

HEDDA   Did you not tell any of the others that you had found it?

TESMAN   Oh, far from it! You can surely understand that, for Eilert's sake, I wouldn't do that.

HEDDA   So no one knows that Eilert Lövborg's manuscript is in your possession?

TESMAN   No. And no one must know it.

HEDDA   Then what did you say to him afterwards?

TESMAN   I didn't talk to him again at all; for when we got in among the streets, he and two or three of the others gave us the slip and disappeared. Fancy that!

HEDDA   Indeed! They must have taken him home then.

TESMAN   Yes, so it would appear. And Brack, too, left us.

HEDDA   And what have you been doing with yourself since?

TESMAN   Well, I and some of the others went home with one of the party, a jolly fellow, and took our morning coffee with him; or perhaps I should rather call it our night coffee—eh? But now, when I have rested a little, and given Eilert, poor fellow, time to have his sleep out, I must take this back to him.

HEDDA [*Holds out her hand for the packet.*]   No—don't give it to him! Not in such a hurry, I mean. Let me read it first.

TESMAN   No, my dearest Hedda, I mustn't, I really mustn't.

HEDDA   You must not?

TESMAN   No—for you can imagine what a state of despair he will be in when he wakens and misses the manuscript. He has no copy of it, you must know! He told me so.

HEDDA [*Looking searchingly at him.*]   Can such a thing not be reproduced? Written over again?

TESMAN   No, I don't think that would be possible. For the inspiration, you see . . .

HEDDA   Yes, yes—I suppose it depends on that . . . [*Lightly.*] But, by the by—here is a letter for you.

TESMAN   Fancy . . . !

HEDDA [*Handing it to him.*]   It came early this morning.

TESMAN   It's from Aunt Julia! What can it be? [*He lays the packet on the other footstool, opens the letter, runs his eye through it, and jumps up.*]   Oh, Hedda—she says that poor Aunt Rina is dying!

HEDDA   Well, we were prepared for that.

TESMAN   And that if I want to see her again, I must make haste. I'll run in to them at once.

HEDDA   [*Suppressing a smile.*]   Will you run?

TESMAN   Oh, my dearest Hedda—if you could only make up your mind to come with me! Just think!

HEDDA   [*Rises and says wearily, repelling the idea.*]   No, no, don't ask me. I will not look upon sickness and death. I loathe all sorts of ugliness.

TESMAN   Well, well, then . . . ! [*Bustling around.*]   My hat . . . ? My overcoat . . . ? Oh, in the hall . . . I do hope I mayn't come too late, Hedda! Eh?

HEDDA   Oh, if you run . . .

[BERTA *appears at the hall door.*]

BERTA   Judge Brack is at the door, and wishes to know if he may come in.

TESMAN   At this time! No, I can't possibly see him.

HEDDA   But I can. [*To* BERTA.]   Ask Judge Brack to come in. [BERTA *goes out.*]

HEDDA   [*Quickly, whispering.*]   The parcel, Tesman! [*She snatches it up from the stool.*]

TESMAN   Yes, give it to me!

HEDDA   No, no, I will keep it till you come back.

[*She goes to the writing table and places it in the bookcase.* TESMAN *stands in a flurry of haste, and cannot get his gloves on.* JUDGE BRACK *enters from the hall.*]

HEDDA   [*Nodding to him.*]   You are an early bird, I must say.

BRACK   Yes, don't you think so? [*To* TESMAN.]   Are you on the move, too?

TESMAN   Yes, I must rush off to my aunts'. Fancy—the invalid one is lying at death's door, poor creature.

BRACK   Dear me, is she indeed? Then on no account let me detain you. At such a critical moment . . .

TESMAN   Yes, I must really rush . . . Good-bye! Good-bye! [*He hastens out by the hall door.*]

HEDDA   [*Approaching.*]   You seem to have made a particularly lively night of it at your rooms, Judge Brack.

BRACK   I assure you I have not had my clothes off, Mrs. Hedda.

HEDDA Not you, either?

BRACK No, as you may see. But what has Tesman been telling you of the night's adventures?

HEDDA Oh, some tiresome story. Only that they went and had coffee somewhere or other.

BRACK I have heard about that coffee party already. Eilert Lövborg was not with them, I fancy?

HEDDA No, they had taken him home before that.

BRACK Tesman too?

HEDDA No, but some of the others, he said.

BRACK [Smiling.] George Tesman is really an ingenuous creature, Mrs. Hedda.

HEDDA Yes, heaven knows he is. Then is there something behind all this?

BRACK Yes, perhaps there may be.

HEDDA Well then, sit down, my dear Judge, and tell your story in comfort.

[She seats herself to the left of the table. BRACK sits near her, at the long side of the table.]

HEDDA Now then?

BRACK I had special reasons for keeping track of my guests— or rather of some of my guests—last night.

HEDDA Of Eilert Lövborg among the rest, perhaps?

BRACK Frankly—yes.

HEDDA Now you make me really curious . . .

BRACK Do you know where he and one or two of the others finished the night, Mrs. Hedda?

HEDDA If it is not quite unmentionable, tell me.

BRACK Oh no, it's not at all unmentionable. Well, they put in an appearance at a particularly animated soirée.

HEDDA Of the lively kind?

BRACK Of the very liveliest . . .

HEDDA Tell me more of this, Judge Brack . . .

BRACK Lövborg, as well as the others, had been invited in advance. I knew all about it. But he had declined the invitation; for now, as you know, he has become a new man.

HEDDA Up at the Elvsteds', yes. But he went after all, then?

BRACK Well, you see, Mrs. Hedda—unhappily the spirit moved him at my rooms last evening . . .

HEDDA Yes, I hear he found inspiration.

BRACK Pretty violent inspiration. Well, I fancy that altered his purpose; for we menfolk are unfortunately not always so firm in our principles as we ought to be.

HEDDA Oh, I am sure you are an exception, Judge Brack. But as to Lövborg . . . ?

BRACK To make a long story short—he landed at last in Mademoiselle Diana's rooms.

HEDDA Mademoiselle Diana's?

BRACK It was Mademoiselle Diana that was giving the *soirée*, to a select circle of her admirers and her lady friends.

HEDDA Is she a red-haired woman?

BRACK Precisely.

HEDDA A sort of a—singer?

BRACK Oh yes—in her leisure moments. And moreover a mighty huntress—of men—Mrs. Hedda. You have no doubt heard of her. Eilert Lövborg was one of her most enthusiastic protectors —in the days of his glory.

HEDDA And how did all this end?

BRACK Far from amicably, it appears. After a most tender meeting, they seem to have come to blows . . .

HEDDA Lövborg and she?

BRACK Yes. He accused her or her friends of having robbed him. He declared that his pocketbook had disappeared—and other things as well. In short, he seems to have made a furious disturbance.

HEDDA And what came of it all?

BRACK It came to a general scrimmage, in which the ladies as well as the gentlemen took part. Fortunately the police at last appeared on the scene.

HEDDA The police too?

BRACK Yes. I fancy it will prove a costly frolic for Eilert Lövborg, crazy being that he is.

HEDDA How so?

BRACK   He seems to have made a violent resistance—to have hit one of the constables on the head and torn the coat off his back. So they had to march him off to the police station with the rest.

HEDDA   How have you learnt all this?

BRACK   From the police themselves.

HEDDA   [Gazing straight before her.]   So that is what happened. Then he had no vine leaves in his hair.

BRACK   Vine leaves, Mrs. Hedda?

HEDDA   [Changing her tone.]   But tell me now, Judge—what is your real reason for tracking out Eilert Lövborg's movements so carefully?

BRACK   In the first place, it could not be entirely indifferent to me if it should appear in the police court that he came straight from my house.

HEDDA   Will the matter come into court then?

BRACK   Of course. However, I should scarcely have troubled so much about that. But I thought that, as a friend of the family, it was my duty to supply you and Tesman with a full account of his nocturnal exploits.

HEDDA   Why so, Judge Brack?

BRACK   Why, because I have a shrewd suspicion that he intends to use you as a sort of blind.

HEDDA   Oh, how can you think such a thing!

BRACK   Good heavens, Mrs. Hedda—we have eyes in our head. Mark my words! This Mrs. Elvsted will be in no hurry to leave town again.

HEDDA   Well, even if there should be anything between them, I suppose there are plenty of other places where they could meet.

BRACK   Not a single home. Henceforth, as before, every respectable house will be closed against Eilert Lövborg.

HEDDA   And so ought mine to be, you mean?

BRACK   Yes. I confess it would be more than painful to me if this personage were to be made free of your house. How superfluous, how intrusive, he would be, if he were to force his way into . . .

HEDDA . . . into the triangle?

BRACK Precisely. It would simply mean that I should find myself homeless.

HEDDA [*Looks at him with a smile.*] So you want to be the one cock in the basket [9]—that is your aim.

BRACK [*Nods slowly and lowers his voice.*] Yes, that is my aim. And for that I will fight—with every weapon I can command.

HEDDA [*Her smile vanishing.*] I see you are a dangerous person—when it comes to the point.

BRACK Do you think so?

HEDDA I am beginning to think so. And I am exceedingly glad to think—that you have no sort of hold over me.

BRACK [*Laughing equivocally.*] Well, well, Mrs. Hedda—perhaps you are right there. If I had, who knows what I might be capable of?

HEDDA Come, come now, Judge Brack! That sounds almost like a threat.

BRACK [*Rising.*] Oh, not at all! The triangle, you know, ought, if possible, to be spontaneously constructed.

HEDDA There I agree with you.

BRACK Well, now I have said all I had to say; and I had better be getting back to town. Good-bye, Mrs. Hedda. [*He goes towards the glass door.*]

HEDDA [*Rising.*] Are you going through the garden?

BRACK Yes, it's a short cut for me.

HEDDA And then it is a back way, too.

BRACK Quite so. I have no objection to back ways. They may be piquant enough at times.

HEDDA When there is shooting practice going on, you mean?

BRACK [*In the doorway, laughing to her.*] Oh, people don't shoot their tame poultry, I fancy.

HEDDA [*Also laughing.*] Oh no, when there is only one cock in the basket . . .

[*They exchange laughing nods of farewell. He goes. She closes the door behind him.* HEDDA, *who has become quite serious, stands*

---

9. A proverbial saying in Norway.

for a moment looking out. Presently she goes and peeps through the curtain over the middle doorway. Then she goes to the writing table, takes LÖVBORG'S *packet out of the bookcase, and is on the point of looking through its contents.* BERTA *is heard speaking loudly in the hall.* HEDDA *turns and listens. Then she hastily locks up the packet in the drawer, and lays the key on the inkstand.* EILERT LÖVBORG, *with his greatcoat on and his hat in his hand, tears open the hall door. He looks somewhat confused and irritated.*]

LÖVBORG [*Looking towards the hall.*]   And I tell you I must and will come in! There!

[*He closes the door, turns, sees* HEDDA, *at once regains his self-control, and bows.*]

HEDDA [*At the writing table.*]   Well, Mr. Lövborg, this is rather a late hour to call for Thea.

LÖVBORG   You mean rather an early hour to call on you. Pray pardon me.

HEDDA   How do you know that she is still here?

LÖVBORG   They told me at her lodgings that she had been out all night.

HEDDA [*Going to the oval table.*]   Did you notice anything about the people of the house when they said that?

LÖVBORG [*Looks inquiringly at her.*]   Notice anything about them?

HEDDA   I mean, did they seem to think it odd?

LÖVBORG [*Suddenly understanding.*]   Oh yes, of course! I am dragging her down with me! However, I didn't notice anything.— I suppose Tesman is not up yet?

HEDDA   No—I think not . . .

LÖVBORG   When did he come home?

HEDDA   Very late.

LÖVBORG   Did he tell you anything?

HEDDA   Yes, I gathered that you had had an exceedingly jolly evening at Judge Brack's.

LÖVBORG   Nothing more?

HEDDA   I don't think so. However, I was so dreadfully sleepy . . .

[MRS. ELVSTED *enters through the curtains of the middle doorway.*]

MRS. ELVSTED [*Going towards him.*] Ah, Lövborg! At last . . . !

LÖVBORG Yes, at last. And too late!

MRS. ELVSTED [*Looks anxiously at him.*] What is too late?

LÖVBORG Everything is too late now. It is all over with me.

MRS. ELVSTED Oh no, no—don't say that!

LÖVBORG You will say the same when you hear . . .

MRS. ELVSTED I won't hear anything!

HEDDA Perhaps you would prefer to talk to her alone? If so, I will leave you.

LÖVBORG No, stay—you too. I beg you to stay.

MRS. ELVSTED Yes, but I won't hear anything, I tell you.

LÖVBORG It is not last night's adventures that I want to talk about.

MRS. ELVSTED What is it then . . . ?

LÖVBORG I want to say that now our ways must part.

MRS. ELVSTED Part!

HEDDA [*Involuntarily.*] I knew it!

LÖVBORG You can be of no more service to me, Thea.

MRS. ELVSTED How can you stand there and say that! No more service to you! Am I not to help you now, as before? Are we not to go on working together?

LÖVBORG Henceforward I shall do no work.

MRS. ELVSTED [*Despairingly.*] Then what am I to do with my life?

LÖVBORG You must try to live your life as if you had never known me.

MRS. ELVSTED But you know I cannot do that!

LÖVBORG Try if you cannot, Thea. You must go home again . . .

MRS. ELVSTED [*In vehement protest.*] Never in this world! Where you are, there will I be also! I will not let myself be driven away like this! I will remain here! I will be with you when the book appears.

HEDDA [*Half aloud, in suspense.*] Ah yes—the book!

LÖVBORG [*Looks at her.*]   My book and Thea's; for that is what it is.

MRS. ELVSTED   Yes, I feel that it is. And that is why I have a right to be with you when it appears! I will see with my own eyes how respect and honor pour in upon you afresh. And the happiness—the happiness—oh, I must share it with you!

LÖVBORG   Thea—our book will never appear.

HEDDA   Ah!

MRS. ELVSTED   Never appear!

LÖVBORG   Can never appear.

MRS. ELVSTED [*In agonized foreboding.*]   Lövborg—what have you done with the manuscript?

HEDDA [*Looks anxiously at him.*]   Yes, the manuscript . . .

MRS. ELVSTED   Where is it?

LÖVBORG   Oh Thea—don't ask me about it!

MRS. ELVSTED   Yes, yes, I will know. I demand to be told at once.

LÖVBORG   The manuscript . . . Well then—I have torn the manuscript into a thousand pieces.

MRS. ELVSTED [*Shrieks.*]   Oh no, no . . . !

HEDDA [*Involuntarily.*]   But that's not . . .

LÖVBORG [*Looks at her.*]   Not true, you think?

HEDDA [*Collecting herself.*]   Oh well, of course—since you say so. But it sounded so improbable . . .

LÖVBORG   It is true, all the same.

MRS. ELVSTED [*Wringing her hands.*]   Oh God—oh God, Hedda—torn his own work to pieces!

LÖVBORG   I have torn my own life to pieces. So why should I not tear my lifework too . . . ?

MRS. ELVSTED   And you did this last night?

LÖVBORG   Yes, I tell you! Tore it into a thousand pieces—and scattered them on the fjord—far out. There there is cool sea water at any rate—let them drift upon it—drift with the current and the wind. And then presently they will sink—deeper and deeper —as I shall, Thea.

MRS. ELVSTED   Do you know, Lövborg, that what you have

HEDDA   No, no . . . But—where is it then?

LÖVBORG   I have destroyed it none the less—utterly destroyed it, Hedda!

HEDDA   I don't understand.

LÖVBORG   Thea said that what I had done seemed to her like a child murder.

HEDDA   Yes, so she said.

LÖVBORG   But to kill his child—that is not the worst thing a father can do to it.

HEDDA   Not the worst?

LÖVBORG   No. I wanted to spare Thea from hearing the worst.

HEDDA   Then what is the worst?

LÖVBORG   Suppose now, Hedda, that a man—in the small hours of the morning—came home to his child's mother after a night of riot and debauchery, and said: "Listen—I have been here and there—in this place and in that. And I have taken our child with me—to this place and to that. And I have lost the child—utterly lost it. The devil knows into what hands it may have fallen—who may have had their clutches on it."

HEDDA   Well—but when all is said and done, you know—this was only a book . . .

LÖVBORG   Thea's pure soul was in that book.

HEDDA   Yes, so I understand.

LÖVBORG   And you can understand, too, that for her and me together no future is possible.

HEDDA   What path do you mean to take then?

LÖVBORG   None. I will only try to make an end of it all—the sooner the better.

HEDDA   [A step nearer him.] Eilert Lövborg—listen to me. Will you not try to—to do it beautifully?

LÖVBORG   Beautifully? [Smiling.] With vine leaves in my hair, as you used to dream in the old days . . . ?

HEDDA   No, no. I have lost my faith in the vine leaves. But beautifully nevertheless! For once in a way! Good-bye! You must go now—and do not come here any more.

LÖVBORG   Good-bye, Mrs. Tesman. And give George Tesman my love. [He is on the point of going.]

HEDDA   No, wait! I must give you a memento to take with you.
[*She goes to the writing table and opens the drawer and the
pistol case; then returns to* LÖVBORG *with one of the pistols.*]

LÖVBORG [*Looks at her.*] This? Is this the memento?

HEDDA [*Nodding slowly.*] Do you recognize it? It was aimed
at you once.

LÖVBORG You should have used it then.

HEDDA Take it—and do you use it now.

LÖVBORG [*Puts the pistol in his breast pocket.*] Thanks!

HEDDA And beautifully, Eilert Lövborg. Promise me that!

LÖVBORG Good-bye, Hedda Gabler.

[*He goes out by the hall door.* HEDDA *listens for a moment at the
door. Then she goes up to the writing table, takes out the packet
of manuscript, peeps under the cover, draws a few of the sheets
half out, and looks at them. Next she goes over and seats herself in the armchair beside the stove, with the packet in her lap.
Presently she opens the stove door, and then the packet.*]

HEDDA [*Throws one of the quires into the fire and whispers to
herself.*] Now I am burning your child, Thea!—Burning it,
curly-locks! [*Throwing one or two more quires into the stove.*]
Your child and Eilert Lövborg's. [*Throws the rest in.*] I am
burning—I am burning your child.

ACT IV

HHHHHHHHHHHHHHHHHH

SCENE: *The same rooms at the* TESMANS'. *It is evening. The drawing room is in darkness. The back room is lighted by the hanging
lamp over the table. The curtains over the glass door are drawn
close.* HEDDA, *dressed in black, walks to and fro in the dark room.
Then she goes into the back room and disappears for a moment
to the left. She is heard to strike a few chords on the piano. Presently she comes in sight again, and returns to the drawing room.*
BERTA *enters from the right, through the inner room, with a lighted*

lamp, which she places on the table in front of the corner settee in the drawing room. Her eyes are red with weeping, and she has black ribbons in her cap. She goes quietly and circumspectly out to the right. HEDDA *goes up to the glass door, lifts the curtain a little aside, and looks out into the darkness. Shortly afterwards,* MISS TESMAN, *in mourning, with a bonnet and veil on, comes in from the hall.* HEDDA *goes towards her and holds out her hand.*

MISS TESMAN   Yes, Hedda, here I am, in mourning and forlorn; for now my poor sister has at last found peace.

HEDDA   I have heard the news already, as you see. Tesman sent me a card.

MISS TESMAN   Yes, he promised me he would. But nevertheless I thought that to Hedda—here in the house of life—I ought myself to bring the tidings of death.

HEDDA   That was very kind of you.

MISS TESMAN   Ah, Rina ought not to have left us just now. This is not the time for Hedda's house to be a house of mourning.

HEDDA   [*Changing the subject.*]   She died quite peacefully, did she not, Miss Tesman?

MISS TESMAN   Oh, her end was so calm, so beautiful. And then she had the unspeakable happiness of seeing George once more—and bidding him good-bye. Has he not come home yet?

HEDDA   No. He wrote that he might be detained. But won't you sit down?

MISS TESMAN   No thank you, my dear, dear Hedda. I should like to, but I have so much to do. I must prepare my dear one for her rest as well as I can. She shall go to her grave looking her best.

HEDDA   Can I not help you in any way?

MISS TESMAN   Oh, you must not think of it! Hedda Tesman must have no hand in such mournful work. Nor let her thoughts dwell on it either—not at this time.

HEDDA   One is not always mistress of one's thoughts . . .

MISS TESMAN   [*Continuing.*]   Ah yes, it is the way of the world. At home we shall be sewing a shroud; and here there will soon be sewing too, I suppose—but of another sort, thank God!

[GEORGE TESMAN *enters by the hall door.*]

HEDDA   Ah, you have come at last!

TESMAN   You here, Aunt Julia? With Hedda? Fancy that!

MISS TESMAN   I was just going, my dear boy. Well, have you done all you promised?

TESMAN   No; I'm really afraid I have forgotten half of it. I must come to you again tomorrow. Today my brain is all in a whirl. I can't keep my thoughts together.

MISS TESMAN   Why, my dear George, you mustn't take it in this way.

TESMAN   Mustn't . . . ? How do you mean?

MISS TESMAN   Even in your sorrow you must rejoice, as I do— rejoice that she is at rest.

TESMAN   Oh yes, yes—you are thinking of Aunt Rina.

HEDDA   You will feel lonely now, Miss Tesman.

MISS TESMAN   Just at first, yes. But that will not last very long, I hope. I daresay I shall soon find an occupant for poor Rina's little room.

TESMAN   Indeed? Who do you think will take it? Eh?

MISS TESMAN   Oh, there's always some poor invalid or other in want of nursing, unfortunately.

HEDDA   Would you really take such a burden upon you again?

MISS TESMAN   A burden! Heaven forgive you, child—it has been no burden to me.

HEDDA   But suppose you had a total stranger on your hands . . .

MISS TESMAN   Oh, one soon makes friends with sick folk; and it's such an absolute necessity for me to have some one to live for. Well, heaven be praised, there may soon be something in *this* house, too, to keep an old aunt busy.

HEDDA   Oh, don't trouble about anything here.

TESMAN   Yes, just fancy what a nice time we three might have together, if . . . ?

HEDDA   If . . . ?

TESMAN   [*Uneasily.*]   Oh, nothing. It will all come right. Let us hope so—eh?

MISS TESMAN   Well, well, I daresay you two want to talk to each other. [*Smiling.*] And perhaps Hedda may have something to tell you too, George. Good-bye! I must go home to Rina. [*Turning at the door.*] How strange it is to think that now Rina is with me and with my poor brother as well!

TESMAN Yes, fancy that, Aunt Julia! Eh? [MISS TESMAN *goes out by the hall door.*]

HEDDA [*Follows* TESMAN *coldly and searchingly with her eyes.*] I almost believe your Aunt Rina's death affects you more than it does your Aunt Julia.

TESMAN Oh, it's not that alone. It's Eilert I am so terribly uneasy about.

HEDDA [*Quickly.*] Is there anything new about him?

TESMAN I looked in at his rooms this afternoon, intending to tell him the manuscript was in safe keeping.

HEDDA Well, did you not find him?

TESMAN No. He wasn't at home. But afterwards I met Mrs. Elvsted, and she told me that he had been here early this morning.

HEDDA Yes, directly after you had gone.

TESMAN And he said that he had torn his manuscript to pieces —eh?

HEDDA Yes, so he declared.

TESMAN Why, good heavens, he must have been completely out of his mind! And I suppose you thought it best not to give it back to him, Hedda?

HEDDA No, he did not get it.

TESMAN But of course you told him that we had it?

HEDDA No. [*Quickly.*] Did you tell Mrs. Elvsted?

TESMAN No; I thought I had better not. But you ought to have told him. Fancy, if, in desperation, he should go and do himself some injury! Let me have the manuscript, Hedda! I will take it to him at once. Where is it?

HEDDA [*Cold and immovable, leaning on the armchair.*] I have not got it.

TESMAN Have not got it? What in the world do you mean?

HEDDA I have burnt it—every line of it.

TESMAN [*With a violent movement of terror.*] Burnt! Burnt Eilert's manuscript!

HEDDA Don't scream so. The servant might hear you.

TESMAN Burnt! Why, good God . . . ! No, no, no! It's impossible!

HEDDA It is so, nevertheless.

TESMAN Do you know what you have done, Hedda? It's unlawful appropriation of lost property. Fancy that! Just ask Judge Brack, and he'll tell you what it is.

HEDDA I advise you not to speak of it—either to Judge Brack, or to any one else.

TESMAN But how could you do anything so unheard of? What put it into your head? What possessed you? Answer me that —eh?

HEDDA [Suppressing an almost imperceptible smile.] I did it for your sake, George.

TESMAN For my sake!

HEDDA This morning, when you told me about what he had read to you . . .

TESMAN Yes, yes—what then?

HEDDA You acknowledged that you envied him his work.

TESMAN Oh, of course I didn't mean that literally.

HEDDA No matter—I could not bear the idea that any one should throw you into the shade.

TESMAN [In an outburst of mingled doubt and joy.] Hedda! Oh, is this true? But—but—I never knew you to show your love like that before. Fancy that!

HEDDA Well, I may as well tell you that—just at this time . . . [Impatiently, breaking off.] No, no; you can ask Aunt Julia. She will tell you, fast enough.

TESMAN Oh, I almost think I understand you, Hedda! [Clasps his hands together.] Great heavens! do you really mean it? Eh?

HEDDA Don't shout so. The servant might hear.

TESMAN [Laughing in irrepressible glee.] The servant! Why, how absurd you are, Hedda. It's only my old Berta! Why, I'll tell Berta myself.

HEDDA [Clenching her hands together in desperation.] Oh, it is killing me—it is killing me, all this!

TESMAN What is, Hedda? Eh?

HEDDA [*Coldly, controlling herself.*] All this—absurdity—
George.

TESMAN Absurdity! Do you see anything absurd in my being
overjoyed at the news! But after all—perhaps I had better not say
anything to Berta.

HEDDA Oh . . . why not that too?

TESMAN No, no, not yet! But I must certainly tell Aunt Julia.
And then that you have begun to call me George too! Fancy that!
Oh, Aunt Julia will be so happy—so happy!

HEDDA When she hears that I have burnt Eilert Lövborg's
manuscript—for your sake?

TESMAN No, by the by—that affair of the manuscript—of
course nobody must know about that. But that you love me so
much, Hedda—Aunt Julia must really share my joy in that! I
wonder, now, whether this sort of thing is usual in young wives?
Eh?

HEDDA I think you had better ask Aunt Julia that question too.

TESMAN I will indeed, some time or other. [*Looks uneasy and
downcast again.*] And yet the manuscript—the manuscript! Good
God! It is terrible to think what will become of poor Eilert now.

[MRS. ELVSTED, *dressed as in the first act, with hat and cloak,
enters by the hall door.*]

MRS. ELVSTED [*Greets them hurriedly, and says in evident
agitation.*] Oh, dear Hedda, forgive my coming again.

HEDDA What is the matter with you, Thea?

TESMAN Something about Eilert Lövborg again—eh?

MRS. ELVSTED Yes! I am dreadfully afraid some misfortune has
happened to him.

HEDDA [*Seizes her arm.*] Ah—do you think so?

TESMAN Why, good Lord—what makes you think that, Mrs.
Elvsted?

MRS. ELVSTED I heard them talking at my boardinghouse—just
as I came in. Oh, the most incredible rumors are afloat about him
today.

TESMAN Yes, fancy, so I heard too! And I can bear witness that
he went straight home to bed last night. Fancy that!

HEDDA Well, what did they say at the boardinghouse?

MRS. ELVSTED Oh, I couldn't make out anything clearly. Either they knew nothing definite, or else . . . They stopped talking when they saw me; and I did not dare to ask.

TESMAN [*Moving about uneasily.*] We must hope—we must hope that you misunderstood them, Mrs. Elvsted.

MRS. ELVSTED No, no; I am sure it was of him they were talking. And I heard something about the hospital or . . .

TESMAN The hospital?

HEDDA No—surely that cannot be!

MRS. ELVSTED Oh, I was in such mortal terror! I went to his lodgings and asked for him there.

HEDDA You could make up your mind to that, Thea!

MRS. ELVSTED What else could I do? I really could bear the suspense no longer.

TESMAN But you didn't find him either—eh?

MRS. ELVSTED No. And the people knew nothing about him. He hadn't been home since yesterday afternoon, they said.

TESMAN Yesterday! Fancy, how could they say that?

MRS. ELVSTED Oh, I am sure something terrible must have happened to him.

TESMAN Hedda dear—how would it be if I were to go and make inquiries . . . ?

HEDDA No, no—don't mix yourself up in this affair.

[JUDGE BRACK, *with his hat in his hand, enters by the hall door, which* BERTA *opens, and closes behind him. He looks grave and bows in silence.*]

TESMAN Oh, is that you, my dear Judge? Eh?

BRACK Yes. It was imperative I should see you this evening.

TESMAN I can see you have heard the news about Aunt Rina?

BRACK Yes, that among other things.

TESMAN Isn't it sad—eh?

BRACK Well, my dear Tesman, that depends on how you look at it.

TESMAN [*Looks doubtfully at him.*] Has anything else happened?

BRACK Yes.

HEDDA [*In suspense.*] Anything sad, Judge Brack?

BRACK That, too, depends on how you look at it, Mrs. Tesman.

MRS. ELVSTED [*Unable to restrain her anxiety.*] Oh! it is something about Eilert Lövborg!

BRACK [*With a glance at her.*] What makes you think that, Madam? Perhaps you have already heard something . . . ?

MRS. ELVSTED [*In confusion.*] No, nothing at all, but . . .

TESMAN Oh, for heaven's sake, tell us!

BRACK [*Shrugging his shoulders.*] Well, I regret to say Eilert Lövborg has been taken to the hospital. He is lying at the point of death.

MRS. ELVSTED [*Shrieks.*] Oh God! oh God . . . !

TESMAN To the hospital! And at the point of death!

HEDDA [*Involuntarily.*] So soon then . . .

MRS. ELVSTED [*Wailing.*] And we parted in anger, Hedda!

HEDDA [*Whispers.*] Thea—Thea—be careful!

MRS. ELVSTED [*Not heeding her.*] I must go to him! I must see him alive!

BRACK It is useless, Madam. No one will be admitted.

MRS. ELVSTED Oh, at least tell me what has happened to him? What is it?

TESMAN You don't mean to say that he has himself . . . Eh?

HEDDA Yes, I am sure he has.

TESMAN Hedda, how can you . . . ?

BRACK [*Keeping his eyes fixed upon her.*] Unfortunately you have guessed quite correctly, Mrs. Tesman.

MRS. ELVSTED Oh, how horrible!

TESMAN Himself, then! Fancy that!

HEDDA Shot himself!

BRACK Rightly guessed again, Mrs. Tesman.

MRS. ELVSTED [*With an effort at self-control.*] When did it happen, Mr. Brack?

BRACK This afternoon—between three and four.

TESMAN But, good Lord, where did he do it? Eh?

BRACK [*With some hesitation.*] Where? Well—I suppose at his lodgings.

MRS. ELVSTED No, that cannot be; for I was there between six and seven.

BRACK   Well then, somewhere else. I don't know exactly. I only know that he was found . . . He had shot himself—in the breast.

MRS. ELVSTED   Oh, how terrible! That he should die like that!

HEDDA   [*To* BRACK.]   Was it in the breast?

BRACK   Yes—as I told you.

HEDDA   Not in the temple?

BRACK   In the breast, Mrs. Tesman.

HEDDA   Well, well—the breast is a good place, too.

BRACK   How do you mean, Mrs. Tesman?

HEDDA   [*Evasively.*]   Oh, nothing—nothing.

TESMAN   And the wound is dangerous, you say—eh?

BRACK   Absolutely mortal. The end has probably come by this time.

MRS. ELVSTED   Yes, yes, I feel it. The end! The end! Oh, Hedda . . . !

TESMAN   But tell me, how have you learnt all this?

BRACK   [*Curtly.*]   Through one of the police. A man I had some business with.

HEDDA   [*In a clear voice.*]   At last a deed worth doing!

TESMAN   [*Terrified.*]   Good heavens, Hedda! what are you saying?

HEDDA   I say there is beauty in this.

BRACK   H'm, Mrs. Tesman . . .

TESMAN   Beauty! Fancy that!

MRS. ELVSTED   Oh, Hedda, how can you talk of beauty in such an act!

HEDDA   Eilert Lövborg has himself made up his account with life. He has had the courage to do—the one right thing.

MRS. ELVSTED   No, you must never think that was how it happened! It must have been in delirium that he did it.

TESMAN   In despair!

HEDDA   That he did not. I am certain of that.

MRS. ELVSTED   Yes, yes! In delirium! Just as when he tore up our manuscript.

BRACK   [*Starting.*]   The manuscript? Has he torn that up?

MRS. ELVSTED   Yes, last night.

TESMAN [*Whispers softly.*] Oh, Hedda, we shall never get over this.

BRACK H'm, very extraordinary.

TESMAN [*Moving about the room.*] To think of Eilert going out of the world in this way! And not leaving behind him the book that would have immortalized his name . . .

MRS. ELVSTED Oh, if only it could be put together again!

TESMAN Yes, if it only could! I don't know what I would not give . . .

MRS. ELVSTED Perhaps it can, Mr. Tesman.

TESMAN What do you mean?

MRS. ELVSTED [*Searches in the pocket of her dress.*] Look here. I have kept all the loose notes he used to dictate from.

HEDDA [*A step forward.*] Ah . . . !

TESMAN You have kept them, Mrs. Elvsted! Eh?

MRS. ELVSTED Yes, I have them here. I put them in my pocket when I left home. Here they still are . . .

TESMAN Oh, do let me see them!

MRS. ELVSTED [*Hands him a bundle of papers.*] But they are in such disorder—all mixed up.

TESMAN Fancy, if we could make something out of them, after all! Perhaps if we two put our heads together . . .

MRS. ELVSTED Oh yes, at least let us try . . .

TESMAN We will manage it! We must! I will dedicate my life to this task.

HEDDA You, George? Your life?

TESMAN Yes, or rather all the time I can spare. My own collections must wait in the meantime. Hedda—you understand, eh? I owe this to Eilert's memory.

HEDDA Perhaps.

TESMAN And so, my dear Mrs. Elvsted, we will give our whole minds to it. There is no use in brooding over what can't be undone—eh? We must try to control our grief as much as possible, and . . .

MRS. ELVSTED Yes, yes, Mr. Tesman, I will do the best I can.

TESMAN Well then, come here. I can't rest until we have looked through the notes. Where shall we sit? Here? No, in there, in the back room. Excuse me, my dear Judge. Come with me, Mrs. Elvsted.

MRS. ELVSTED Oh, if only it were possible!

[TESMAN *and* MRS. ELVSTED *go into the back room. She takes off her hat and cloak. They both sit at the table under the hanging lamp, and are soon deep in an eager examination of the papers.* HEDDA *crosses to the stove and sits in the armchair. Presently* BRACK *goes up to her.*]

HEDDA [*In a low voice.*] Oh, what a sense of freedom it gives one, this act of Eilert Lövborg's.

BRACK Freedom, Mrs. Hedda? Well, of course, it is a release for him . . .

HEDDA I mean for me. It gives me a sense of freedom to know that a deed of deliberate courage is still possible in this world— a deed of spontaneous beauty.

BRACK [*Smiling.*] H'm—my dear Mrs. Hedda . . .

HEDDA Oh, I know what you are going to say. For you are a kind of specialist, too, like—you know!

BRACK [*Looking hard at her.*] Eilert Lövborg was more to you than perhaps you are willing to admit to yourself. Am I wrong?

HEDDA I don't answer such questions. I only know that Eilert Lövborg has had the courage to live his life after his own fashion. And then—the last great act, with its beauty! Ah! that he should have the will and the strength to turn away from the banquet of life—so early.

BRACK I am sorry, Mrs. Hedda, but I fear I must dispel an amiable illusion.

HEDDA Illusion?

BRACK Which could not have lasted long in any case.

HEDDA What do you mean?

BRACK Eilert Lövborg did not shoot himself—voluntarily.

HEDDA Not voluntarily!

BRACK No. The thing did not happen exactly as I told it.

HEDDA [*In suspense.*] Have you concealed something? What is it?

BRACK For poor Mrs. Elvsted's sake I idealized the facts a little.

HEDDA What are the facts?

BRACK   First, that he is already dead.

HEDDA   At the hospital?

BRACK   Yes—without regaining consciousness.

HEDDA   What more have you concealed?

BRACK   This—the event did not happen at his lodgings.

HEDDA   Oh, that can make no difference.

BRACK   Perhaps it may. For I must tell you—Eilert Lövborg was found shot in—in Mademoiselle Diana's boudoir.

HEDDA   [Makes a motion as if to rise, but sinks back again.] That is impossible, Judge Brack! He cannot have been there again today.

BRACK   He was there this afternoon. He went there, he said, to demand the return of something which they had taken from him. Talked wildly about a lost child . . .

HEDDA   Ah—so that was why . . .

BRACK   I thought probably he meant his manuscript; but now I hear he destroyed that himself. So I suppose it must have been his pocketbook.

HEDDA   Yes, no doubt. And there—there he was found?

BRACK   Yes, there. With a pistol in his breast pocket, discharged. The ball had lodged in a vital part.

HEDDA   In the breast—yes.

BRACK   No—in the bowels.

HEDDA   [Looks up at him with an expression of loathing.] That, too! Oh, what curse is it that makes everything I touch turn ludicrous and mean?

BRACK   There is one point more, Mrs. Hedda—another disagreeable feature in the affair.

HEDDA   And what is that?

BRACK   The pistol he carried . . .

HEDDA   [Breathless.] Well? What of it?

BRACK   He must have stolen it.

HEDDA   [Leaps up.] Stolen it! That is not true! He did not steal it!

BRACK   No other explanation is possible. He must have stolen it . . . Hush!

[TESMAN *and* MRS. ELVSTED *have risen from the table in the back room, and come into the drawing room.*]

TESMAN [*With the papers in both his hands.*] Hedda, dear, it is almost impossible to see under that lamp. Think of that!

HEDDA Yes, I am thinking.

TESMAN Would you mind our sitting at your writing table —eh?

HEDDA If you like. [*Quickly.*] No, wait! Let me clear it first!

TESMAN Oh, you needn't trouble, Hedda. There is plenty of room.

HEDDA No, no, let me clear it, I say! I will take these things in and put them on the piano. There!

[*She has drawn out an object, covered with sheet music, from under the bookcase, places several other pieces of music upon it, and carries the whole into the inner room, to the left.* TESMAN *lays the scraps of paper on the writing table, and moves the lamp there from the corner table. He and* MRS. ELVSTED *sit down and proceed with their work.* HEDDA *returns.*]

HEDDA [*Behind* MRS. ELVSTED'S *chair, gently ruffing her hair.*] Well, my sweet Thea, how goes it with Eilert Lövborg's monument?

MRS. ELVSTED [*Looks dispiritedly up at her.*] Oh, it will be terribly hard to put in order.

TESMAN We must manage it. I am determined. And arranging other people's papers is just the work for me.

[HEDDA *goes over to the stove, and seats herself on one of the footstools.* BRACK *stands over her, leaning on the armchair.*]

HEDDA [*Whispers.*] What did you say about the pistol?

BRACK [*Softly.*] That he must have stolen it.

HEDDA Why stolen it?

BRACK Because every other explanation ought to be impossible, Mrs. Hedda.

HEDDA Indeed?

BRACK [*Glances at her.*] Of course, Eilert Lövborg was here this morning. Was he not?

HEDDA Yes.

BRACK Were you alone with him?

HEDDA   Part of the time.

BRACK   Did you not leave the room whilst he was here?

HEDDA   No.

BRACK   Try to recollect. Were you not out of the room a moment?

HEDDA   Yes, perhaps just a moment—out in the hall.

BRACK   And where was your pistol case during that time?

HEDDA   I had it locked up in . . .

BRACK   Well, Mrs. Hedda?

HEDDA   The case stood there on the writing table.

BRACK   Have you looked since, to see whether both the pistols are there?

HEDDA   No.

BRACK   Well, you need not. I saw the pistol found in Lövborg's pocket, and I knew it at once as the one I had seen yesterday—and before, too.

HEDDA   Have you it with you?

BRACK   No, the police have it.

HEDDA   What will the police do with it?

BRACK   Search till they find the owner.

HEDDA   Do you think they will succeed?

BRACK   [Bends over her and whispers.]   No, Hedda Gabler—not so long as I say nothing.

HEDDA   [Looks frightened at him.]   And if you do not say nothing—what then?

BRACK   [Shrugs his shoulders.]   There is always the possibility that pistol was stolen.

HEDDA   [Firmly.]   Death rather than that.

BRACK   [Smiling.]   People say such things—but they don't do them.

HEDDA   [Without replying.]   And supposing the pistol was not stolen, and the owner is discovered? What then?

BRACK   Well, Hedda—then comes the scandal.

HEDDA   The scandal!

BRACK   Yes, the scandal—of which you are so mortally afraid. You will, of course, be brought before the court—both you and Mademoiselle Diana. She will have to explain how the thing happened—whether it was an accidental shot or murder. Did the pistol go off as he was trying to take it out of his pocket, to threaten her with? Or did she tear the pistol out of his hand, shoot him, and push it back into his pocket? That would be quite like her; for she is an able-bodied young person, this same Mademoiselle Diana.

HEDDA　But I have nothing to do with all this repulsive business.

BRACK　No. But you will have to answer the question: Why did you give Eilert Lövborg the pistol? And what conclusions will people draw from the fact that you did give it to him?

HEDDA　[Lets her head sink.]　That is true. I did not think of that.

BRACK　Well, fortunately, there is no danger, so long as I say nothing.

HEDDA　[Looks up at him.]　So I am in your power, Judge Brack. You have me at your beck and call, from this time forward.

BRACK　[Whispers softly.]　Dearest Hedda—believe me—I shall not abuse my advantage.

HEDDA　I am in your power none the less. Subject to your will and your demands. A slave, a slave then! [Rises impetuously.] No, I cannot endure the thought of that! Never!

BRACK　[Looks half-mockingly at her.]　People generally get used to the inevitable.

HEDDA　[Returns his look.]　Yes, perhaps. [She crosses to the writing table. Suppressing an involuntary smile, she imitates TESMAN's intonations.]　Well? Are you getting on, George? Eh?

TESMAN　Heaven knows, dear. In any case it will be the work of months.

HEDDA　[As before.]　Fancy that! [Passes her hands softly through MRS. ELVSTED's hair.]　Doesn't it seem strange to you, Thea? Here are you sitting with Tesman—just as you used to sit with Eilert Lövborg?

MRS. ELVSTED　Ah, if I could only inspire your husband in the same way!

HEDDA　Oh, that will come, too—in time.

TESMAN　Yes, do you know, Hedda—I really think I begin to

feel something of the sort. But won't you go and sit with Brack again?

HEDDA Is there nothing I can do to help you two?

TESMAN No, nothing in the world. [*Turning his head.*] I trust to you to keep Hedda company, my dear Brack.

BRACK [*With a glance at* HEDDA.] With the very greatest of pleasure.

HEDDA Thanks. But I am tired this evening. I will go in and lie down a little on the sofa.

TESMAN Yes, do, dear—eh?

[HEDDA *goes into the back room and draws the curtains. A short pause. Suddenly she is heard playing a wild dance on the piano.*]

MRS. ELVSTED [*Starts from her chair.*] Oh—what is that?

TESMAN [*Runs to the doorway.*] Why, my dearest Hedda—don't play dance music tonight! Just think of Aunt Rina! And of Eilert, too!

HEDDA [*Puts her head out between the curtains.*] And of Aunt Julia. And of all the rest of them. After this, I will be quiet. [*Closes the curtains again.*]

TESMAN [*At the writing table.*] It's not good for her to see us at this distressing work. I'll tell you what, Mrs. Elvsted—you shall take the empty room at Aunt Julia's, and then I will come over in the evenings, and we can sit and work there—eh?

HEDDA [*In the inner room.*] I hear what you are saying, Tesman. But how am *I* to get through the evenings out here?

TESMAN [*Turning over the papers.*] Oh, I daresay Judge Brack will be so kind as to look in now and then, even though I am out.

BRACK [*In the armchair, calls out gaily.*] Every blessed evening, with all the pleasure in life, Mrs. Tesman! We shall get on capitally together, we two!

HEDDA [*Speaking loud and clear.*] Yes, don't you flatter yourself we will, Judge Brack? Now that you are the one cock in the basket . . .

[*A shot is heard within.* TESMAN, MRS. ELVSTED, *and* BRACK *leap to their feet.*]

TESMAN Oh, now she is playing with those pistols again.

[*He throws back the curtains and runs in, followed by* MRS. ELVSTED. HEDDA *lies stretched on the sofa, lifeless. Confusion and cries.* BERTA *enters in alarm from the right.*]

TESMAN [*Shrieks to* BRACK.]   Shot herself! Shot herself in the temple! Fancy that!

BRACK [*Half-fainting in the armchair.*]   Good God!—people don't do such things.

BERNARD SHAW

Pygmalion

CAST

HENRY HIGGINS

COLONEL PICKERING

FREDDY EYNSFORD HILL

ALFRED DOOLITTLE

A BYSTANDER

ANOTHER ONE

ELIZA DOOLITTLE

MRS EYNSFORD HILL

MISS EYNSFORD HILL

MRS HIGGINS

MRS PEARCE

PARLORMAID

SCENE: *London.*

PREFACE TO PYGMALION

As will be seen later on, Pygmalion needs, not a preface, but a sequel, which I have supplied in its due place.

The English have no respect for their language, and will not teach their children to speak it. They cannot spell it because they have nothing to spell it with but an old foreign alphabet of which only the consonants—and not all of them—have any agreed speech value. Consequently no man can teach himself what it should sound like from reading it; and it is impossible for an Englishman to open his mouth without making some other Englishman despise him. Most European languages are now accessible in black and white to foreigners: English and French are not thus accessible even to Englishmen and Frenchmen. The reformer we need most today is an energetic enthusiast: that is why I have made such a one the hero of a popular play.

There have been heroes of that kind crying in the wilderness for many years past. When I became interested in the subject towards the end of the eighteen-seventies, the illustrious Alexander Melville Bell, the inventor of Visible Speech, had emigrated to Canada, where his son invented the telephone; but Alexander J. Ellis was still a London Patriarch, with an impressive head always covered by a velvet skull cap, for which he would apologize to public meetings in a very courtly manner. He and Tito Pagliardini, another phonetic veteran, were men whom it was impossible to dislike. Henry Sweet, then a young man, lacked their sweetness of character: he was about as conciliatory to conventional mortals as Ibsen or Samuel Butler. His great ability as a phonetician (he was, I think, the best of them all at his job) would have entitled him to high official recognition, and perhaps enabled him to popularize his subject, but for his Satanic contempt for all academic dignitaries and persons in general who thought more of Greek than of phonetics. Once, in the days when the Imperial Institute rose in South Kensington, and Joseph Chamberlain was booming the Empire, I induced the editor of a leading monthly review to commission an article from Sweet on the imperial importance of his subject. When it arrived, it contained nothing but a savagely derisive attack on a professor of language and literature whose chair Sweet regarded as proper to a phonetic expert only. The article, being libellous, had to be returned as impossible; and I had to renounce my dream of dragging its author into the limelight. When I met him afterwards, for the first time for many years, I found to my astonishment that he, who had been a quite tolerably presentable young man, had actually managed by sheer scorn to alter his personal appearance until he had become a sort of walking repudiation of Oxford and all its traditions. It must have been largely in his own despite that he was squeezed into something called a Readership of phonetics there. The future of phonetics rests probably with his pupils who all swore by him; but nothing could bring the man himself into any sort of compliance with the university to which he nevertheless clung by divine right in an intensely Oxonian way. I daresay his papers, if he has left any, include some satires that may be published without too destructive results fifty years hence. He was, I believe, not in the least an ill-natured man: very much the opposite, I should say; but he would not suffer fools gladly; and to him all scholars who were not rabid phoneticians were fools.

Those who knew him will recognize in my third act the allusion to the Current Shorthand in which he used to write postcards. It may be acquired from a four and sixpenny manual published by the Clarendon Press. The postcards which Mrs Higgins describes are such as I have received from Sweet. I would decipher a sound which a cockney would represent by *zerr,* and a Frenchman by *seu,* and then write demanding with some heat what on earth it meant. Sweet, with boundless contempt for my stupidity, would reply that it not only meant but obviously was the word Result, as no other word containing that sound, and capable of making sense with the context, existed in any language spoken on earth. That

less expert mortals should require fuller indications was beyond
Sweet's patience. Therefore, though the whole point of his Current
Shorthand is that it can express every sound in the language
perfectly, vowels as well as consonants, and that your hand has
to make no stroke except the easy and current ones with which
you write m, n, and u, l, p, and q, scribbling them at whatever
angle comes easiest to you, his unfortunate determination to make
this remarkable and quite legible script serve also as a shorthand
reduced it in his own practice to the most inscrutable of crypto-
grams. His true objective was the provision of a full, accurate,
legible script for our language; but he was led past that by his
contempt for the popular Pitman system of shorthand, which he
called the Pitfall system. The triumph of Pitman was a triumph of
business organization: there was a weekly paper to persuade you
to learn Pitman: there were cheap textbooks and exercise books
and transcripts of speeches for you to copy, and schools where
experienced teachers coached you up to the necessary proficiency.
Sweet could not organize his market in that fashion. He might
as well have been the Sybil who tore up the leaves of prophecy
that nobody would attend to. The four and sixpenny manual,
mostly in his lithographed handwriting, that was never vulgarly
advertised, may perhaps some day be taken up by a syndicate and
pushed upon the public as *The Times* pushed the *Encyclopædia
Britannica*; but until then it will certainly not prevail against Pitman. I have bought three copies of it during my lifetime; and I
am informed by the publishers that its cloistered existence is still
a steady and healthy one. I actually learned the system two several
times; and yet the shorthand in which I am writing these lines is
Pitman's. And the reason is, that my secretary cannot transcribe
Sweet, having been perforce taught in the schools of Pitman. In
America I could use the commercially organized Gregg shorthand,
which has taken a hint from Sweet by making its letters writable
(current, Sweet would have called them) instead of having to be
geometrically drawn like Pitman's; but all these systems, including
Sweet's, are spoilt by making them available for verbatim report-
ing, in which complete and exact spelling and word division are
impossible. A complete and exact phonetic script is neither prac-

ticable nor necessary for ordinary use; but if we enlarge our alphabet to the Russian size, and make our spelling as phonetic as Spanish, the advance will be prodigious.

Pygmalion Higgins is not a portrait of Sweet, to whom the adventure of Eliza Doolittle would have been impossible; still, as will be seen, there are touches of Sweet in the play. With Higgins's physique and temperament Sweet might have set the Thames on fire. As it was, he impressed himself professionally on Europe to an extent that made his comparative personal obscurity, and the failure of Oxford to do justice to his eminence, a puzzle to foreign specialists in his subject. I do not blame Oxford, because I think Oxford is quite right in demanding a certain social amenity from its nurslings (heaven knows it is not exorbitant in its requirement!); for although I well know how hard it is for a man of genius with a seriously underrated subject to maintain serene and kindly relations with the men who underrate it, and who keep all the best places for less important subjects which they profess without originality and sometimes without much capacity for them, still, if he overwhelms them with wrath and disdain, he cannot expect them to heap honors on him.

Of the later generations of phoneticians I know little. Among them towered Robert Bridges, to whom perhaps Higgins may owe his Miltonic sympathies, though here again I must disclaim all portraiture. But if the play makes the public aware that there are such people as phoneticians, and that they are among the most important people in England at present, it will serve its turn.

I wish to boast that Pygmalion has been an extremely successful play, both on stage and screen, all over Europe and North America as well as at home. It is so intensely and deliberately didactic, and its subject is esteemed so dry, that I delight in throwing at the heads of the wiseacres who repeat the parrot cry that art should never be didactic. It goes to prove my contention that great art can never be anything else.

Finally, and for the encouragement of people troubled with accents that cut them off from all high employment, I may add that the change wrought by Professor Higgins in the flower girl is neither impossible nor uncommon. The modern concierge's daughter who fulfills her ambition by playing the Queen of Spain in Ruy Blas at the Théâtre Français is only one of the many thousands of men and women who have sloughed off their native dialects and acquired a new tongue. Our West End shop assistants and domestic servants are bilingual. But the thing has to be done scientifically, or the last state of the aspirant may be worse than the first. An honest slum dialect is more tolerable than the attempts of phonetically untaught persons to imitate the plutocracy. Ambitious flower girls who read this play must not imagine that they can pass themselves off as fine ladies by untutored imitation. They must learn their alphabet over again, and differently, from a phonetic expert. Imitation will only make them ridiculous.

Note for Technicians: A complete representation of the play as printed in this edition is technically possible only on the cinema screen or on stages furnished with exceptionally elaborate machinery. For ordinary theatrical use the scenes separated by rows of asterisks are to be omitted.

In the dialogue an e upside down indicates the indefinite vowel, sometimes called obscure or neutral, for which, though it is one of the commonest sounds in English speech, our wretched alphabet has no letter.

ACT I

SCENE: *London at 11:15 p.m. Torrents of heavy summer rain. Cab whistles blowing frantically in all directions. Pedestrians running for shelter into the portico of St Paul's church (not Wren's cathedral but Inigo Jones's church in Covent Garden vegetable market), among them a lady and her daughter in evening dress. All are peering out gloomily at the rain, except one man with his back turned to the rest, wholly preoccupied with a notebook in which he is writing.*

The church clock strikes the first quarter.

THE DAUGHTER [*In the space between the central pillars, close to the one on her left.*]   I'm getting chilled to the bone. What can Freddy be doing all this time? He's been gone twenty minutes.

THE MOTHER [*On her daughter's right.*]   Not so long. But he ought to have got us a cab by this.

A BYSTANDER [*On the lady's right.*]   He wont get no cab not until half-past eleven, missus, when they come back after dropping their theatre fares.

THE MOTHER   But we must have a cab. We cant stand here until half-past eleven. It's too bad.

THE BYSTANDER   Well, it aint my fault, missus.

THE DAUGHTER   If Freddy had a bit of gumption, he would have got one at the theatre door.

THE MOTHER   What could he have done, poor boy?

THE DAUGHTER   Other people got cabs. Why couldnt he?

[*Freddy rushes in out of the rain from Southampton Street side, and comes between them closing a dripping umbrella. He is a young man of twenty, in evening dress, very wet round the ankles.*]

THE DAUGHTER   Well, havnt you got a cab?

FREDDY   Theres not one to be had for love or money.

THE MOTHER   Oh, Freddy, there must be one. You cant have tried.

THE DAUGHTER   It's too tiresome. Do you expect us to go and get one ourselves?

FREDDY   I tell you theyre all engaged. The rain was so sudden: nobody was prepared; and everybody had to take a cab. Ive been to Charing Cross one way and nearly to Ludgate Circus the other; and they were all engaged.

THE MOTHER   Did you try Trafalgar Square?

FREDDY   There wasnt one at Trafalgar Square.

THE DAUGHTER   Did you try?

FREDDY   I tried as far as Charing Cross Station. Did you expect me to walk to Hammersmith?

THE DAUGHTER   You havnt tried at all.

THE MOTHER   You really are very helpless, Freddy. Go again; and dont come back until you have found a cab.

FREDDY   I shall simply get soaked for nothing.

THE DAUGHTER   And what about us? Are we to stay here all night in this draught, with next to nothing on? You selfish pig . . .

FREDDY   Oh, very well: I'll go, I'll go. [*He opens his umbrella and dashes off Strandwards, but comes into collision with a flower girl who is hurrying in for shelter, knocking her basket out of her hands. A blinding flash of lightning, followed instantly by a rattling peal of thunder, orchestrates the incident.*]

THE FLOWER GIRL   Nah then, Freddy: look wh' y' gowin, deah.

FREDDY   Sorry. [*He rushes off.*]

THE FLOWER GIRL   [*Picking up her scattered flowers and replacing them in the basket.*]   Theres menners f' yer! Tə-oo banches o voylets trod into the mad. [*She sits down on the plinth of the column, sorting her flowers, on the lady's right. She is not at all a romantic figure. She is perhaps eighteen, perhaps twenty, hardly older. She wears a little sailor hat of black straw that has long been exposed to the dust and soot of London and has seldom if ever been brushed. Her hair needs washing rather badly: its mousy color can hardly be natural. She wears a shoddy black coat*] *that reaches nearly to her knees and is shaped to her waist. She has a brown skirt with a coarse apron. Her boots are much the worse for wear. She is no doubt as clean as she can afford to be; but compared to the ladies she is very dirty. Her features are no worse than theirs; but their condition leaves something to be desired; and she needs the services of a dentist.*]

THE MOTHER   How do you know that my son's name is Freddy, pray?

THE FLOWER GIRL   Ow, eez yə-ooa san, is e? Wal, fewd dan y' də-ooty bawmz a mather should, eed now bettern to spawl a pore gel's flahrzn than ran awy athaht pyin. Will ye-oo py me f'them? [*Here, with apologies, this desperate attempt to represent her dialect without a phonetic alphabet must be abandoned as unintelligible outside London.*]

THE DAUGHTER   Do nothing of the sort, mother. The idea!

THE MOTHER   Please allow me, Clara. Have you any pennies?

THE DAUGHTER   No. Ive nothing smaller than sixpence.

THE FLOWER GIRL [*Hopefully.*]   I can give you change for a tanner, kind lady.

THE MOTHER [*To* CLARA.]   Give it to me. [CLARA *parts reluctantly.*]   Now [*to the girl*]   this is for your flowers.

THE FLOWER GIRL   Thank you kindly, lady.

THE DAUGHTER   Make her give you the change. These things are only a penny a bunch.

THE MOTHER   Do hold your tongue, Clara. [*To the girl.*] You can keep the change.

THE FLOWER GIRL   Oh, thank you, lady.

THE MOTHER   Now tell me how you know that young gentleman's name.

THE FLOWER GIRL   I didnt.

THE MOTHER   I heard you call him by it. Dont try to deceive me.

THE FLOWER GIRL [*Protesting.*]   Who's trying to deceive you? I called him Freddy or Charlie same as you might yourself if you was talking to a stranger and wished to be pleasant.

THE DAUGHTER Sixpence thrown away! Really, mamma, you might have spared Freddy that. [*She retreats in disgust behind the pillar.*]

[*An elderly gentleman of the amiable military type rushes into the shelter, and closes a dripping umbrella. He is in the same plight as* FREDDY, *very wet about the ankles. He is in evening dress, with a light overcoat. He takes the place left vacant by the daughter.*]

THE GENTLEMAN Phew!

THE MOTHER [*To the gentleman.*] Oh, sir, is there any sign of its stopping?

THE GENTLEMAN I'm afraid not. It started worse than ever about two minutes ago. [*He goes to the plinth beside the flower girl; puts up his foot on it; and stoops to turn down his trouser ends.*]

THE MOTHER Oh dear! [*She retires sadly and joins her daughter.*]

THE FLOWER GIRL [*Taking advantage of the military gentleman's proximity to establish friendly relations with him.*] If it's worse, it's a sign it's nearly over. So cheer up, Captain; and buy a flower off a poor girl.

THE GENTLEMAN I'm sorry. I havnt any change.

THE FLOWER GIRL I can give you change, Captain.

THE GENTLEMAN For a sovereign? Ive nothing less.

THE FLOWER GIRL Garn! Oh do buy a flower off me, Captain. I can change a half-a-crown. Take this for tuppence.

THE GENTLEMAN Now dont be troublesome: theres a good girl. [*Trying his pockets.*] I really havnt any change—Stop: heres three hapence, if thats any use to you. [*He retreats to the other pillar.*]

THE FLOWER GIRL [*Disappointed, but thinking three half-pence better than nothing.*] Thank you, sir.

THE BYSTANDER [*To the girl.*] You be careful: give him a flower for it. Theres a bloke here behind taking down every blessed word youre saying. [*All turn to the man who is taking notes.*]

THE FLOWER GIRL [*Springing up terrified.*] I aint done nothing wrong by speaking to the gentleman. Ive a right to sell flowers if I keep off the kerb. [*Hysterically.*] I'm a respectable girl: so help me, I never spoke to him except to ask him to buy a flower off me.

General hubbub, mostly sympathetic to the flower girl, but deprecating her excessive sensibility. Cries of Dont start hollerin. Who's hurting you? Nobody's going to touch you. Whats the good of fussing? Steady on. Easy easy, etc., *come from the elderly staid spectators, who pat her comfortingly. Less patient ones bid her shut her head, or ask her roughly what is wrong with her. A remoter group, not knowing what the matter is, crowd in and increase the noise with question and answer:* Whats the row? Whatshe do? Where is he? A tec taking her down. What! him? Yes: him over there: Took money off the gentleman, etc.

THE FLOWER GIRL [*Breaking through them to the gentleman, crying wildly.*] Oh, sir, dont let him charge me. You dunno what it means to me. Theyll take away my character and drive me on the streets for speaking to gentlemen. They . . .

THE NOTE TAKER [*Coming forward on her right, the rest crowding after him.*] There! there! there! there! who's hurting you, you silly girl? What do you take me for?

THE BYSTANDER It's aw rawt: e's a gentleman: look at his bə-oots. [*Explaining to the note taker.*] She thought you was a copper's nark, sir.

THE NOTE TAKER [*With quick interest.*] Whats a copper's nark?

THE BYSTANDER [*Inapt at definition.*] It's a—well, it's a copper's nark, as you might say. What else would you call it? A sort of informer.

THE FLOWER GIRL [*Still hysterical.*] I take my Bible oath I never said a word . . .

THE NOTE TAKER [*Overbearing but good-humored.*] Oh, shut up, shut up. Do I look like a policeman?

THE FLOWER GIRL [*Far from reassured.*] Then what did you take down my words for? How do I know whether you took me down right? You just show me what youve wrote about me. [*The note taker opens his book and holds it steadily under her nose, though the pressure of the mob trying to read it over his shoulders would upset a weaker man.*] Whats that? That aint proper writing. I cant read that.

THE NOTE TAKER I can. [*Reads, reproducing her pronunciation exactly.*] "Cheer ap, Keptin; n' baw ya flahr orf a pore gel."

THE FLOWER GIRL [*Much distressed.*] It's because I called him Captain. I meant no harm. [*To the gentleman.*] Oh, sir, dont let him lay a charge agen me for a word like that. You . . .

THE GENTLEMAN Charge! I make no charge. [*To the note taker.*] Really, sir, if you are a detective, you need not begin protecting me against molestation by young women until I ask you. Anybody could see that the girl meant no harm.

THE BYSTANDERS GENERALLY [*Demonstrating against police espionage.*] Course they could. What business is it of yours? You mind your own affairs. He wants a promotion, he does. Taking down people's words! Girl never said a word to him. What harm if she did? Nice thing a girl cant shelter from the rain without being insulted, etc., etc., etc. [*She is conducted by the more sympathetic demonstrators back to her plinth, where she resumes her seat and struggles with her emotion.*]

THE BYSTANDER He aint a tec. He's a bloming busybody: thats what he is. I tell you, look at his bə-oots.

THE NOTE TAKER [*Turning on him genially.*] And how are all your people down at Selsey?

THE BYSTANDER [*Suspiciously.*] Who told you my people come from Selsey?

THE NOTE TAKER Never you mind. They did. [*To the girl.*] How do you come to be up so far east? You were born in Lisson Grove.

THE FLOWER GIRL [*Appalled.*] Oh, what harm is there in my leaving Lisson Grove? It wasn't fit for a pig to live in; and I had to pay four-and-six a week. [*In tears.*] Oh, boo—hoo—oo—

THE NOTE TAKER Live where you like; but stop that noise.

THE GENTLEMAN [*To the girl.*] Come, come! he cant touch you: you have a right to live where you please.

A SARCASTIC BYSTANDER [*Thrusting himself between the note*

taker and the gentleman.]   Park Lane, for instance. I'd like to go into the Housing Question with you, I would.

THE FLOWER GIRL [*Subsiding into a brooding melancholy over her basket, and talking very low-spiritedly to herself.*]   I'm a good girl, I am.

THE SARCASTIC BYSTANDER [*Not attending to her.*]   Do you know where I come from?

THE NOTE TAKER [*promptly.*]   Hoxton.

[*Titterings. Popular interest in the note taker's performance increases.*]

THE SARCASTIC ONE [*Amazed.*]   Well, who said I didnt? Bly me! you know everything, you do.

THE FLOWER GIRL [*Still nursing her sense of injury.*]   Aint no call to meddle with me, he aint.

THE BYSTANDER [*To her.*]   Of course he aint. Dont you stand it from him. [*To the note taker.*]   See here: what call have you to know about people what never offered to meddle with you?

THE FLOWER GIRL   Let him say what he likes. I dont want to have no truck with him.

THE BYSTANDER   You take us for dirt under your feet, dont you? Catch you taking liberties with a gentleman!

THE SARCASTIC BYSTANDER   Yes: tell him where he come from if you want to go fortune-telling.

THE NOTE TAKER   Cheltenham, Harrow, Cambridge, and India.

THE GENTLEMAN   Quite right.

Great laughter. Reaction in the note taker's favor. Exclamations of He knows all about it. Told him proper. Hear him tell the toff where he come from? etc.

THE GENTLEMAN   May I ask, sir, do you do this for your living at a music hall?

THE NOTE TAKER   Ive thought of that. Perhaps I shall some day.

[*The rain has stopped; and the persons on the outside of the crowd begin to drop off.*]

THE FLOWER GIRL [*Resenting the reaction.*] He's no gentleman, he aint, to interfere with a poor girl.

THE DAUGHTER [*Out of patience, pushing her way rudely to the front and displacing the gentleman, who politely retires to the other side of the pillar.*] What on earth is Freddy doing? I shall get pneumownia if I stay in this draught any longer.

THE NOTE TAKER [*To himself, hastily making a note of her pronunciation of "monia".*] Earlscourt.

THE DAUGHTER [*Violently.*] Will you please keep your impertinent remarks to yourself.

THE NOTE TAKER Did I say that out loud? I didnt mean to. I beg your pardon. Your mother's Epsom, unmistakably.

THE MOTHER [*Advancing between the daughter and the note taker.*] How very curious! I was brought up in Largelady Park, near Epsom.

THE NOTE TAKER [*Uproariously amused.*] Ha! Ha! What a devil of a name! Excuse me. [*To the daughter.*] You want a cab, do you?

THE DAUGHTER Dont dare speak to me.

THE MOTHER Oh please, please, Clara. [*Her daughter repudiates her with an angry shrug and retires haughtily.*] We should be so grateful to you, sir, if you found us a cab. [*The note taker produces a whistle.*] Oh, thank you. [*She joins her daughter.*]

[*The note taker blows a piercing blast.*]

THE SARCASTIC BYSTANDER There! I knowed he was a plainclothes copper.

THE BYSTANDER That aint a police whistle: thats a sporting whistle.

THE FLOWER GIRL [*Still preoccupied with her wounded feelings.*] He's no right to take away my character. My character is the same to me as any lady's.

THE NOTE TAKER I dont know whether youve noticed it; but the rain stopped about two minutes ago.

THE BYSTANDER So it has. Why didnt you say so before? and us losing our time listening to your silliness! [*He walks off towards the Strand.*]

THE SARCASTIC BYSTANDER I can tell where you come from. You come from Anwell. Go back there.

THE NOTE TAKER [*Helpfully.*] Hanwell.

THE SARCASTIC BYSTANDER [*Affecting great distinction of speech.*] Thenk you, teacher. Haw haw! So long. [*He touches his hat with mock respect and strolls off.*]

THE FLOWER GIRL Frightening people like that! How would he like it himself?

THE MOTHER It's quite fine now, Clara. We can walk to a motor bus. Come. [*She gathers her skirts above her ankles and hurries off towards the Strand.*]

THE DAUGHTER But the cab . . . [*Her mother is out of hearing.*] Oh, how tiresome! [*She follows angrily.*]

[*All the rest have gone except the note taker, the gentleman, and the flower girl, who sits arranging her basket, and still pitying herself in murmurs.*]

THE FLOWER GIRL Poor girl! Hard enough for her to live without being worrited and chivied.

THE GENTLEMAN [*Returning to his former place on the note taker's left.*] How do you do it, if I may ask?

THE NOTE TAKER Simply phonetics. The science of speech. Thats my profession: also my hobby. Happy is the man who can make a living by his hobby! You can spot an Irishman or a Yorkshireman by his brogue. I can place any man within six miles. I can place him within two miles in London. Sometimes within two streets.

THE FLOWER GIRL Ought to be ashamed of himself, unmanly coward!

THE GENTLEMAN But is there a living in that?

THE NOTE TAKER Oh yes. Quite a fat one. This is an age of upstarts. Men begin in Kentish Town with £80 a year, and end in Park Lane with a hundred thousand. They want to drop Kentish Town; but they give themselves away every time they open their mouths. Now I can teach them . . .

THE FLOWER GIRL Let him mind his own business and leave a poor girl . . .

THE NOTE TAKER [*Explosively.*] Woman: cease this detestable boohooing instantly; or else seek the shelter of some other place of worship.

THE FLOWER GIRL [*With feeble defiance.*] Ive a right to be here if I like, same as you.

THE NOTE TAKER A woman who utters such depressing and disgusting sounds has no right to be anywhere—no right to live. Remember that you are a human being with a soul and the divine gift of articulate speech: that your native language is the language of Shakespear and Milton and The Bible; and dont sit there crooning like a bilious pigeon.

THE FLOWER GIRL [*Quite overwhelmed, looking up at him in mingled wonder and deprecation without daring to raise her head.*] Ah-ah-ah-ow-ow-ow-oo!

THE NOTE TAKER [*Whipping out his book.*] Heavens! what a sound! [*He writes; then holds out the book and reads, reproducing her vowels exactly.*] Ah-ah-ah-ow-ow-ow-oo!

THE FLOWER GIRL [*Tickled by the performance, and laughing in spite of herself.*] Garn!

THE NOTE TAKER You see this creature with her kerbstone English: the English that will keep her in the gutter to the end of her days. Well, sir, in three months I could pass that girl off as a duchess at an ambassador's garden party. I could even get her a place as lady's maid or shop assistant, which requires better English.

THE FLOWER GIRL Whats that you say?

THE NOTE TAKER Yes, you squashed cabbage leaf, you disgrace to the noble architecture of these columns, you incarnate insult to the English language: I could pass you off as the Queen of Sheba. [*To the gentleman.*] Can you believe that?

THE GENTLEMAN Of course I can. I am myself a student of Indian dialects; and . . .

THE NOTE TAKER [*Eagerly.*] Are you? Do you know Colonel Pickering, the author of Spoken Sanscrit?

THE GENTLEMAN I am Colonel Pickering. Who are you?

THE NOTE TAKER Henry Higgins, author of Higgins's Universal Alphabet.

PICKERING [*With enthusiasm.*] I came from India to meet you.

HIGGINS I was going to India to meet you.

PICKERING Where do you live?

HIGGINS 27A Wimpole Street. Come and see me tomorrow.

PICKERING I'm at the Carlton. Come with me now and lets have a jaw over some supper.

HIGGINS Right you are.

THE FLOWER GIRL [*To* PICKERING, *as he passes her.*] Buy a flower, kind gentleman. I'm short for my lodging.

PICKERING I really havnt any change. I'm sorry. [*He goes away.*]

HIGGINS [*Shocked at the girl's mendacity.*] Liar. You said you could change half-a-crown.

THE FLOWER GIRL [*Rising in desperation.*] You ought to be stuffed with nails, you ought. [*Flinging the basket at his feet.*] Take the whole blooming basket for sixpence.

[*The church clock strikes the second quarter.*]

HIGGINS [*Hearing in it the voice of God, rebuking him for his Pharisaic want of charity to the poor girl.*] A reminder. [*He raises his hat solemnly; then throws a handful of money into the basket and follows* PICKERING.]

THE FLOWER GIRL [*Picking up a half-crown.*] Ah-ow-ooh! [*Picking up a couple of florins.*] Aaah-ow-ooh! [*Picking up several coins.*] Aaaaah-ow-ooh! [*Picking up a half-sovereign.*] Aaaaaaaaaaa-ow-ooh!!!

FREDDY [*Springing out of a taxicab.*] Got one at last. Hallo! [*To the girl.*] Where are the two ladies that were here?

THE FLOWER GIRL They walked to the bus when the rain stopped.

FREDDY And left me with a cab on my hands! Damnation!

THE FLOWER GIRL [*With grandeur.*] Never mind, young man. I'm going home in a taxi. [*She sails off to the cab. The driver puts his hand behind him and holds the door firmly shut against her. Quite understanding his mistrust, she shows him her handful of money.*] A taxi fare aint no object to me, Charlie. [*He grins and opens the door.*] Here. What about the basket?

THE TAXIMAN Give it here. Tuppence extra.

LIZA No: I dont want nobody to see it. [*She crushes it into the cab and gets in, continuing the conversation through the window.*] Goodbye, Freddy.

FREDDY [*Dazedly raising his hat.*] Goodbye.

TAXIMAN Where to?

LIZA Bucknam Pellis [Buckingham Palace].

TAXIMAN What d'ye mean—Bucknam Pellis?

LIZA Dont you know where it is? In the Green Park, where the King lives. Goodbye, Freddy. Dont let me keep you standing there. Goodbye.

FREDDY Goodbye. [*He goes.*]

TAXIMAN Here? Whats this about Bucknam Pellis? What business have you at Bucknam Pellis?

LIZA Of course I havnt none. But I wasnt going to let him know that. You drive me home.

TAXIMAN And wheres home?

LIZA Angel Court, Drury Lane, next Meiklejohn's oil shop.

TAXIMAN That sounds more like it, Judy. [*He drives off.*]

*　　*　　*　　*　　*　　*

Let us follow the taxi to the entrance to Angel Court, a narrow little archway between two shops, one of them Meiklejohn's oil shop. When it stops there, Eliza gets out, dragging her basket with her.

LIZA How much?

TAXIMAN [*Indicating the taximeter.*] Cant you read? A shilling.

LIZA A shilling for two minutes!!

TAXIMAN Two minutes or ten: it's all the same.

LIZA Well, I dont call it right.

TAXIMAN Ever been in a taxi before?

LIZA [*With dignity.*] Hundreds and thousands of times, young man.

TAXIMAN [*Laughing at her.*] Good for you, Judy. Keep the shilling, darling, with best love from all at home. Good luck! [*He drives off.*]

LIZA [*Humiliated.*]   Impidence!

[*She picks up the basket and trudges up the alley with it to her lodging: a small room with very old wall paper hanging loose in the damp places. A broken pane in the window is mended with paper. A portrait of a popular actor and a fashion plate of ladies' dresses, all wildly beyond poor Eliza's means, both torn from newspapers, are pinned up on the wall. A birdcage hangs in the window; but its tenant died long ago: it remains as a memorial only.*

These are the only visible luxuries: the rest is the irreducible minimum of poverty's needs: a wretched bed heaped with all sorts of coverings that have any warmth in them, a draped packing case with a basin and jug on it and a little looking glass over it, a chair and table, the refuse of some suburban kitchen, and an American alarm clock on the shelf above the unused fireplace: the whole lighted with a gas lamp with a penny in the slot meter. Rent: four shillings a week.]

Here Eliza, chronically weary, but too excited to go to bed, sits, counting her new riches and dreaming and planning what to do with them, until the gas goes out, when she enjoys for the first time the sensation of being able to put in another penny without grudging it. This prodigal mood does not extinguish her gnawing sense of the need for economy sufficiently to prevent her from calculating that she can dream and plan in bed more cheaply and warmly than sitting up without a fire. So she takes off her shawl and skirt and adds them to the miscellaneous bedclothes. Then she kicks off her shoes and gets into bed without any further change.

ACT II

SCENE: *Next day at 11 A.M.* HIGGINS's *laboratory in Wimpole Street. It is a room on the first floor, looking on the street, and was meant for the drawing room. The double doors are in the middle of the back wall; and persons entering find in the corner to their right two tall file cabinets at right angles to one another against the walls. In this corner stands a flat writing table, on which are a phonograph, a laryngoscope, a row of tiny organ pipes with a bellows, a set of lamp chimneys for singing flames with burners attached to a gas plug in the wall by an indiarubber tube, several tuning forks of different sizes, a life-size image of half a human head, showing in section the vocal organs, and a box containing a supply of wax cylinders for the phonograph.*

Further down the room, on the same side, is a fireplace, with a comfortable leather-covered easy-chair at the side of the hearth nearest the door, and a coal scuttle. There is a clock on the mantlepiece. Between the fireplace and the phonograph table is a stand for newspapers.

On the other side of the central door, to the left of the visitor, is a cabinet of shallow drawers. On it is a telephone and the telephone directory. The corner beyond, and most of the side wall, is occupied by a grand piano, with the keyboard at the end furthest from the door, and a bench for the players extending the full length of the keyboard. On the piano is a dessert dish heaped with fruit and sweets, mostly chocolates.

The middle of the room is clear. Besides the easy-chair, the piano bench, and two chairs at the phonograph table, there is one stray chair. It stands near the fireplace. On the walls, engravings: mostly Piranesis and mezzotint portraits. No paintings.

PICKERING *is seated at the table, putting down some cards and a tuning fork which he has been using.* HIGGINS *is standing up*

*near him, closing two or three file drawers which are hanging out.
He appears in the morning light as a robust, vital, appetizing sort
of man of forty or thereabouts, dressed in a professional looking
black frock-coat with a white linen collar and black silk tie. He
is of energetic, scientific type, heartily, even violently interested
in everything that can be studied as a scientific subject, and careless about himself and other people, including their feelings. He
is, in fact, but for his years and size, rather like a very impetuous
baby "taking notice" eagerly and loudly, and requiring almost as
much watching to keep him out of unintended mischief. His
manner varies from genial bullying when he is in a good humor
to stormy petulance when anything goes wrong; but he is so entirely frank and void of malice that he remains likeable even in
his least reasonable moments.*

HIGGINS [*As he shuts the last drawer.*]   Well, I think thats the
whole show.

PICKERING   It's really amazing. I havnt taken half of it in,
you know.

HIGGINS   Would you like to go over any of it again?

PICKERING [*Rising and coming to the fireplace, where he plants
himself with his back to the fire.*]   No, thank you: not now. I'm
quite done up for this morning.

HIGGINS [*Following him, and standing beside him on his left.*]
Tired of listening to sounds?

PICKERING   Yes. It's a fearful strain. I rather fancied myself
because I can pronounce twenty-four distinct vowel sounds; but
your hundred and thirty beat me. I cant hear a bit of difference
between most of them.

HIGGINS [*Chuckling, and going over to the piano to eat sweets.*]
Oh, that comes with practice. You hear no difference at first; but
you keep on listening, and presently you find theyre all as different as A from B. [MRS PEARCE *looks in: she is* HIGGINS's *housekeeper.*]   Whats the matter?

MRS PEARCE [*Hesitating, evidently perplexed.*]   A young
woman asks to see you, sir.

HIGGINS   A young woman! What does she want?

MRS PEARCE Well, sir, she says youll be glad to see her when you know what she's come about. She's quite a common girl, sir. Very common indeed. I should have sent her away, only I thought perhaps you wanted her to talk into your machines. I hope Ive not done wrong; but really you see such queer people sometimes— youll excuse me, I'm sure, sir . . .

HIGGINS Oh, thats all right, Mrs Pearce. Has she an interesting accent?

MRS PEARCE Oh, something dreadful, sir, really. I dont know how you can take an interest in it.

HIGGINS [To PICKERING.] Lets have her up. Show her up, Mrs Pearce. [He rushes across to his working table and picks out a cylinder to use on the phonograph.]

MRS PEARCE [Only half resigned to it.] Very well, sir. It's for you to say. [She goes downstairs.]

HIGGINS This is rather a bit of luck. I'll show you how I make records. We'll set her talking; and I'll take it down first in Bell's Visible Speech; then in broad Romic; and then we'll get her on the phonograph so that you can turn her on as often as you like with the written transcript before you.

MRS PEARCE [Returning.] This is the young woman, sir.

[The flower girl enters in state. She has a hat with three ostrich feathers, orange, sky-blue, and red. She has a nearly clean apron, and the shoddy coat has been tidied a little. The pathos of this deplorable figure, with its innocent vanity and consequential air, touches PICKERING, who has already straightened himself in the presence of MRS PEARCE. But as to HIGGINS, the only distinction he makes between men and women is that when he is neither bullying nor exclaiming to the heavens against some feather-weight cross, he coaxes women as a child coaxes its nurse when it wants to get anything out of her.]

HIGGINS [Brusquely, recognizing her with unconcealed disappointment, and at once, babylike, making an intolerable grievance of it.] Why, this is the girl I jotted down last night. She's no use: Ive got all the records I want of the Lisson Grove lingo; and I'm not going to waste another cylinder on it. [To the girl.] Be off with you: I dont want you.

THE FLOWER GIRL Dont you be so saucy. You aint heard what I come for yet. [*To* MRS PEARCE, *who is waiting at the door for further instructions.*] Did you tell him I come in a taxi?

MRS PEARCE Nonsense, girl! what do you think a gentleman like Mr Higgins cares what you came in?

THE FLOWER GIRL Oh, we are proud! He aint above giving lessons, not him: I heard him say so. Well, I aint come here to ask for any compliment; and if my money's not good enough I can go elsewhere.

HIGGINS Good enough for what?

THE FLOWER GIRL Good enough for yǝ-oo. Now you know, don't you? I've come to have lessons, I am. And to pay for em tǝ-oo: make no mistake.

HIGGINS [*Stupent.*] Well!!! [*Recovering his breath with a gasp.*] What do you expect me to say to you?

THE FLOWER GIRL Well, if you was a gentleman, you might ask me to sit down, I think. Dont I tell you I'm bringing you business?

HIGGINS Pickering: shall we ask this baggage to sit down, or shall we throw her out of the window?

THE FLOWER GIRL [*Running away in terror to the piano, where she turns at bay.*] Ah-ah-oh-ow-ow-ow-oo! [*Wounded and whimpering.*] I wont be called a baggage when Ive offered to pay like any lady.

[*Motionless, the two men stare at her from the other side of the room, amazed.*]

PICKERING [*Gently.*] But what is it you want?

THE FLOWER GIRL I want to be a lady in a flower shop stead of sellin at the corner of Tottenham Court Road. But they wont take me unless I can talk more genteel. He said he could teach me. Well, here I am ready to pay him—not asking any favor— and he treats me zif I was dirt.

MRS PEARCE How can you be such a foolish ignorant girl as to think you could afford to pay Mr Higgins?

THE FLOWER GIRL Why shouldnt I? I know what lessons cost as well as you do; and I'm ready to pay.

HIGGINS How much?

THE FLOWER GIRL [*Coming back to him, triumphant.*] Now youre talking! I thought youd come off it when you saw a chance of getting back a bit of what you chucked at me last night. [*Confidentially.*] Youd had a drop in, hadnt you?

HIGGINS [*Peremptorily.*] Sit down.

THE FLOWER GIRL Oh, if youre going to make a compliment of it . . .

HIGGINS [*Thundering at her.*] Sit down.

MRS PEARCE [*Severely.*] Sit down, girl. Do as youre told.

THE FLOWER GIRL Ah-ah-ah-ow-ow-oo! [*She stands, half rebellious, half bewildered.*]

PICKERING [*Very courteous.*] Wont you sit down? [*He places the stray chair near the hearthrug between himself and* HIGGINS.]

LIZA [*Coyly.*] Dont mind if I do. [*She sits down.* PICKERING *returns to the hearthrug.*]

HIGGINS Whats your name?

THE FLOWER GIRL Liza Doolittle.

HIGGINS [*Declaiming gravely.*]

> Eliza, Elizabeth, Betsy and Bess,
> They went to the woods to get a bird's nes':

PICKERING They found a nest with four eggs in it:

HIGGINS They took one apiece, and left three in it.

[*They laugh heartily at their own fun.*]

LIZA Oh, dont be silly.

MRS PEARCE [*Placing herself behind* ELIZA'S *chair.*] You mustnt speak to the gentleman like that.

LIZA Well, why wont he speak sensible to me?

HIGGINS Come back to business. How much do you propose to pay me for the lessons?

LIZA Oh, I know whats right. A lady friend of mine gets French lessons for eighteenpence an hour from a real French gentleman. Well, you wouldnt have the face to ask me the same for teaching me my own language as you would for French; so I wont give more than a shilling. Take it or leave it.

HIGGINS [*Walking up and down the room, rattling his keys*

and his cash in his pockets.] You know, Pickering, if you consider a shilling, not as a simple shilling, but as a percentage of this girl's income, it works out as fully equivalent to sixty or seventy guineas from a millionaire.

PICKERING How so?

HIGGINS Figure it out. A millionaire has about £150 a day. She earns about half-a-crown.

LIZA [*Haughtily.*] Who told you I only . . .

HIGGINS [*Continuing.*] She offers me two-fifths of her day's income for a lesson. Two-fifths of a millionaire's income for a day would be somewhere about £60. It's handsome. By George, it's enormous! it's the biggest offer I ever had.

LIZA [*Rising, terrified.*] Sixty pounds! What are you talking about? I never offered you sixty pounds. Where would I get . . .

HIGGINS Hold your tongue.

LIZA [*Weeping.*] But I aint got sixty pounds. Oh . . .

MRS PEARCE Dont cry, you silly girl. Sit down. Nobody is going to touch your money.

HIGGINS Somebody is going to touch you, with a broomstick, if you dont stop snivelling. Sit down.

LIZA [*Obeying slowly.*] Ah-ah-ah-ow-oo-o! One would think you was my father.

HIGGINS If I decide to teach you, I'll be worse than two fathers to you. Here! [*He offers her his silk handkerchief.*]

LIZA Whats this for?

HIGGINS To wipe your eyes. To wipe any part of your face that feels moist. Remember: thats your handkerchief; and thats your sleeve. Dont mistake the one for the other if you wish to become a lady in a shop.

[LIZA, *utterly bewildered, stares helplessly at him.*]

MRS PEARCE It's no use talking to her like that, Mr Higgins: she doesnt understand you. Besides, youre quite wrong: she doesnt do it that way at all. [*She takes the handkerchief.*]

LIZA [*Snatching it.*] Here! You give me that handkerchief. He gev it to me, not to you.

PICKERING [*Laughing.*] He did. I think it must be regarded as her property, Mrs Pearce.

MRS PEARCE [*Resigning herself.*] Serve you right, Mr Higgins.

PICKERING Higgins: I'm interested. What about the ambassador's garden party? I'll say youre the greatest teacher alive if you make that good. I'll bet you all the expenses of the experiment you cant do it. And I'll pay for the lessons.

LIZA Oh, you are real good. Thank you, Captain.

HIGGINS [*Tempted, looking at her.*] It's almost irresistible. She's so deliciously low—so horribly dirty . . .

LIZA [*Protesting extremely.*] Ah-ah-ah-ah-ow-ow-oo-oo!!! I aint dirty: I washed my face and hands afore I come, I did.

PICKERING Youre certainly not going to turn her head with flattery, Higgins.

MRS PEARCE [*Uneasy.*] Oh, dont say that, sir: theres more ways than one of turning a girl's head; and nobody can do it better than Mr Higgins, though he may not always mean it. I do hope, sir, you wont encourage him to do anything foolish.

HIGGINS [*Becoming excited as the idea grows on him.*] What is life but a series of inspired follies? The difficulty is to find them to do. Never lose a chance: it doesnt come every day. I shall make a duchess of this draggletailed guttersnipe.

LIZA [*Strongly deprecating this view of her.*] Ah-ah-ah-ow-ow-oo!

HIGGINS [*Carried away.*] Yes: in six months—in three if she has a good ear and a quick tongue—I'll take her anywhere and pass her off as anything. We'll start today: now! this moment! Take her away and clean her, Mrs Pearce. Monkey Brand, if it wont come off any other way. Is there a good fire in the kitchen?

MRS PEARCE [*Protesting.*] Yes; but . . .

HIGGINS [*Storming on.*] Take all her clothes off and burn them. Ring up Whitely or somebody for new ones. Wrap her up in brown paper til they come.

LIZA Youre no gentleman, youre not, to talk of such things. I'm a good girl, I am; and I know what the like of you are, I do.

HIGGINS We want none of your Lisson Grove prudery here, young woman. Youve got to learn to behave like a duchess. Take her away, Mrs Pearce. If she gives you any trouble, wallop her.

LIZA [*Springing up and running between* PICKERING *and* MRS PEARCE *for protection.*] No! I'll call the police, I will.

MRS PEARCE But Ive no place to put her.

HIGGINS Put her in the dustbin.

LIZA Ah-ah-ah-ow-ow-oo!

PICKERING Oh come, Higgins! be reasonable.

MRS PEARCE [*Resolutely.*] You must be reasonable, Mr Higgins: really you must. You cant walk over everybody like this.

[HIGGINS, *thus scolded, subsides. The hurricane is succeeded by a zephyr of amiable surprise.*]

HIGGINS [*With professional exquisiteness of modulation.*] I walk over everybody! My dear Mrs Pearce, my dear Pickering, I never had the slightest intention of walking over anyone. All I propose is that we should be kind to this poor girl. We must help her to prepare and fit herself for her new station in life. If I did not express myself clearly it was because I did not wish to hurt her delicacy, or yours.

[LIZA, *reassured, steals back to her chair.*]

MRS PEARCE [*To* PICKERING.] Well, did you ever hear anything like that, sir?

PICKERING [*Laughing heartily.*] Never, Mrs Pearce: never.

HIGGINS [*Patiently.*] Whats the matter?

MRS PEARCE Well, the matter is, sir, that you cant take a girl up like that as if you were picking up a pebble on the beach.

HIGGINS Why not?

MRS PEARCE Why not! But you dont know anything about her. What about her parents? She may be married.

LIZA Garn!

HIGGINS There! As the girl very properly says, Garn! Married indeed! Dont you know that a woman of that class looks a worn out drudge of fifty a year after she's married?

LIZA Whood marry me?

HIGGINS [*Suddenly resorting to the most thrillingly beautiful low tones in his best elocutionary style.*] By George, Eliza, the streets will be strewn with the bodies of men shooting themselves for your sake before Ive done with you.

MRS PEARCE Nonsense, sir. You mustnt talk like that to her.

LIZA [*Rising and squaring herself determinedly.*] I'm going away. He's off his chump, he is. I dont want no balmies teaching me.

HIGGINS [*Wounded in his tenderest point by her insensibility to his elocution.*] Oh, indeed! I'm mad, am I? Very well, Mrs Pearce: you neednt order the new clothes for her. Throw her out.

LIZA [*Whimpering.*] Nah-ow. You got no right to touch me.

MRS PEARCE You see now what comes of being saucy. [*Indicating the door.*] This way, please.

LIZA [*Almost in tears.*] I didnt want no clothes. I wouldnt have taken them. [*She throws away the handkerchief.*] I can buy my own clothes.

HIGGINS [*Deftly retrieving the handkerchief and intercepting her on her reluctant way to the door.*] Youre an ungrateful wicked girl. This is my return for offering to take you out of the gutter and dress you beautifully and make a lady of you.

MRS PEARCE Stop, Mr Higgins. I wont allow it. It's you that are wicked. Go home to your parents, girl; and tell them to take better care of you.

LIZA I aint got no parents. They told me I was big enough to earn my own living and turned me out.

MRS PEARCE Wheres your mother?

LIZA I aint got no mother. Her that turned me out was my sixth stepmother. But I done without them. And I'm a good girl, I am.

HIGGINS Very well, then, what on earth is all this fuss about? The girl doesnt belong to anybody—is no use to anybody but me. [*He goes to* MRS PEARCE *and begins coaxing.*] You can adopt her, Mrs Pearce: I'm sure a daughter would be a great amusement to you. Now dont make any more fuss. Take her downstairs; and . . .

MRS PEARCE But whats to become of her? Is she to be paid anything? Do be sensible, sir.

HIGGINS Oh, pay her whatever is necessary: put it down in the housekeeping book. [*Impatiently.*] What on earth will she want with money? She'll have her food and her clothes. She'll only drink if you give her money.

LIZA [*Turning on him.*]   Oh you are a brute. It's a lie: nobody ever saw the sign of liquor on me. [*To* PICKERING.]   Oh, sir: youre a gentleman: dont let him speak to me like that.

PICKERING [*In good-humored remonstrance.*]   Does it occur to you, Higgins, that the girl has some feelings?

HIGGINS [*Looking critically at her.*]   Oh no, I dont think so. Not any feelings that we need bother about. [*Cheerily.*]   Have you, Eliza?

LIZA   I got my feelings same as anyone else.

HIGGINS [*To* PICKERING, *reflectively.*]   You see the difficulty?

PICKERING   Eh? What difficulty?

HIGGINS   To get her to talk grammar. The mere pronunciation is easy enough.

LIZA   I dont want to talk grammar. I want to talk like a lady in a flowershop.

MRS PEARCE   Will you please keep to the point, Mr Higgins. I want to know on what terms the girl is to be here. Is she to have any wages? And what is to become of her when youve finished your teaching? You must look ahead a little.

HIGGINS [*Impatiently.*]   Whats to become of her if I leave her in the gutter? Tell me that, Mrs Pearce.

MRS PEARCE   Thats her own business, not yours, Mr Higgins.

HIGGINS   Well, when Ive done with her, we can throw her back into the gutter; and then it will be her own business again; so thats all right.

LIZA   Oh, youve no feeling heart in you: you dont care for nothing but yourself. [*She rises and takes the floor resolutely.*] Here! Ive had enough of this. I'm going. [*Making for the door.*] You ought to be ashamed of yourself, you ought.

HIGGINS [*Snatching a chocolate cream from the piano, his eyes suddenly beginning to twinkle with mischief.*]   Have some chocolates, Eliza.

LIZA [*Halting, tempted.*]   How do I know what might be in them? Ive heard of girls being drugged by the like of you.

[HIGGINS *whips out his penknife; cuts a chocolate in two; puts one half into his mouth and bolts it; and offers her the other half.*]

HIGGINS   Pledge of good faith, Eliza. I eat one half: you eat the other. [LIZA *opens her mouth to retort: he pops the half chocolate into it.*] You shall have boxes of them, barrels of them, every day. You shall live on them. Eh?

LIZA [*Who has disposed of the chocolate after being nearly choked by it.*] I wouldnt have ate it, only I'm too ladylike to take it out of my mouth.

HIGGINS   Listen, Eliza. I think you said you came in a taxi.

LIZA   Well, what if I did? Ive as good a right to take a taxi as anyone else.

HIGGINS   You have, Eliza; and in future you shall have as many taxis as you want. You shall go up and down and round the town in a taxi every day. Think of that, Eliza.

MRS PEARCE   Mr Higgins: youre tempting the girl. It's not right. She should think of the future.

HIGGINS   At her age! Nonsense! Time enough to think of the future when you havnt any future to think of. No, Eliza: do as this lady does: think of other people's futures; but never think of your own. Think of chocolates, and taxis, and gold, and diamonds.

LIZA   No: I dont want no gold and no diamonds. I'm a good girl, I am. [*She sits down again, with an attempt at dignity.*]

HIGGINS   You shall remain so, Eliza, under the care of Mrs Pearce. And you shall marry an officer in the Guards, with a beautiful mustache: the son of a marquis, who will disinherit him for marrying you, but will relent when he sees your beauty and goodness . . .

PICKERING   Excuse me, Higgins; but I really must interfere. Mrs Pearce is quite right. If this girl is to put herself in your hands for six months for an experiment in teaching, she must understand thoroughly what she's doing.

HIGGINS   How can she? She's incapable of understanding anything. Besides, do any of us understand what we are doing? If we did, would we ever do it?

PICKERING   Very clever, Higgins; but not to the present point. [*To* ELIZA.]   Miss Doolittle . . .

LIZA [*Overwhelmed.*]   Ah-ah-ow-oo!

HIGGINS   There! Thats all youll get out of Eliza. Ah-ah-ow-oo!

No use explaining. As a military man you ought to know that. Give her her orders: thats enough for her. Eliza: you are to live here for the next six months, learning how to speak beautifully, like a lady in a florist's shop. If youre good and do whatever youre told, you shall sleep in a proper bedroom, and have lots to eat, and money to buy chocolates and take rides in taxis. If youre naughty and idle you will sleep in the back kitchen among the black beetles, and be walloped by Mrs Pearce with a broomstick. At the end of six months you shall go to Buckingham Palace in a carriage, beautifully dressed. If the King finds out youre not a lady, you will be taken by the police to the Tower of London, where your head will be cut off as a warning to other presumptuous flower girls. If you are not found out, you shall have a present of seven-and-sixpence to start life with as a lady in a shop. If you refuse this offer you will be a most ungrateful wicked girl; and the angels will weep for you. [To PICKERING.]   Now are you satisfied, Pickering? [To MRS PEARCE.]   Can I put it more plainly and fairly, Mrs Pearce?

MRS PEARCE [Patiently.]   I think youd better let me speak to the girl properly in private. I dont know that I can take charge of her or consent to the arrangement at all. Of course I know you dont mean her any harm; but when you get what you call interested in people's accents, you never think or care what may happen to them or you. Come with me, Eliza.

HIGGINS   Thats all right. Thank you, Mrs Pearce. Bundle her off to the bathroom.

LIZA [Rising reluctantly and suspiciously.]   Youre a great bully, you are. I wont stay here if I dont like. I wont let nobody wallop me. I never asked to go to Bucknam Palace, I didnt. I was never in trouble with the police, not me. I'm a good girl . . .

MRS PEARCE   Dont answer back, girl. You dont understand the gentleman. Come with me. [She leads the way to the door, and holds it open for ELIZA.]

LIZA [As she goes out.]   Well, what I say is right. I wont go near the King, not if I'm going to have my head cut off. If I'd known what I was letting myself in for, I wouldnt have come here. I always been a good girl; and I never offered to say a word to him; and I dont owe him nothing; and I dont care; and I wont be put upon; and I have my feelings the same as anyone else . . .

[MRS PEARCE *shuts the door; and* ELIZA's *plaints are no longer audible.*]

*　　　*　　　*　　　*　　　*　　　*

Eliza is taken upstairs to the third floor greatly to her surprise; for she expected to be taken down to the scullery. There Mrs Pearce opens a door and takes her into a spare bedroom.

MRS PEARCE　I will have to put you here. This will be your bedroom.

LIZA　O-h, I couldn't sleep here, missus. It's too good for the likes of me. I should be afraid to touch anything. I aint a duchess yet, you know.

MRS PEARCE　You have got to make yourself as clean as the room: then you wont be afraid of it. And you must call me Mrs Pearce, not missus. [*She throws open the door of the dressing-room, now modernized as a bathroom.*]

LIZA　Gawd! whats this? Is this where you wash clothes? Funny sort of copper I call it.

MRS PEARCE　It is not a copper. This is where we wash ourselves, Eliza, and where I am going to wash you.

LIZA　You expect me to get into that and wet myself all over! Not me. I should catch my death. I knew a woman did it every Saturday night; and she died of it.

MRS PEARCE　Mr Higgins has the gentlemen's bathroom downstairs; and he has a bath every morning, in cold water.

LIZA　Ugh! He's made of iron, that man.

MRS PEARCE　If you are to sit with him and the Colonel and be taught you will have to do the same. They wont like the smell of you if you dont. But you can have the water as hot as you like. There are two taps: hot and cold.

LIZA　[*Weeping.*]　I couldnt. I dursnt. Its not natural: it would kill me. Ive never had a bath in my life: not what youd call a proper one.

MRS PEARCE　Well, dont you want to be clean and sweet and

decent, like a lady? You know you cant be a nice girl inside if youre a dirty slut outside.

LIZA   Boohoo!!!!

MRS PEARCE   Now stop crying and go back into your room and take off all your clothes. Then wrap yourself in this [*taking down a gown from its peg and handing it to her*]   and come back to me. I will get the bath ready.

LIZA   [*All tears.*]   I cant. I wont. I'm not used to it. Ive never took off all my clothes before. It's not right: it's not decent.

MRS PEARCE   Nonsense, child. Dont you take off all your clothes every night when you go to bed?

LIZA   [*Amazed.*]   No. Why should I? I should catch my death. Of course I take off my skirt.

MRS PEARCE   Do you mean that you sleep in the underclothes you wear in the daytime?

LIZA   What else have I to sleep in?

MRS PEARCE   You will never do that again as long as you live here. I will get you a proper nightdress.

LIZA   Do you mean change into cold things and lie awake shivering half the night? You want to kill me, you do.

MRS PEARCE   I want to change you from a frowzy slut to a clean respectable girl fit to sit with the gentlemen in the study. Are you going to trust me and do what I tell you or be thrown out and sent back to your flower basket?

LIZA   But you dont know what the cold is to me. You dont know how I dread it.

MRS PEARCE   Your bed won't be cold here: I will put a hot water bottle in it. [*Pushing her into the bedroom.*]   Off with you and undress.

LIZA   Oh, if only I'd known what a dreadful thing it is to be clean I'd never have come. I didnt know when I was well off. I . . . [MRS PEARCE *pushes her through the door, but leaves it partly open lest her prisoner should take to flight.*]

[MRS PEARCE *puts on a pair of white rubber sleeves, and fills the bath, mixing hot and cold, and testing the result with the bath thermometer. She perfumes it with a handful of bath salts and*

*adds a palmful of mustard. She then takes a formidable looking
long handled scrubbing brush and soaps it profusely with a ball
of scented soap.*]

[ELIZA *comes back with nothing on but the bath gown huddled
tightly round her, a piteous spectacle of abject terror.*]

MRS PEARCE   Now come along. Take that thing off.

LIZA   Oh I couldnt, Mrs Pearce: I reely couldnt. I never done
such a thing.

MRS PEARCE   Nonsense. Here: step in and tell me whether its
hot enough for you.

LIZA   Ah-oo! Ah-oo! It's too hot.

MRS PEARCE [*Deftly snatching the gown away and throwing
ELIZA down on her back.*]   It wont hurt you. [*She sets to work
with the scrubbing brush.*]

[ELIZA'S *screams are heartrending.*]

*   *   *   *   *   *

Meanwhile the Colonel has been having it out with Higgins
about Eliza. Pickering has come from the hearth to the chair and
seated himself astride of it with his arms on the back to cross-
examine him.

PICKERING   Excuse the straight question, Higgins. Are you a
man of good character where women are concerned?

HIGGINS [*Moodily.*]   Have you ever met a man of good character where women are concerned?

PICKERING   Yes: very frequently.

HIGGINS [*Dogmatically, lifting himself on his hands to the level
of the piano, and sitting on it with a bounce.*]   Well, I havnt.
I find that the moment I let a woman make friends with me, she
becomes jealous, exacting, suspicious, and a damned nuisance. I
find that the moment I let myself make friends with a woman, I
become selfish and tyrannical. Women upset everything. When
you let them into your life, you find that the woman is driving
at one thing and youre driving at another.

PICKERING   At what, for example?

HIGGINS [*Coming off the piano restlessly.*]   Oh, Lord knows!

I suppose the woman wants to live her own life; and the man wants to live his; and each tries to drag the other on to the wrong track. One wants to go north and the other south; and the result is that both have to go east, though they both hate the east wind. [*He sits down on the bench at the keyboard.*] So here I am, a confirmed old bachelor, and likely to remain so.

PICKERING [*Rising and standing over him gravely.*] Come, Higgins! You know what I mean. If I'm to be in this business I shall feel responsible for that girl. I hope it's understood that no advantage is to be taken of her position.

HIGGINS What! That thing! Sacred, I assure you. [*Rising to explain.*] You see, she'll be a pupil; and teaching would be impossible unless pupils were sacred. Ive taught scores of American millionairesses how to speak English: the best looking women in the world. I'm seasoned. They might as well be blocks of wood. *I* might as well be a block of wood. It's . . .

[MRS PEARCE *opens the door. She has* ELIZA's *hat in her hand.* PICKERING *retires to the easy-chair at the hearth and sits down.*]

HIGGINS [*Eagerly.*] Well, Mrs Pearce: is it all right?

MRS PEARCE [*At the door.*] I just wish to trouble you with a word, if I may, Mr Higgins.

HIGGINS Yes, certainly. Come in. [*She comes forward.*] Dont burn that, Mrs Pearce. I'll keep it as a curiosity. [*He takes the hat.*]

MRS PEARCE Handle it carefully, sir, please. I had to promise her not to burn it; but I had better put it in the oven for a while.

HIGGINS [*Putting it down hastily on the piano.*] Oh! thank you. Well, what have you to say to me?

PICKERING Am I in the way?

MRS PEARCE Not in the least, sir. Mr Higgins: will you please be very particular what you say before the girl?

HIGGINS [*Sternly.*] Of course. I'm always particular about what I say. Why do you say this to me?

MRS PEARCE [*Unmoved.*] No, sir: youre not at all particular when youve mislaid anything or when you get a little impatient. Now it doesnt matter before me: I'm used to it. But you really must not swear before the girl.

HIGGINS [*Indignantly.*] I swear! [*Most emphatically.*] I never swear. I detest the habit. What the devil do you mean?

MRS PEARCE [*Stolidly.*] Thats what I mean, sir. You swear a great deal too much. I dont mind your damning and blasting, and what the devil and where the devil and who the devil . . .

HIGGINS Mrs Pearce: this language from your lips! Really!

MRS PEARCE [*Not to be put off.*] . . . but there is a certain word I must ask you not to use. The girl used it herself when she began to enjoy the bath. It begins with the same letter as bath. She knows no better: she learnt it at her mother's knee. But she must not hear it from your lips.

HIGGINS [*Loftily.*] I cannot charge myself with having ever uttered it, Mrs Pearce. [*She looks at him steadfastly. He adds, hiding an uneasy conscience with a judicial air.*] Except perhaps in a moment of extreme and justifiable excitement.

MRS PEARCE Only this morning, sir, you applied it to your boots, to the butter, and to the brown bread.

HIGGINS Oh, that! Mere alliteration, Mrs Pearce, natural to a poet.

MRS PEARCE Well, sir, whatever you choose to call it, I beg you not to let the girl hear you repeat it.

HIGGINS Oh, very well, very well. Is that all?

MRS PEARCE No, sir. We shall have to be very particular with this girl as to personal cleanliness.

HIGGINS Certainly. Quite right. Most important.

MRS PEARCE I mean not to be slovenly about her dress or untidy in leaving things about.

HIGGINS [*Going to her solemnly.*] Just so, I intended to call your attention to that. [*He passes on to* PICKERING, *who is enjoying the conversation immensely*.] It is these little things that matter, Pickering. Take care of the pence and the pounds will take care of themselves is as true of personal habits as of money. [*He comes to anchor on the hearthrug, with the air of a man in an unassailable position.*]

MRS PEARCE Yes, sir. Then might I ask you not to come down to breakfast in your dressing gown, or at any rate not to use it as a napkin to the extent you do, sir. And if you would be so good as not to eat everything off the same plate, and to remember not to put the porridge saucepan out of your hand on the clean tablecloth, it would be a better example to the girl. You know you nearly choked yourself with a fishbone in a jam only last week.

HIGGINS [*Routed from the hearthrug and drifting back to the piano.*] I may do these things sometimes in absence of mind; but surely I dont do them habitually. [*Angrily.*] By the way: my dressing gown smells most damnably of benzine.

MRS PEARCE No doubt it does, Mr Higgins. But if you will wipe your fingers . . .

HIGGINS [*Yelling.*] Oh very well, very well: I'll wipe them in my hair in future.

MRS PEARCE I hope youre not offended, Mr Higgins.

HIGGINS [*Shocked at finding himself thought capable of an unamiable sentiment.*] Not at all, not at all. Youre quite right, Mrs Pearce: I shall be particularly careful before the girl. Is that all?

MRS PEARCE No, sir. Might she use some of those Japanese dresses you brought from abroad? I really cant put her back into her old things.

HIGGINS Certainly. Anything you like. Is that all?

MRS PEARCE Thank you, sir. Thats all. [*She goes out.*]

HIGGINS You know, Pickering, that woman has the most extraordinary ideas about me. Here I am, a shy, diffident sort of man. Ive never been able to feel really grown-up and tremendous, like other chaps. And yet she's firmly persuaded that I'm an arbitrary overbearing bossing kind of person. I cant account for it.

[MRS PEARCE *returns.*]

MRS PEARCE If you please, sir, the trouble's beginning already. Theres a dustman downstairs, Alfred Doolittle, wants to see you. He says you have his daughter here.

PICKERING [*Rising.*] Phew! I say!

HIGGINS [*Promptly.*] Send the blackguard up.

MRS PEARCE Oh, very well, sir. [*She goes out.*]

PICKERING He may not be a blackguard, Higgins.

HIGGINS Nonsense. Of course he's a blackguard.

PICKERING Whether he is or not, I'm afraid we shall have some trouble with him.

HIGGINS [*Confidently.*] Oh no: I think not. If theres any trouble he shall have it with me, not I with him. And we are sure to get something interesting out of him.

PICKERING About the girl?

HIGGINS No. I mean his dialect.

PICKERING Oh!

MRS PEARCE [*At the door.*] Doolittle, sir. [*She admits Doolittle and retires.*]

[ALFRED *is an elderly but vigorous dustman, clad in the costume of his profession, including a hat with a back brim covering his neck and shoulders. He has well-marked and rather interesting features, and seems equally free from fear and conscience. He has a remarkably expressive voice, the result of a habit of giving vent to his feelings without reserve. His present pose is that of wounded honor and stern resolution.*]

DOOLITTLE [*At the door, uncertain which of the two gentlemen is his man.*] Professor Iggins?

HIGGINS Here. Good morning. Sit down.

DOOLITTLE Morning, Governor. [*He sits down magisterially.*] I come about a very serious matter, Governor.

HIGGINS [*to* PICKERING.] Brought up in Hounslow. Mother Welsh, I should think. [DOOLITTLE *opens his mouth, amazed.* HIGGINS *continues.*] What do you want, Doolittle?

DOOLITTLE [*Menacingly.*] I want my daughter: thats what I want. See?

HIGGINS Of course you do. Youre her father, arnt you? You dont suppose anyone else wants her, do you? I'm glad to see you have some spark of family feeling left. She's upstairs. Take her away at once.

DOOLITTLE [*Rising, fearfully taken aback.*] What!

HIGGINS Take her away. Do you suppose I'm going to keep your daughter for you?

DOOLITTLE [*Remonstrating.*] Now, now, look here, Governor. Is this reasonable? Is it fairity to take advantage of a man like this? The girl belongs to me. You got her. Where do I come in? [*He sits down again.*]

HIGGINS Your daughter had the audacity to come to my house

and ask me to teach her how to speak properly so that she could get a place in a flowershop. This gentleman and my housekeeper have been here all the time. [*Bullying him.*] How dare you come here and attempt to blackmail me? You sent her here on purpose.

DOOLITTLE [*Protesting.*]   No, Governor.

HIGGINS   You must have. How else could you possibly know that she is here?

DOOLITTLE   Dont take a man up like that, Governor.

HIGGINS   The police shall take you up. This is a plant—a plot to extort money by threats. I shall telephone for the police. [*He goes resolutely to the telephone and opens the directory.*]

DOOLITTLE   Have I asked you for a brass farthing? I leave it to the gentleman here: have I said a word about money?

HIGGINS [*Throwing the book aside and marching down on* DOOLITTLE *with a poser.*]   What else did you come for?

DOOLITTLE [*Sweetly.*]   Well, what would a man come for? Be human, Governor.

HIGGINS [*Disarmed.*]   Alfred: did you put her up to it?

DOOLITTLE   So help me, Governor, I never did. I take my Bible oath I aint seen the girl these two months past.

HIGGINS   Then how did you know she was here?

DOOLITTLE [*"Most musical, most melancholy."*]   I'll tell you, Governor, if youll only let me get a word in. I'm willing to tell you. I'm wanting to tell you. I'm waiting to tell you.

HIGGINS   Pickering: this chap has a certain natural gift of rhetoric. Observe the rhythm of his native woodnotes wild. "I'm willing to tell you: I'm wanting to tell you: I'm waiting to tell you." Sentimental rhetoric! thats the Welsh strain in him. It also accounts for his mendacity and dishonesty.

PICKERING   Oh, please, Higgins: I'm west country myself. [*To* DOOLITTLE.]   How did you know the girl was here if you didnt send her?

DOOLITTLE   It was like this, Governor. The girl took a boy in the taxi to give him a jaunt. Son of her landlady, he is. He hung about on the chance of her giving him another ride home. Well, she sent him back for her luggage when she heard you was willing for her to stop here. I met the boy at the corner of Long Acre and Endell Street.

HIGGINS   Public house. Yes?

DOOLITTLE   The poor man's club, Governor: why shouldnt I?

PICKERING   Do let him tell his story, Higgins.

DOOLITTLE   He told me what was up. And I ask you, what was my feelings and my duty as a father? I says to the boy, "You bring me the luggage," I says . . .

PICKERING   Why didnt you go for it yourself?

DOOLITTLE   Landlady wouldnt have trusted me with it, Governor. She's that kind of woman: you know. I had to give the boy a penny afore he trusted me with it, the little swine. I brought it to her just to oblige you like, and make myself agreeable. Thats all.

HIGGINS   How much luggage?

DOOLITTLE   Musical instrument, Governor. A few pictures, a trifle of jewelry, and a birdcage. She said she didnt want no clothes. What was I to think from that, Governor? I ask you as a parent what was I to think?

HIGGINS   So you came to rescue her from worse than death, eh?

DOOLITTLE   [Appreciatively: relieved at being so well understood.]   Just so, Governor. Thats right.

PICKERING   But why did you bring her luggage if you intended to take her away?

DOOLITTLE   Have I said a word about taking her away? Have I now?

HIGGINS   [Determinedly.]   Youre going to take her away, double quick. [He crosses to the hearth and rings the bell.]

DOOLITTLE   [Rising.]   No, Governor. Dont say that. I'm not the man to stand in my girl's light. Heres a career opening for her, as you might say; and . . .

[MRS PEARCE opens the door and awaits orders.]

HIGGINS   Mrs. Pearce: this is Eliza's father. He has come to take her away. Give her to him. [He goes back to the piano, with an air of washing his hands of the whole affair.]

DOOLITTLE   No. This is a misunderstanding. Listen here . . .

MRS PEARCE   He cant take her away, Mr Higgins: how can he? You told me to burn her clothes.

DOOLITTLE   Thats right. I cant carry the girl through the streets like a blooming monkey, can I? I put it to you.

HIGGINS   You have put it to me that you want your daughter. Take your daughter. If she has no clothes go out and buy her some.

DOOLITTLE   [*Desperate.*]   Wheres the clothes she come in? Did I burn them or did your missus here?

MRS PEARCE   I am the housekeeper, if you please. I have sent for some clothes for your girl. When they come you can take her away. You can wait in the kitchen. This way, please.

[DOOLITTLE, *much troubled, accompanies her to the door; then hesitates; finally turns confidentially to* HIGGINS.]

DOOLITTLE   Listen here, Governor. You and me is men of the world, aint we?

HIGGINS   Oh! Men of the world, are we? Youd better go, Mrs Pearce.

MRS PEARCE   I think so, indeed, sir. [*She goes, with dignity.*]

PICKERING   The floor is yours, Mr Doolittle.

DOOLITTLE   [*To* PICKERING.]   I thank you, Governor. [*To* HIGGINS, *who takes refuge on the piano bench, a little overwhelmed by the proximity of his visitor; for* DOOLITTLE *has a professional flavor of dust about him.*]   Well, the truth is, Ive taken a sort of fancy to you, Governor; and if you want the girl, I'm not so set on having her back home again but what I might be open to an arrangement. Regarded in the light of a young woman, she's a fine handsome girl. As a daughter she's not worth her keep; and so I tell you straight. All I ask is my rights as a father; and youre the last man alive to expect me to let her go for nothing; for I can see youre one of the straight sort, Governor. Well, whats a five-pound note to you? and whats Eliza to me? [*He turns to his chair and sits down judicially.*]

PICKERING   I think you ought to know, Doolittle, that Mr Higgins's intentions are entirely honorable.

DOOLITTLE   Course they are, Governor. If I thought they wasnt, I'd ask fifty.

HIGGINS [*Revolted.*] Do you mean to say that you would sell your daughter for £50?

DOOLITTLE Not in a general way I would; but to oblige a gentleman like you I'd do a good deal, I do assure you.

PICKERING Have you no morals, man?

DOOLITTLE [*Unabashed.*] Cant afford them, Governor. Neither could you if you was as poor as me. Not that I mean any harm, you know. But if Liza is going to have a bit out of this, why not me too?

HIGGINS [*Troubled.*] I dont know what to do, Pickering. There can be no question that as a matter of morals it's a positive crime to give this chap a farthing. And yet I feel a sort of rough justice in his claim.

DOOLITTLE Thats it, Governor. Thats all I say. A father's heart, as it were.

PICKERING Well, I know the feeling; but really it seems hardly right . . .

DOOLITTLE Dont say that, Governor. Dont look at it that way. What am I, Governors both? I ask you, what am I? I'm one of the undeserving poor: thats what I am. Think of what that means to a man. It means that he's up agen middle-class morality all the time. If theres anything going, and I put in for a bit of it, it's always the same story: "Youre undeserving; so you cant have it." But my needs is as great as the most deserving widow's that ever got money out of six different charities in one week for the death of the same husband. I dont need less than a deserving man: I need more. I dont eat less hearty than him; and I drink a lot more. I want a bit of amusement, cause I'm a thinking man. I want cheerfulness and a song and a band when I feel low. Well, they charge me just the same for everything as they charge the deserving. What is middle-class morality? Just an excuse for never giving me anything. Therefore, I ask you, as two gentlemen, not to play that game on me. I'm playing straight with you. I aint pretending to be deserving. I'm undeserving; and I mean to go on being undeserving. I like it; and thats the truth. Will you take advantage of a man's nature to do him out of the price of his own daughter what he's brought up and fed and clothed by the sweat of his brow until she's growed big enough to be interesting to you two gentlemen? Is five pounds unreasonable? I put it to you; and I leave it to you.

HIGGINS [*Rising, and going over to* PICKERING.] Pickering: if we were to take this man in hand for three months, he could choose between a seat in the Cabinet and a popular pulpit in Wales.

PICKERING What do you say to that, Doolittle?

DOOLITTLE Not me, Governor, thank you kindly. Ive heard all the preachers and all the prime ministers—for I'm a thinking man and game for politics or religion or social reform same as all the other amusements—and I tell you it's a dog's life any way you look at it. Undeserving poverty is my line. Taking one station in society with another, it's—it's—well, it's the only one that has any ginger in it, to my taste.

HIGGINS I suppose we must give him a fiver.

PICKERING He'll make a bad use of it, I'm afraid.

DOOLITTLE Not me, Governor, so help me I wont. Dont you be afraid that I'll save it and spare it and live idle on it. There wont be a penny of it left by Monday: I'll have to go to work same as if I'd never had it. It wont pauperize me, you bet. Just one good spree for myself and the missus, giving pleasure to ourselves and employment to others, and satisfaction to you to think it's not been throwed away. You couldnt spend it better.

HIGGINS [*Taking out his pocketbook and coming between* DOOLITTLE *and the piano.*] This is irresistible. Lets give him ten. [*He offers two notes to the dustman.*]

DOOLITTLE No, Governor. She wouldn't have the heart to spend ten; and perhaps I shouldnt neither. Ten pounds is a lot of money: it makes a man feel prudent like; and then goodbye to happiness. You give me what I ask you, Governor: not a penny more, and not a penny less.

PICKERING Why dont you marry that missus of yours? I rather draw the line at encouraging that sort of immorality.

DOOLITTLE Tell her so, Governor: tell her so. I'm willing. It's me that suffers by it. Ive no hold on her. I got to be agreeable to her. I got to give her presents. I got to buy her clothes something sinful. I'm a slave to that woman, Governor, just because I'm not her lawful husband. And she knows it too. Catch her marrying me! Take my advice, Governor: marry Eliza while she's young and dont know no better. If you dont you'll be sorry for it after. If you do, she'll be sorry for it after; but better her than you, because youre a man, and she's only a woman and dont know how to be happy anyhow.

HIGGINS Pickering: if we listen to this man another minute, we shall have no convictions left. [*To* DOOLITTLE.] Five pounds I think you said.

DOOLITTLE Thank you kindly, Governor.

HIGGINS Youre sure you wont take ten?

DOOLITTLE Not now. Another time, Governor.

HIGGINS [*Handing him a five-pound note.*] Here you are.

DOOLITTLE Thank you, Governor. Good morning. [*He hurries to the door, anxious to get away with his booty. When he opens it he is confronted with a dainty and exquisitely clean young Japanese lady in a simple blue cotton kimono printed cunningly with small white jasmine blossoms.* MRS PEARCE *is with her. He gets out of her way deferentially and apologizes.*] Beg pardon, miss.

THE JAPANESE LADY Garn! Dont you know your own daughter?

DOOLITTLE	*Exclaiming*	Bly me! it's Eliza!
HIGGINS	*simul-*	Whats that? This!
PICKERING	*taneously.*	By Jove!

LIZA Dont I look silly?

HIGGINS Silly?

MRS PEARCE [*At the door.*] Now, Mr Higgins, please dont say anything to make the girl conceited about herself.

HIGGINS [*Conscientiously.*] Oh! Quite right, Mrs Pearce. [*To* ELIZA.] Yes: damned silly.

MRS PEARCE Please, sir.

HIGGINS [*Correcting himself.*] I mean extremely silly.

LIZA I should look all right with my hat on. [*She takes up her hat; puts it on; and walks across the room to the fireplace with a fashionable air.*]

HIGGINS   A new fashion, by George! And it ought to look horrible!

DOOLITTLE [*With fatherly pride.*]   Well, I never thought she'd clean up as good looking as that, Governor. She's a credit to me, aint she?

LIZA   I tell you, it's easy to clean up here. Hot and cold water on tap, just as much as you like, there is. Woolly towels, there is; and a towel horse so hot, it burns your fingers. Soft brushes to scrub yourself, and a wooden bowl of soap smelling like primroses. Now I know why ladies is so clean. Washing's a treat for them. Wish they could see what it is for the like of me!

HIGGINS   I'm glad the bathroom met with your approval.

LIZA   It didnt: not all of it; and I dont care who hears me say it. Mrs Pearce knows.

HIGGINS   What was wrong, Mrs Pearce?

MRS PEARCE [*Blandly.*]   Oh, nothing, sir. It doesnt matter.

LIZA   I had a good mind to break it. I didnt know which way to look. But I hung a towel over it, I did.

HIGGINS   Over what?

MRS PEARCE   Over the looking glass, sir.

HIGGINS   Doolittle: you have brought your daughter up too strictly.

DOOLITTLE   Me! I never brought her up at all, except to give her a lick of a strap now and again. Dont put it on me, Governor. She aint accustomed to it, you see: thats all. But she'll soon pick up your free-and-easy ways.

LIZA   I'm a good girl, I am; and I wont pick up no free-and-easy ways.

HIGGINS   Eliza: if you say again that youre a good girl, your father shall take you home.

LIZA   Not him. You dont know my father. All he come here for was to touch you for some money to get drunk on.

DOOLITTLE   Well, what else would I want money for? To put into the plate in church, I suppose. [*She puts out her tongue at him. He is so incensed by this that* PICKERING *presently finds it necessary to step between them.*]   Dont you give me none of your lip; and dont let me hear you giving this gentleman any of it neither, or youll hear from me about it. See?

HIGGINS Have you any further advice to give her before you go, Doolittle? Your blessing, for instance.

DOOLITTLE No, Governor: I aint such a mug as to put up my children to all I know myself. Hard enough to hold them in without that. If you want Eliza's mind improved, Governor, you do it yourself with a strap. So long, gentlemen. [*He turns to go.*]

HIGGINS [*Impressively.*] Stop. Youll come regularly to see your daughter. It's your duty, you know. My brother is a clergyman; and he could help you in your talks with her.

DOOLITTLE [*Evasively.*] Certainly, I'll come, Governor. Not just this week, because I have a job at a distance. But later on you may depend on me. Afternoon, gentlemen. Afternoon, maam. [*He touches his hat to* MRS PEARCE, *who disdains the salutation and goes out. He winks at* HIGGINS, *thinking him probably a fellow-sufferer from* MRS PEARCE's *difficult disposition, and follows her.*]

LIZA Don't you believe the old liar. He'd as soon you set a bulldog on him as a clergyman. You wont see him again in a hurry.

HIGGINS I dont want to, Eliza. Do you?

LIZA Not me. I dont want never to see him again, I dont. He's a disgrace to me, he is, collecting dust, instead of working at his trade.

PICKERING What is his trade, Eliza?

LIZA Taking money out of other people's pockets into his own. His proper trade's a navvy; and he works at it sometimes too—for exercise—and earns good money at it. Aint you going to call me Miss Doolittle any more?

PICKERING I beg your pardon, Miss Doolittle. It was a slip of the tongue.

LIZA Oh, I dont mind; only it sounded so genteel. I should just like to take a taxi to the corner of Tottenham Court Road and get out there and tell it to wait for me, just to put the girls in their place a bit. I wouldnt speak to them, you know.

PICKERING   Better wait til we get you something really fashionable.

HIGGINS   Besides, you shouldnt cut your old friends now that you have risen in the world. Thats what we call snobbery.

LIZA   You dont call the like of them my friends now, I should hope. Theyve took it out of me often enough with their ridicule when they had the chance; and now I mean to get a bit of my own back. But if I'm to have fashionable clothes, I'll wait. I should like to have some. Mrs Pearce says youre going to give me some to wear in bed at night different to what I wear in the daytime; but it do seem a waste of money when you could get something to show. Besides, I never could fancy changing into cold things on a winter night.

MRS PEARCE   [Coming back.]   Now, Eliza. The new things have come for you to try on.

LIZA   Ah-ow-oo-ooh! [She rushes out.]

MRS PEARCE   [Following her.]   Oh, don't rush about like that, girl. [She shuts the door behind her.]

HIGGINS   Pickering: we have taken on a stiff job.

PICKERING   [With conviction.]   Higgins: we have.

*   *   *   *   *   *

There seems to be some curiosity as to what Higgins's lessons to Eliza were like. Well, here is a sample: the first one.

Picture Eliza, in her new clothes, and feeling her inside put out of step by a lunch, dinner, and breakfast of a kind to which it is unaccustomed, seated with Higgins and the Colonel in the study, feeling like a hospital out-patient at a first encounter with the doctors.

Higgins, constitutionally unable to sit still, discomposes her still more by striding restlessly about. But for the reassuring presence and quietude of her friend the Colonel she would run for her life, even back to Drury Lane.

HIGGINS   Say your alphabet.

LIZA   I know my alphabet. Do you think I know nothing? I dont need to be taught like a child.

HIGGINS [*Thundering.*]   Say your alphabet.

PICKERING   Say it, Miss Doolittle. You will understand presently. Do what he tells you; and let him teach you in his own way.

LIZA   Oh well, if you put it like that—Ahyee, bəyee, cəyee, dəyee . . .

HIGGINS [*With the roar of a wounded lion.*]   Stop. Listen to this, Pickering. This is what we pay for as elementary education. This unfortunate animal has been locked up for nine years in school at our expense to teach her to speak and read the language of Shakespear and Milton. And the result is Ahyee, Bə-yee, Cə-yee, Də-yee. [*To Eliza.*]   Say A, B, C, D.

LIZA [*Almost in tears.*]   But I'm sayin it. Ahyee, Bəyee, Cə-yee . . .

HIGGINS   Stop. Say a cup of tea.

LIZA   A cáppətə-ee.

HIGGINS   Put your tongue forward until it squeezes against the top of your lower teeth. Now say cup.

LIZA   C-c-c—I cant. C-Cup.

PICKERING   Good. Splendid, Miss Doolittle.

HIGGINS   By Jupiter, she's done it the first shot. Pickering: we shall make a duchess of her. [*To* ELIZA.]   Now do you think you could possibly say tea? Not tə-yee, mind: if you ever say bə-yee cə-yee də-yee again you shall be dragged round the room three times by the hair of your head. [*Fortissimo.*]   T, T, T, T.

LIZA [*Weeping.*]   I cant hear no difference cep that it sounds more genteel-like when you say it.

HIGGINS   Well, if you can hear that difference, what the devil are you crying for? Pickering: give her a chocolate.

PICKERING   No, no. Never mind crying a little, Miss Doolittle: you are doing very well; and the lessons wont hurt. I promise you I wont let him drag you round the room by your hair.

HIGGINS   Be off with you to Mrs Pearce and tell her about it. Think about it. Try to do it by yourself: and keep your tongue well forward in your mouth instead of trying to roll it up and swallow it. Another lesson at half-past four this afternoon. Away with you.

[ELIZA, *still sobbing, rushes from the room.*]

And that is the sort of ordeal poor Eliza has to go through for months before we meet her again on her first appearance in London society of the professional class.

ACT III

SCENE: *It is* MRS HIGGINS's *at-home day. Nobody has yet arrived. Her drawing room, in a flat on Chelsea Embankment, has three windows looking on the river; and the ceiling is not so lofty as it would be in an older house of the same pretension. The windows are open, giving access to a balcony with flowers in pots. If you stand with your face to the windows, you have the fireplace on your left and the door in the right-hand wall close to the corner nearest the windows.*

MRS HIGGINS *was brought up on Morris and Burne Jones; and her room, which is very unlike her son's room in Wimpole Street, is not crowded with furniture and little tables and nicknacks. In the middle of the room there is a big ottoman; and this, with the carpet, the Morris wallpapers, and the Morris chintz window curtains and brocade covers of the ottoman and its cushions, supply all the ornament, and are much too handsome to be hidden by odds and ends of useless things. A few good oil paintings from the exhibitions in the Grosvenor Gallery thirty years ago (the Burne Jones, not the Whistler side of them) are on the walls. The only landscape is a Cecil Lawson on the scale of a Rubens. There is a portrait of* MRS HIGGINS *as she was when she defied the fashion in her youth in one of the beautiful Rossettian costumes which, when caricatured by people who did not understand, led to the absurdities of popular estheticism in the eighteen-seventies.*

In the corner diagonally opposite the door MRS HIGGINS, *now over sixty and long past taking the trouble to dress out of the fashion, sits writing at an elegantly simple writing table with a bell button within reach of her hand. There is a Chippendale chair further back in the room between her and the window nearest her side. At the other side of the room, further forward, is an Elizabethan chair roughly carved in the taste of Inigo Jones. On the same side a piano in a decorated case. The corner between the fireplace and the window is occupied by a divan cushioned in Morris chintz.*

It is between four and five in the afternoon.

The door is opened violently; and HIGGINS *enters with his hat on.*

MRS HIGGINS [*Dismayed.*] Henry! [*Scolding him.*] What are you doing here today? It is my at-home day: you promised not to come. [*As he bends to kiss her, she takes his hat off, and presents it to him.*]

HIGGINS Oh bother! [*He throws the hat down on the table.*]

MRS HIGGINS Go home at once.

HIGGINS [*Kissing her.*] I know, mother. I came on purpose.

MRS HIGGINS But you mustnt. I'm serious, Henry. You offend all my friends: they stop coming whenever they meet you.

HIGGINS Nonsense! I know I have no small talk; but people dont mind. [*He sits on the settee.*]

MRS HIGGINS Oh! dont they? Small talk indeed! What about your large talk? Really, dear, you mustnt stay.

HIGGINS I must. Ive a job for you. A phonetic job.

MRS HIGGINS No use, dear. I'm sorry; but I cant get round your vowels; and though I like to get pretty postcards in your patent shorthand, I always have to read the copies in ordinary writing you so thoughtfully send me.

HIGGINS Well, this isnt a phonetic job.

MRS HIGGINS You said it was.

HIGGINS Not your part of it. Ive picked up a girl.

MRS HIGGINS Does that mean that some girl has picked you up?

HIGGINS Not at all. I dont mean a love affair.

MRS HIGGINS What a pity!

HIGGINS Why?

MRS HIGGINS Well, you never fall in love with anyone under

forty-five. When will you discover that there are some rather nice-looking young women about?

HIGGINS Oh, I can't be bothered with young women. My idea of a lovable woman is somebody as like you as possible. I shall never get into the way of seriously liking young women: some habits lie too deep to be changed. [*Rising abruptly and walking about, jingling his money and his keys in his trouser pockets.*] Besides, theyre all idiots.

MRS HIGGINS Do you know what you would do if you really loved me, Henry?

HIGGINS Oh bother! What? Marry, I suppose.

MRS HIGGINS No. Stop fidgeting and take your hands out of your pockets. [*With a gesture of despair, he obeys and sits down again.*] Thats a good boy. Now tell me about the girl.

HIGGINS She's coming to see you.

MRS HIGGINS I dont remember asking her.

HIGGINS You didnt. I asked her. If youd known her you wouldnt have asked her.

MRS HIGGINS Indeed! Why?

HIGGINS Well, it's like this. She's a common flower girl. I picked her off the kerbstone.

MRS HIGGINS And invited her to my at-home!

HIGGINS [*Rising and coming to her to coax her.*] Oh, thatll be all right. Ive taught her to speak properly; and she has strict orders as to her behavior. She's to keep to two subjects: the weather and everybody's health—Fine day and How do you do, you know—and not to let herself go on things in general. That will be safe.

MRS HIGGINS Safe! To talk about our health! about our insides! perhaps about our outsides! How could you be so silly, Henry?

HIGGINS [*Impatiently.*] Well, she must talk about something. [*He controls himself and sits down again.*] Oh, she'll be all right: dont you fuss. Pickering is in it with me. Ive a sort of bet on that I'll pass her off as a duchess in six months. I started on her some months ago; and she's getting on like a house on fire. I shall win my bet. She has a quick ear; and she's easier to teach than my middle-class pupils because she's had to learn a complete new language. She talks English almost as you talk French.

MRS HIGGINS   Thats satisfactory, at all events.

HIGGINS   Well, it is and it isnt.

MRS HIGGINS   What does that mean?

HIGGINS   You see, Ive got her pronunciation all right; but you have to consider not only how a girl pronounces, but what she pronounces; and that's where . . .

[*They are interrupted by the parlormaid, announcing guests.*]

THE PARLORMAID   Mrs and Miss Eynsford Hill. [*She withdraws.*]

HIGGINS   Oh Lord! [*He rises; snatches his hat from the table; and makes for the door; but before he reaches it his mother introduces him.*]

[MRS *and* MISS EYNSFORD HILL *are the mother and daughter who sheltered from the rain in Covent Garden. The mother is well bred, quiet, and has the habitual anxiety of straitened means. The daughter has acquired a gay air of being very much at home in society: the bravado of genteel poverty.*]

MRS EYNSFORD HILL [*To* MRS HIGGINS.]   How do you do? [*They shake hands.*]

MISS EYNSFORD HILL   How d'you do? [*She shakes.*]

MRS HIGGINS [*Introducing.*]   My son Henry.

MRS EYNSFORD HILL   Your celebrated son! I have so longed to meet you, Professor Higgins.

HIGGINS [*Glumly, making no movement in her direction.*] Delighted. [*He backs against the piano and bows brusquely.*]

MISS EYNSFORD HILL [*Going to him with confident familiarity.*] How do you do?

HIGGINS [*Staring at her.*]   Ive seen you before somewhere. I havnt the ghost of a notion where; but Ive heard your voice. [*Drearily.*]   It doesnt matter. Youd better sit down.

MRS HIGGINS   I'm sorry to say that my celebrated son has no manners. You mustnt mind him.

MISS EYNSFORD HILL [*Gaily.*]   I don't. [*She sits in the Elizabethan chair.*]

MRS EYNSFORD HILL [*A little bewildered.*]   Not at all. [*She sits on the ottoman between her daughter and* MRS HIGGINS, *who has turned her chair away from the writing table.*]

HIGGINS   Oh, have I been rude? I didnt mean to be.

[*He goes to the central window, through which, with his back to the company, he contemplates the river and the flowers in Battersea Park on the opposite bank as if they were a frozen desert.*]

[*The parlormaid returns, ushering in* PICKERING.]

THE PARLORMAID   Colonel Pickering. [*She withdraws.*]

PICKERING   How do you do, Mrs Higgins?

MRS HIGGINS   So glad youve come. Do you know Mrs Eynsford Hill—Miss Eynsford Hill? [*Exchange of bows. The* COLONEL *brings the Chippendale chair a little forward between* MRS HILL *and* MRS HIGGINS, *and sits down.*]

PICKERING   Has Henry told you what weve come for?

HIGGINS [*Over his shoulder.*]   We were interrupted: damn it!

MRS HIGGINS   Oh Henry, Henry, really!

MRS EYNSFORD HILL [*Half rising.*]   Are we in the way?

MRS HIGGINS [*Rising and making her sit down again.*]   No, no. You couldnt have come more fortunately: we want you to meet a friend of ours.

HIGGINS [*Turning hopefully.*]   Yes, by George! We want two or three people. Youll do as well as anybody else.

[*The parlormaid returns, ushering* FREDDY.]

THE PARLORMAID   Mr Eynsford Hill.

HIGGINS [*Almost audibly, past endurance.*]   God of Heaven! another of them.

FREDDY [*Shaking hands with* MRS HIGGINS.]   Ahdedo?

MRS HIGGINS   Very good of you to come. [*Introducing.*]   Colonel Pickering.

FREDDY [*Bowing.*]   Ahdedo?

MRS HIGGINS   I dont think you know my son, Professor Higgins.

FREDDY [*Going to* HIGGINS.]   Ahdedo?

HIGGINS [*Looking at him much as if he were a pickpocket.*] I'll take my oath Ive met you before somewhere. Where was it?

FREDDY   I dont think so.

HIGGINS [*Resignedly.*]   It doesnt matter, anyhow. Sit down.

[*He shakes* FREDDY's *hand, and almost slings him on to the ottoman with his face to the window; then comes round to the other side of it.*]

HIGGINS   Well, here we are, anyhow! [*He sits down on the ottoman next* MRS EYNSFORD HILL, *on her left.*]   And now, what the devil are we going to talk about until Eliza comes?

MRS HIGGINS   Henry: you are the life and soul of the Royal Society's soirées; but really youre rather trying on more commonplace occasions.

HIGGINS   Am I? Very sorry. [*Beaming suddenly.*]   I suppose I am, you know. [*Uproariously.*]   Ha, ha!

MISS EYNSFORD HILL [*Who considers* HIGGINS *quite eligible matrimonially.*]   I sympathize. I havnt any small talk. If people would only be frank and say what they really think!

HIGGINS [*Relapsing into gloom.*]   Lord forbid!

MRS EYNSFORD HILL [*Taking up her daughter's cue.*]   But why?

HIGGINS   What they think they ought to think is bad enough, Lord knows; but what they really think would break up the whole show. Do you suppose it would be really agreeable if I were to come out now with what I really think?

MISS EYNSFORD HILL [*Gaily.*]   Is it so very cynical?

HIGGINS   Cynical! Who the dickens said it was cynical? I mean it wouldnt be decent.

MRS EYNSFORD HILL [*Seriously.*]   Oh! I'm sure you dont mean that, Mr Higgins.

HIGGINS   You see, we're all savages, more or less. We're supposed to be civilized and cultured—to know all about poetry and philosophy and art and science, and so on; but how many of us know even the meaning of these names? [*To* MISS HILL.]   What do you know of poetry? [*To* MRS HILL.]   What do you know of science? [*Indicating* FREDDY.]   What does he know of art or science or anything else? What the devil do you imagine I know of philosophy?

MRS HIGGINS [*Warningly.*]   Or of manners, Henry?

THE PARLORMAID [*Opening the door.*]   Miss Doolittle. [*She withdraws.*]

HIGGINS [*Rising hastily and running to* MRS HIGGINS.]   Here she is, mother. [*He stands on tiptoe and makes signs over his mother's head to* ELIZA *to indicate to her which lady is her hostess.*]

[ELIZA, *who is exquisitely dressed, produces an impression of* *such remarkable distinction and beauty as she enters that they all* *rise, quite fluttered. Guided by* HIGGINS's *signals, she comes to* MRS HIGGINS *with studied grace.*]

LIZA [*Speaking with pedantic correctness of pronunciation and* *great beauty of tone.*] How do you do, Mrs Higgins? [*She gasps* *slightly in making sure of the H in Higgins, but is quite success-* *ful.*] Mr Higgins told me I might come.

MRS HIGGINS [*Cordially.*] Quite right: I'm very glad indeed to see you.

PICKERING How do you do, Miss Doolittle?

LIZA [*Shaking hands with him.*] Colonel Pickering, is it not?

MRS EYNSFORD HILL I feel sure we have met before, Miss Doolittle. I remember your eyes.

LIZA How do you do? [*She sits down on the ottoman grace-* *fully in the place just left vacant by* HIGGINS.]

MRS EYNSFORD HILL [*Introducing.*] My daughter Clara.

LIZA How do you do?

CLARA [*Impulsively.*] How do you do? [*She sits down on the* *ottoman beside* ELIZA, *devouring her with her eyes.*]

FREDDY [*Coming to their side of the ottoman.*] Ive certainly had the pleasure.

MRS EYNSFORD HILL [*Introducing.*] My son Freddy.

LIZA How do you do?

[FREDDY *bows and sits down in the Elizabethan chair, infatu-* *ated.*]

HIGGINS [*Suddenly.*] By George, yes: it all comes back to me! [*They stare at him.*] Covent Garden! [*Lamentably.*] What a damned thing!

MRS HIGGINS Henry, please! [*He is about to sit on the edge of* *the table.*] Dont sit on my writing table: youll break it.

HIGGINS [*Sulkily.*] Sorry.

[*He goes to the divan, stumbling into the fender and over the* *fire-irons on his way; extricating himself with muttered impreca-* *tions; and finishing his disastrous journey by throwing himself so* *impatiently on the divan that he almost breaks it.* MRS HIGGINS *looks at him, but controls herself and says nothing.*]

[*A long and painful pause ensues.*]

MRS HIGGINS [*At last, conversationally.*] Will it rain, do you think?

LIZA The shallow depression in the west of these islands is likely to move slowly in an easterly direction. There are no indications of any great change in the barometrical situation.

FREDDY Ha! ha! how awfully funny!

LIZA What is wrong with that, young man? I bet I got it right.

FREDDY Killing!

MRS EYNSFORD HILL I'm sure I hope it wont turn cold. Theres so much influenza about. It runs right through our whole family regularly every spring.

LIZA [*Darkly.*] My aunt died of influenza: so they said.

MRS EYNSFORD HILL [*Clicks her tongue sympathetically.*]!!!

LIZA [*In the same tragic tone.*] But it's my belief they done the old woman in.

MRS HIGGINS [*Puzzled.*] Done her in?

LIZA Y-e-e-e-es, Lord love you! Why should she die of influenza? She come through diphtheria right enough the year before. I saw her with my own eyes. Fairly blue with it, she was. They all thought she was dead; but my father he kept ladling gin down her throat til she came to so sudden that she bit the bowl off the spoon.

MRS EYNSFORD HILL [*Startled.*] Dear me!

LIZA [*Piling up the indictment.*] What call would a woman with that strength in her have to die of influenza? What become of her new straw hat that should have come to me? Somebody pinched it; and what I say is, them as pinched it done her in.

MRS EYNSFORD HILL What does doing her in mean?

HIGGINS [*Hastily.*] Oh, thats the new small talk. To do a person in means to kill them.

MRS EYNSFORD HILL [*To* ELIZA, *horrified.*] You surely dont believe that your aunt was killed!

LIZA Do I not! Them she lived with would have killed her for a hat pin, let alone a hat.

MRS EYNSFORD HILL But it cant have been right for your

father to pour spirits down her throat like that. It might have killed her.

LIZA   Not her. Gin was mother's milk to her. Besides, he'd poured so much down his own throat that he knew the good of it.

MRS EYNSFORD HILL   Do you mean that he drank?

LIZA   Drank! My word! Something chronic.

MRS EYNSFORD HILL   How dreadful for you!

LIZA   Not a bit. It never did him no harm what I could see. But then he did not keep it up regular. [*Cheerfully.*]   On the burst, as you might say, from time to time. And always more agreeable when he had a drop in. When he was out of work, my mother used to give him fourpence and tell him to go out and not come back until he'd drunk himself cheerful and loving-like. Theres lots of women has to make their husbands drunk to make them fit to live with. [*Now quite at her ease.*]   You see, it's like this. If a man has a bit of conscience, it always takes him when he's sober; and then it makes him low-spirited. A drop of booze just takes that off and makes him happy. [*To* FREDDY, *who is in convulsions of suppressed laughter.*]   Here! what are you sniggering at?

FREDDY   The new small talk. You do it so awfully well.

LIZA   If I was doing it proper, what was you laughing at? [*To* HIGGINS.]   Have I said anything I oughtnt?

MRS HIGGINS [*Interposing.*]   Not at all, Miss Doolittle.

LIZA   Well, thats a mercy, anyhow. [*Expansively.*]   What I always say is . . .

HIGGINS [*Rising and looking at his watch.*]   Ahem!

LIZA [*Looking round at him; taking the hint; and rising.*] Well: I must go. [*They all rise.* FREDDY *goes to the door.*]   So pleased to have met you. Goodbye. [*She shakes hands with* MRS HIGGINS.]

MRS HIGGINS   Goodbye.

LIZA   Goodbye, Colonel Pickering.

PICKERING   Goodbye, Miss Doolittle. [*They shake hands.*]

LIZA [*Nodding to the others.*]   Goodbye, all.

FREDDY [*Opening the door for her.*]   Are you walking across the Park, Miss Doolittle? If so . . .

LIZA [*With perfectly elegant diction.*] Walk! Not bloody likely. [*Sensation.*] I am going in a taxi. [*She goes out.*]

[PICKERING *gasps and sits down.* FREDDY *goes out on the balcony to catch another glimpse of* ELIZA.]

MRS EYNSFORD HILL [*Suffering from shock.*] Well, I really cant get used to the new ways.

CLARA [*Throwing herself discontentedly into the Elizabethan chair.*] Oh, it's all right, mamma, quite right. People will think we never go anywhere or see anybody if you are so old-fashioned.

MRS EYNSFORD HILL I daresay I am very old-fashioned; but I do hope you wont begin using that expression, Clara. I have got accustomed to hear you talking about men as rotters, and calling everything filthy and beastly; though I do think it horrible and unladylike. But this last is really too much. Dont you think so, Colonel Pickering?

PICKERING Dont ask me. Ive been away in India for several years; and manners have changed so much that I sometimes dont know whether I'm at a respectable dinnertable or in a ship's fore-castle.

CLARA It's all a matter of habit. Theres no right or wrong in it. Nobody means anything by it. And it's so quaint, and gives such a smart emphasis to things that are not in themselves very witty. I find the new small talk delightful and quite innocent.

MRS EYNSFORD HILL [*Rising.*] Well, after that, I think it's time for us to go.

[PICKERING *and* HIGGINS *rise.*]

CLARA [*Rising.*] Oh yes: we have three at-homes to go to still. Goodbye, Mrs Higgins. Goodbye, Colonel Pickering. Goodbye, Professor Higgins.

HIGGINS [*Coming grimly at her from the divan, and accompanying her to the door.*] Goodbye. Be sure you try on that small talk at the three at-homes. Dont be nervous about it. Pitch it in strong.

CLARA [*All smiles.*] I will. Goodbye. Such nonsense, all this early Victorian prudery!

HIGGINS [*Tempting her.*] Such damned nonsense!

CLARA Such bloody nonsense!

MRS EYNSFORD HILL [*Convulsively.*] Clara!

CLARA Ha! ha! [*She goes out radiant, conscious of being thoroughly up to date, and is heard descending the stairs in a stream of silvery laughter.*]

FREDDY [*To the heavens at large.*] Well, I ask you . . . [*He gives it up, and comes to* MRS HIGGINS.] Goodbye.

MRS HIGGINS [*Shaking hands.*] Goodbye. Would you like to meet Miss Doolittle again?

FREDDY [*Eagerly.*] Yes, I should, most awfully.

MRS HIGGINS Well, you know my days.

FREDDY Yes. Thanks awfully. Goodbye. [*He goes out.*]

MRS EYNSFORD HILL Goodbye, Mr Higgins.

HIGGINS Goodbye. Goodbye.

MRS EYNSFORD HILL [*To* PICKERING.] It's no use. I shall never be able to bring myself to use that word.

PICKERING Dont. It's not compulsory, you know. Youll get on quite well without it.

MRS EYNSFORD HILL Only, Clara is so down on me if I am not positively reeking with the latest slang. Goodbye.

PICKERING Goodbye. [*They shake hands.*]

MRS EYNSFORD HILL [*To* MRS HIGGINS.] You mustnt mind Clara. [PICKERING, *catching from her lowered tone that this is not meant for him to hear, discreetly joins* HIGGINS *at the window.*] We're so poor! and she gets so few parties, poor child! She doesnt quite know. [MRS HIGGINS, *seeing that her eyes are moist, takes her hand sympathetically and goes with her to the door.*] But the boy is nice. Dont you think so?

MRS HIGGINS Oh, quite nice. I shall always be delighted to see him.

MRS EYNSFORD HILL Thank you, dear. Goodbye. [*She goes out.*]

HIGGINS [*Eagerly.*] Well? Is Eliza presentable? [*He swoops on his mother and drags her to the ottoman, where she sits down in* ELIZA's *place with her son on her left.*]

[PICKERING *returns to his chair on her right.*]

MRS HIGGINS You silly boy, of course she's not presentable. She's a triumph of your art and of her dressmaker's; but if you suppose for a moment that she doesnt give herself away in every sentence she utters, you must be perfectly cracked about her.

PICKERING   But dont you think something might be done? I mean something to eliminate the sanguinary element from her conversation.

MRS HIGGINS   Not as long as she is in Henry's hands.

HIGGINS [*Aggrieved.*]   Do you mean that my language is improper?

MRS HIGGINS   No, dearest: it would be quite proper—say on a canal barge; but it would not be proper for her at a garden party.

HIGGINS [*Deeply injured.*]   Well I must say . . .

PICKERING [*Interrupting him.*]   Come, Higgins: you must learn to know yourself. I havnt heard such language as yours since we used to review the volunteers in Hyde Park twenty years ago.

HIGGINS [*Sulkily.*]   Oh, well, if you say so, I suppose I dont always talk like a bishop.

MRS HIGGINS [*Quieting* HENRY *with a touch.*]   Colonel Pickering: will you tell me what is the exact state of things in Wimpole Street?

PICKERING [*Cheerfully: as if this completely changed the subject.*]   Well, I have come to live there with Henry. We work together at my Indian Dialects; and we think it more convenient . . .

MRS HIGGINS   Quite so. I know all about that: it's an excellent arrangement. But where does this girl live?

HIGGINS   With us, of course. Where should she live?

MRS HIGGINS   But on what terms? Is she a servant? If not, what is she?

PICKERING [*Slowly.*]   I think I know what you mean, Mrs Higgins.

HIGGINS   Well, dash me if I do! Ive had to work at the girl every day for months to get her to her present pitch. Besides, she's useful. She knows where my things are, and remembers my appointments and so forth.

MRS HIGGINS   How does your housekeeper get on with her?

HIGGINS   Mrs Pearce? Oh, she's jolly glad to get so much taken off her hands; for before Eliza came, she used to have to find things and remind me of my appointments. But she's got some silly bee in her bonnet about Eliza. She keeps saying "You dont think, sir": doesnt she, Pick?

PICKERING   Yes: thats the formula. "You dont think, sir." Thats the end of every conversation about Eliza.

HIGGINS   As if I ever stop thinking about the girl and her confounded vowels and consonants. I'm worn out, thinking about her, and watching her lips and her teeth and her tongue, not to mention her soul, which is the quaintest of the lot.

MRS HIGGINS   You certainly are a pretty pair of babies, playing with your live doll.

HIGGINS   Playing! The hardest job I ever tackled: make no mistake about that, mother. But you have no idea how frightfully interesting it is to take a human being and change her into a quite different human being by creating a new speech for her. It's filling up the deepest gulf that separates class from class and soul from soul.

PICKERING   [*Drawing his chair closer to* MRS HIGGINS *and bending over to her eagerly.*]   Yes: it's enormously interesting. I assure you, Mrs Higgins, we take Eliza very seriously. Every week— every day almost—there is some new change. [*Closer again.*] We keep records of every stage—dozens of gramophone disks and photographs . . .

HIGGINS   [*Assailing her at the other ear.*]   Yes, by George: it's the most absorbing experiment I ever tackled. She regularly fills our lives up: doesnt she, Pick?

PICKERING   We're always talking Eliza.

HIGGINS   Teaching Eliza.

PICKERING   Dressing Eliza.

MRS HIGGINS   What!

HIGGINS   Inventing new Elizas.

HIGGINS	[*Speaking together.*]	You know, she has the most extraordinary quickness of ear:
PICKERING		I assure you, my dear Mrs Higgins, that girl

HIGGINS	[*Speaking together.*]	just like a parrot. Ive tried her with every
PICKERING		is a genius. She can play the piano quite beautifully.
HIGGINS		possible sort of sound that a human being can make—
PICKERING		We have taken her to classical concerts and to music
HIGGINS		Continental dialects, African dialects, Hottentot
PICKERING		halls; and it's all the same to her: she plays everything
HIGGINS		clicks, things it took me years to get hold of; and
PICKERING		she hears right off when she comes home, whether it's
HIGGINS		she picks them up like a shot, right away, as if she had
PICKERING		Beethoven and Brahms or Lehar and Lionel Monckton;
HIGGINS		been at it all her life.
PICKERING		though six months ago, she'd never as much as touched a piano . . .

MRS HIGGINS [*Putting her fingers in her ears, as they are by this time shouting one another down with an intolerable noise.*] Sh-sh-sh—sh! [*They stop.*]

PICKERING   I beg your pardon. [*He draws his chair back apologetically.*]

HIGGINS   Sorry. When Pickering starts shouting nobody can get a word in edgeways.

MRS HIGGINS   Be quiet, Henry. Colonel Pickering: dont you realize that when Eliza walked in Wimpole Street, something walked in with her?

PICKERING   Her father did. But Henry soon got rid of him.

MRS HIGGINS   It would have been more to the point if her mother had. But as her mother didnt something else did.

PICKERING   But what?

MRS HIGGINS   [Unconsciously dating herself by the word.]   A problem.

PICKERING   Oh, I see. The problem of how to pass her off as a lady.

HIGGINS   I'll solve that problem. Ive half solved it already.

MRS HIGGINS   No, you two infinitely stupid male creatures: the problem of what is to be done with her afterwards.

HIGGINS   I dont see anything in that. She can go her own way, with all the advantages I have given her.

MRS HIGGINS   The advantages of that poor woman who was here just now! The manners and habits that disqualify a fine lady from earning her own living without giving her a fine lady's income! Is that what you mean?

PICKERING   [Indulgently, being rather bored.]   Oh, that will be all right, Mrs Higgins. [He rises to go.]

HIGGINS   [Rising also.]   We'll find her some light employment.

PICKERING   She's happy enough. Dont you worry about her. Goodbye. [He shakes hands as if he were consoling a frightened child, and makes for the door.]

HIGGINS   Anyhow, theres no good bothering now. The thing's done. Goodbye, mother. [He kisses her, and follows PICKERING.]

PICKERING   [Turning for a final consolation.]   There are plenty of openings. We'll do whats right. Goodbye.

HIGGINS   [To PICKERING as they go out together.]   Lets take her to the Shakespear exhibition at Earls Court.

PICKERING   Yes: lets. Her remarks will be delicious.

HIGGINS   She'll mimic all the people for us when we get home.

PICKERING   Ripping. [Both are heard laughing as they go downstairs.]

MRS HIGGINS   [Rises with an impatient bounce, and returns to her work at the writing table. She sweeps a litter of disarranged papers out of the way; snatches a sheet of paper from her station-

ery case; and tries resolutely to write. At the third time she gives it up; flings down her pen; grips the table angrily and exclaims.]
Oh, men! men!! men!!!

*   *   *   *   *   *

Clearly Eliza will not pass as a duchess yet; and Higgins's bet remains unwon. But the six months are not yet exhausted; and just in time Eliza does actually pass as a princess. For a glimpse of how she did it imagine an Embassy in London one summer evening after dark. The hall door has an awning and a carpet across the sidewalk to the kerb, because a grand reception is in progress. A small crowd is lined up to see the guests arrive.

A Rolls-Royce car drives up. Pickering in evening dress, with medals and orders, alights, and hands out Eliza, in opera cloak, evening dress, diamonds, fan, flowers and all accessories. Higgins follows. The car drives off; and the three go up the steps and into the house, the door opening for them as they approach.

Inside the house they find themselves in a spacious hall from which the grand staircase rises. On the left are the arrangements for the gentlemen's cloaks. The male guests are depositing their hats and wraps there.

On the right is a door leading to the ladies' cloakroom. Ladies are going in cloaked and coming out in splendor. Pickering whispers to Eliza and points out the ladies' room. She goes into it. Higgins and Pickering take off their overcoats and take tickets for them from the attendant.

One of the guests, occupied in the same way, has his back turned. Having taken his ticket, he turns round and reveals himself as an important looking young man with an astonishingly hairy face. He has an enormous mustache, flowing out into luxuriant whiskers. Waves of hair cluster on his brow. His hair is cropped closely at the back, and glows with oil. Otherwise he is very smart. He wears several worthless orders. He is evidently a foreigner, guessable as a whiskered Pandour from Hungary; but in spite of the ferocity of his mustache he is amiable and genially voluble.

Recognizing Higgins, he flings his arms wide apart and approaches him enthusiastically.

WHISKERS   Maestro, maestro! [*He embraces* HIGGINS *and kisses him on both cheeks.*]   You remember me?

HIGGINS   No I dont. Who the devil are you?

WHISKERS   I am your pupil: your first pupil, your best and greatest pupil. I am little Nepommuck, the marvelous boy. I have made your name famous throughout Europe. You teach me phonetic. You cannot forget ME.

HIGGINS   Why dont you shave?

NEPOMMUCK   I have not your imposing appearance, your chin, your brow. Nobody notice me when I shave. Now I am famous: they call me Hairy Faced Dick.

HIGGINS   And what are you doing here among all these swells?

NEPOMMUCK   I am interpreter. I speak 32 languages. I am indispensable at these international parties. You are great cockney specialist: you place a man anywhere in London the moment he open his mouth. I place any man in Europe.

[*A footman hurries down the grand staircase and comes to* NEPOMMUCK.]

FOOTMAN   You are wanted upstairs. Her Excellency cannot understand the Greek gentleman.

NEPOMMUCK   Thank you, yes, immediately.

[*The footman goes and is lost in the crowd.*]

NEPOMMUCK [*To* HIGGINS.]   This Greek diplomatist pretends he cannot speak nor understand English. He cannot deceive me. He is the son of a Clerkenwell watchmaker. He speaks English so villainously that he dare not utter a word of it without betraying his origin. I help him to pretend; but I make him pay through the nose. I make them all pay. Ha ha! [*He hurries upstairs.*]

PICKERING   Is this fellow really an expert? Can he find out Eliza and blackmail her?

HIGGINS   We shall see. If he finds her out I lose my bet.

[ELIZA *comes from the cloakroom and joins them.*]

PICKERING   Well, Eliza, now for it. Are you ready?

LIZA   Are you nervous, Colonel?

PICKERING   Frightfully. I feel exactly as I felt before my first battle. It's the first time that frightens.

LIZA   It is not the first time for me, Colonel. I have done this fifty times—hundreds of times—in my little piggery in Angel Court in my daydreams. I am in a dream now. Promise me not to let Professor Higgins wake me; for if he does I shall forget everything and talk as I used to in Drury Lane.

PICKERING   Not a word, Higgins. [*To* ELIZA.]   Now, ready?

LIZA   Ready.

PICKERING   Go.

[*They mount the stairs,* HIGGINS *last.* PICKERING *whispers to the footman on the first landing.*]

FIRST LANDING FOOTMAN   Miss Doolittle, Colonel Pickering, Professor Higgins.

SECOND LANDING FOOTMAN   Miss Doolittle, Colonel Pickering, Professor Higgins.

[*At the top of the staircase the Ambassador and his wife, with* NEPOMMUCK *at her elbow, are receiving.*]

HOSTESS [*Taking* ELIZA's *hand.*]   How d'ye do?

HOST [*Same play.*]   How d'ye do? How d'ye do, Pickering?

LIZA [*With a beautiful gravity that awes her hostess.*]   How do you do? [*She passes on to the drawing room.*]

HOSTESS   Is that your adopted daughter, Colonel Pickering? She will make a sensation.

PICKERING   Most kind of you to invite her for me. [*He passes on.*]

HOSTESS [*To* NEPOMMUCK.]   Find out all about her.

NEPOMMUCK [*Bowing.*]   Excellency . . . [*He goes into the crowd.*]

HOST   How d'ye do, Higgins? You have a rival here tonight. He introduced himself as your pupil. Is he any good?

HIGGINS   He can learn a language in a fortnight—knows dozens of them. A sure mark of a fool. As a phonetician, no good whatever.

HOSTESS   How d'ye do, Professor?

HIGGINS   How do you do? Fearful bore for you this sort of thing. Forgive my part in it. [*He passes on.*]

In the drawing room and its suite of salons the reception is in full swing. Eliza passes through. She is so intent on her ordeal that she walks like a somnambulist in a desert instead of a débutante in a fashionable crowd. They stop talking to look at her, admiring her dress, her jewels, and her strangely attractive self. Some of the younger ones at the back stand on their chairs to see.

The Host and Hostess come in from the staircase and mingle with their guests. Higgins, gloomy and contemptuous of the whole business, comes into the group where they are chatting.

HOSTESS   Ah, here is Professor Higgins: he will tell us. Tell us all about the wonderful young lady, Professor.

HIGGINS   [*Almost morosely.*]   What wonderful young lady?

HOSTESS   You know very well. They tell me there has been nothing like her in London since people stood on their chairs to look at Mrs Langtry.

[NEPOMMUCK *joins the group, full of news.*]

HOSTESS   Ah, here you are at last, Nepommuck. Have you found out all about the Doolittle lady?

NEPOMMUCK   I have found out all about her. She is a fraud.

HOSTESS   A fraud! Oh no.

NEPOMMUCK   YES, yes. She cannot deceive me. Her name cannot be Doolittle.

HIGGINS   Why?

NEPOMMUCK   Because Doolittle is an English name. And she is not English.

HOSTESS   Oh, nonsense! She speaks English perfectly.

NEPOMMUCK   Too perfectly. Can you show me any English woman who speaks English as it should be spoken? Only foreigners who have been taught to speak it speak it well.

HOSTESS   Certainly she terrified me by the way she said How d'ye do. I had a schoolmistress who talked like that; and I was mortally afraid of her. But if she is not English what is she?

NEPOMMUCK   Hungarian.

ALL THE REST Hungarian!

NEPOMMUCK Hungarian. And of royal blood. I am Hungarian. My blood is royal.

HIGGINS Did you speak to her in Hungarian?

NEPOMMUCK I did. She was very clever. She said "Please speak to me in English: I do not understand French." French! She pretend not to know the difference between Hungarian and French. Impossible: she knows both.

HIGGINS And the blood royal? How did you find that out?

NEPOMMUCK Instinct, maestro, instinct. Only the Magyar races can produce that air of the divine right, those resolute eyes. She is a princess.

HOST What do you say, Professor?

HIGGINS I say an ordinary London girl out of the gutter and taught to speak by an expert. I place her in Drury Lane.

NEPOMMUCK Ha ha ha! Oh, maestro, maestro, you are mad on the subject of cockney dialects. The London gutter is the whole world for you.

HIGGINS [To the HOSTESS.] What does your Excellency say?

HOSTESS Oh, of course I agree with Nepommuck. She must be a princess at least.

HOST Not necessarily legitimate, of course. Morganatic perhaps. But that is undoubtedly her class.

HIGGINS I stick to my opinion.

HOSTESS Oh, you are incorrigible.

[The group breaks up, leaving HIGGINS isolated. PICKERING joins him.]

PICKERING Where is Eliza? We must keep an eye on her.

[ELIZA joins them.]

LIZA I dont think I can bear much more. The people all stare so at me. An old lady has just told me that I speak exactly like Queen Victoria. I am sorry if I have lost your bet. I have done my best; but nothing can make me the same as these people.

PICKERING You have not lost it, my dear. You have won it ten times over.

HIGGINS Let us get out of this. I have had enough of chattering to these fools.

PICKERING   Eliza is tired; and I am hungry. Let us clear out and have supper somewhere.

ACT IV

SCENE: *The Wimpole Street laboratory. Midnight. Nobody in the room. The clock on the mantelpiece strikes twelve. The fire is not alight: it is a summer night.*

Presently HIGGINS *and* PICKERING *are heard on the stairs.*

HIGGINS [*Calling down to* PICKERING.]   I say, Pick: lock up, will you? I shant be going out again.

PICKERING   Right. Can Mrs Pearce go to bed? We dont want anything more, do we?

HIGGINS   Lord, no!

[ELIZA *opens the door and is seen on the lighted landing in all the finery in which she has just won* HIGGINS's *bet for him. She comes to the hearth, and switches on the electric lights there. She is tired: her pallor contrasts strongly with her dark eyes and hair; and her expression is almost tragic. She takes off her cloak; puts her fan and gloves on the piano; and sits down on the bench, brooding and silent.* HIGGINS, *in evening dress, with overcoat and hat, comes in, carrying a smoking jacket which he has picked up downstairs. He takes off the hat and overcoat; throws them carelessly on the newspaper stand; disposes of his coat in the same way; puts on the smoking jacket; and throws himself wearily into the easy-chair at the hearth.* PICKERING, *similarly attired, comes in. He also takes off his hat and overcoat, and is about to throw them on* HIGGINS's *when he hesitates.*]

PICKERING   I say: Mrs Pearce will row if we leave these things lying about in the drawing room.

HIGGINS   Oh, chuck them over the bannisters into the hall. She'll find them there in the morning and put them away all right. She'll think we were drunk.

PICKERING We are, slightly. Are there any letters?

HIGGINS I didnt look. [PICKERING *takes the overcoats and hats and goes downstairs.* HIGGINS *begins half singing half yawning an air from La Fanciulla del Golden West. Suddenly he stops and exclaims.*] I wonder where the devil my slippers are!

[ELIZA *looks at him darkly; then rises suddenly and leaves the room.* HIGGINS *yawns again, and resumes his song.* PICKERING *returns, with the contents of the letter box in his hand.*]

PICKERING Only circulars, and this coroneted billet-doux for you. [*He throws the circulars into the fender, and posts himself on the hearthrug, with his back to the grate.*]

HIGGINS [*Glancing at the billet-doux.*] Moneylender. [*He throws the letter after the circulars.*]

[ELIZA *returns with a pair of large down-at-heel slippers. She places them on the carpet before* HIGGINS, *and sits as before without a word.*]

HIGGINS [*Yawning again.*] Oh Lord! What an evening! What a crew! What a silly tomfoolery! [*He raises his shoe to unlace it, and catches sight of the slippers. He stops unlacing and looks at them as if they had appeared there of their own accord.*] Oh! theyre there, are they?

PICKERING [*Stretching himself.*] Well, I feel a bit tired. It's been a long day. The garden party, a dinner party, and the reception! Rather too much of a good thing. But youve won your bet, Higgins. Eliza did the trick, and something to spare, eh?

HIGGINS [*Fervently.*] Thank God it's over!

[ELIZA *flinches violently; but they take no notice of her; and she recovers herself and sits stonily as before.*]

PICKERING Were you nervous at the garden party? *I* was. Eliza didnt seem a bit nervous.

HIGGINS Oh, she wasnt nervous. I knew she'd be all right. No: it's the strain of putting the job through all these months that has told on me. It was interesting enough at first, while we were at the phonetics; but after that I got deadly sick of it. If I hadnt backed myself to do it I should have chucked the whole thing up two months ago. It was a silly notion: the whole thing has been a bore.

PICKERING Oh come! the garden party was frightfully excit-
ing. My heart began beating like anything.

HIGGINS Yes, for the first three minutes. But when I saw we
were going to win hands down, I felt like a bear in a cage, hanging about doing nothing. The dinner was worse: sitting gorging
there for over an hour, with nobody but a damned fool of a
fashionable woman to talk to! I tell you, Pickering, never again
for me. No more artificial duchesses. The whole thing has been
simple purgatory.

PICKERING Youve never been broken in properly to the social
routine. [*Strolling over to the piano.*] I rather enjoy dipping into
it occasionally myself: it makes me feel young again. Anyhow,
it was a great success: an immense success. I was quite frightened
once or twice because Eliza was doing it so well. You see, lots of
the real people cant do it at all: theyre such fools that they think
style comes by nature to people in their position; and so they
never learn. Theres always something professional about doing
a thing superlatively well.

HIGGINS Yes: thats what drives me mad: the silly people
dont know their own silly business. [*Rising.*] However, it's
over and done with; and now I can go to bed at last without
dreading tomorrow.

[ELIZA's *beauty becomes murderous.*]

PICKERING I think I shall turn in too. Still, it's been a great
occasion: a triumph for you. Goodnight. [*He goes.*]

HIGGINS [*Following him.*] Goodnight. [*Over his shoulder,
at the door.*] Put out the lights, Eliza; and tell Mrs Pearce not
to make coffee for me in the morning: I'll take tea. [*He goes
out.*]

[ELIZA *tries to control herself and feel indifferent as she rises
and walks across to the hearth to switch off the lights. By the
time she gets there she is on the point of screaming. She sits
down in* HIGGINS's *chair and holds on hard to the arms. Finally
she gives way and flings herself furiously on the floor, raging.*]

HIGGINS [*In despairing wrath outside.*] What the devil have
I done with my slippers? [*He appears at the door.*]

LIZA [*Snatching up the slippers, and hurling them at him one after the other with all her force.*] There are your slippers. And there. Take your slippers; and may you never have a day's luck with them!

HIGGINS [*Astounded.*] What on earth . . . ! [*He comes to her.*] Whats the matter? Get up. [*He pulls her up.*] Anything wrong?

LIZA [*Breathless.*] Nothing wrong—with you. Ive won your bet for you, havnt I? Thats enough for you. *I* dont matter, I suppose.

HIGGINS You won my bet! You! Presumptuous insect! *I* won it. What did you throw those slippers at me for?

LIZA Because I wanted to smash your face. I'd like to kill you, you selfish brute. Why didnt you leave me where you picked me out of—in the gutter? You thank God it's all over, and that now you can throw me back again there, do you? [*She crisps her fingers frantically.*]

HIGGINS [*Looking at her in cool wonder.*] The creature is nervous, after all.

LIZA [*Gives a suffocated scream of fury, and instinctively darts her nails at his face.*]!!

HIGGINS [*Catching her wrists.*] Ah! would you? Claws in, you cat. How dare you show your temper to me? Sit down and be quiet. [*He throws her roughly into the easy-chair.*]

LIZA [*Crushed by superior strength and weight.*] Whats to become of me? Whats to become of me?

HIGGINS How the devil do I know whats to become of you? What does it matter what becomes of you?

LIZA You dont care. I know you dont care. You wouldnt care if I was dead. I'm nothing to you—not so much as them slippers.

HIGGINS [*Thundering.*] Those slippers.

LIZA [*With bitter submission.*] Those slippers. I didnt think it made any difference now.

[*A pause. ELIZA hopeless and crushed. HIGGINS a little uneasy.*]

HIGGINS [*In his loftiest manner.*] Why have you begun going on like this? May I ask whether you complain of your treatment here?

LIZA No.

HIGGINS Has anybody behaved badly to you? Colonel Pickering? Mrs Pearce? Any of the servants?

LIZA No.

HIGGINS I presume you dont pretend that I have treated you badly?

LIZA No.

HIGGINS I am glad to hear it. [He moderates his tone.] Perhaps youre tired after the strain of the day. Will you have a glass of champagne? [He moves towards the door.]

LIZA No. [Recollecting her manners.] Thank you.

HIGGINS [Good-humored again.] This has been coming on you for some days. I suppose it was natural for you to be anxious about the garden party. But thats all over now. [He pats her kindly on the shoulder. She writhes.] Theres nothing more to worry about.

LIZA No. Nothing more for you to worry about. [She suddenly rises and gets away from him by going to the piano bench, where she sits and hides her face.] Oh God! I wish I was dead.

HIGGINS [Staring after her in sincere surprise.] Why? In heaven's name, why? [Reasonably, going to her.] Listen to me, Eliza. All this irritation is purely subjective.

LIZA I dont understand. I'm too ignorant.

HIGGINS It's only imagination. Low spirits and nothing else. Nobody's hurting you. Nothing's wrong. You go to bed like a good girl and sleep it off. Have a little cry and say your prayers: that will make you comfortable.

LIZA I heard your prayers. "Thank God it's all over!"

HIGGINS [Impatiently.] Well, dont you thank God it's all over? Now you are free and can do what you like.

LIZA [Pulling herself together in desperation.] What am I fit for? What have you left me fit for? Where am I to go? What am I to do? Whats to become of me?

HIGGINS [Enlightened, but not at all impressed.] Oh, thats whats worrying you, is it? [He thrusts his hands into his pockets, and walks about in his usual manner, rattling the contents of his pockets, as if condescending to a trivial subject out of pure kind-

ness.] I shouldnt bother about it if I were you. I should imagine you wont have much difficulty in settling yourself somewhere or other, though I hadnt quite realized that you were going away. [*She looks quickly at him: he does not look at her, but examines the dessert stand on the piano and decides that he will eat an apple.*] You might marry, you know. [*He bites a large piece out of the apple and munches it noisily.*] You see, Eliza, all men are not confirmed old bachelors like me and the Colonel. Most men are the marrying sort (poor devils!); and youre not bad-looking: it's quite a pleasure to look at you sometimes—not now, of course, because youre crying and looking as ugly as the very devil; but when youre all right and quite yourself, youre what I should call attractive. That is, to the people in the marrying line, you understand. You go to bed and have a good nice rest; and then get up and look at yourself in the glass; and you wont feel so cheap.

[ELIZA *again looks at him, speechless, and does not stir. The look is quite lost on him: he eats his apple with a dreamy expression of happiness, as it is quite a good one.*]

HIGGINS [*A genial afterthought occurring to him.*] I daresay my mother could find some chap or other who would do very well.

LIZA We were above that at the corner of Tottenham Court Road.

HIGGINS [*Waking up.*] What do you mean?

LIZA I sold flowers. I didnt sell myself. Now youve made a lady of me I'm not fit to sell anything else. I wish youd left me where you found me.

HIGGINS [*Slinging the core of the apple decisively into the grate.*] Tosh, Eliza. Dont you insult human relations by dragging all this cant about buying and selling into it. You neednt marry the fellow if you dont like him.

LIZA What else am I to do?

HIGGINS Oh, lots of things. What about your old idea of a florist's shop? Pickering could set you up in one: he has lots of money. [*Chuckling.*] He'll have to pay for all those togs you have been wearing today; and that, with the hire of the jewelry, will make a big hole in two hundred pounds. Why, six months ago you would have thought it the millennium to have a flower shop of your own. Come! youll be all right. I must clear off to bed: I'm devilish sleepy. By the way, I came down for something: I forget what it was.

LIZA Your slippers.

HIGGINS Oh yes, of course. You shied them at me. [*He picks them up, and is going out when she rises and speaks to him.*]

LIZA Before you go, sir . . .

HIGGINS [*Dropping the slippers in his surprise at her calling him Sir.*] Eh?

LIZA Do my clothes belong to me or to Colonel Pickering?

HIGGINS [*Coming back into the room as if her question were the very climax of unreason.*] What the devil use would they be to Pickering?

LIZA He might want them for the next girl you pick up to experiment on.

HIGGINS [*Shocked and hurt.*] Is that the way you feel towards us?

LIZA I dont want to hear anything more about that. All I want to know is whether anything belongs to me. My own clothes were burnt.

HIGGINS But what does it matter? Why need you start bothering about that in the middle of the night?

LIZA I want to know what I may take away with me. I dont want to be accused of stealing.

HIGGINS [*Now deeply wounded.*] Stealing! You shouldnt have said that, Eliza. That shows a want of feeling.

LIZA I'm sorry. I'm only a common ignorant girl; and in my station I have to be careful. There cant be any feelings between the like of you and the like of me. Please will you tell me what belongs to me and what doesnt?

HIGGINS [*Very sulky.*] You may take the whole damned houseful if you like. Except the jewels. Theyre hired. Will that satisfy you? [*He turns on his heel and is about to go in extreme dudgeon.*]

LIZA [*Drinking in his emotion like nectar, and nagging him to provoke a further supply.*] Stop, please. [*She takes off her*

jewels.]   Will you take these to your room and keep them safe?
I dont want to run the risk of their being missing.

HIGGINS [*Furious.*]   Hand them over. [*She puts them into his
hands.*]   If these belonged to me instead of to the jeweler, I'd
ram them down your ungrateful throat. [*He perfunctorily thrusts
them into his pockets, unconsciously decorating himself with the
protruding ends of the chains.*]

LIZA [*Taking a ring off.*]   This ring isnt the jeweler's: it's the
one you bought me in Brighton. I dont want it now. [HIGGINS
*dashes the ring violently into the fireplace, and turns on her so
threateningly that she crouches over the piano with her hands
over her face, and exclaims.*]   Dont you hit me.

HIGGINS   Hit you! You infamous creature, how dare you accuse
me of such a thing? It is you who have hit me. You have wounded
me to the heart.

LIZA [*Thrilling with hidden joy.*]   I'm glad. Ive got a little of
my own back, anyhow.

HIGGINS [*With dignity, in his finest professional style.*]   You
have caused me to lose my temper: a thing that has hardly ever
happened to me before. I prefer to say nothing more tonight. I am
going to bed.

LIZA [*Pertly.*]   Youd better leave a note for Mrs Pearce about
the coffee; for she wont be told by me.

HIGGINS [*Formally.*]   Damn Mrs Pearce; and damn the coffee;
and damn you; and [*wildly*] damn my own folly in having lav-
ished my hard-earned knowledge and the treasure of my regard
and intimacy on a heartless guttersnipe. [*He goes out with impressive decorum, and spoils it by slamming the door savagely.*]

[ELIZA *goes down on her knees on the hearthrug to look for the
ring. When she finds it she considers for a moment what to do
with it. Finally she flings it down on the dessert stand and goes
upstairs in a tearing rage.*]

*   *   *   *   *   *

The furniture of Eliza's room has been increased by a big wardrobe and a sumptuous dressing table. She comes in and switches

on the electric light. She goes to the wardrobe; opens it; and pulls out a walking dress, a hat, and a pair of shoes, which she throws on the bed. She takes off her evening dress and shoes; then takes a padded hanger from the wardrobe; adjusts it carefully in the evening dress; and hangs it in the wardrobe, which she shuts with a slam. She puts on her walking shoes, her walking dress, and hat. She takes her wrist watch from the dressing table and fastens it on. She pulls on her gloves; takes her vanity bag; and looks into it to see that her purse is there before hanging it on her wrist. She makes for the door. Every movement expresses her furious resolution.

She takes a last look at herself in the glass.

She suddenly puts out her tongue at herself; then leaves the room, switching off the electric light at the door.

Meanwhile, in the street outside, Freddy Eynsford Hill, love-lorn, is gazing up at the second floor, in which one of the windows is still lighted.

The light goes out.

FREDDY Goodnight, darling, darling, darling.

[ELIZA *comes out, giving the door a considerable bang behind her.*]

LIZA Whatever are you doing here?

FREDDY Nothing. I spend most of my nights here. It's the only place where I'm happy. Dont laugh at me, Miss Doolittle.

LIZA Dont you call me Miss Doolittle, do you hear? Liza's good enough for me. [*She breaks down and grabs him by the shoulders.*] Freddy: you dont think I'm a heartless guttersnipe, do you?

FREDDY Oh no, no, darling: how can you imagine such a thing? You are the loveliest, dearest . . .

[*He loses all self-control and smothers her with kisses. She, hungry for comfort, responds. They stand there in one another's arms. An elderly police constable arrives.*]

CONSTABLE [*Scandalized.*] Now then! Now then!! Now then!!!

[*They release one another hastily.*]

FREDDY Sorry, constable. Weve only just become engaged. [*They run away.*]

The constable shakes his head, reflecting on his own courtship and on the vanity of human hopes. He moves off in the opposite direction with slow professional steps.

The flight of the lovers takes them to Cavendish Square. There they halt to consider their next move.

LIZA [*Out of breath.*] He didnt half give me a fright, that copper. But you answered him proper.

FREDDY I hope I havent taken you out of your way. Where were you going?

LIZA To the river.

FREDDY What for?

LIZA To make a hole in it.

FREDDY [*Horrified.*] Eliza, darling. What do you mean? Whats the matter?

LIZA Never mind. It doesnt matter now. Theres nobody in the world now but you and me, is there?

FREDDY Not a soul.

[*They indulge in another embrace, and are again surprised by a much younger constable.*]

SECOND CONSTABLE Now then, you two! Whats this? Where do you think you are? Move along here, double quick.

FREDDY As you say, sir, double quick.

They run away again, and are in Hanover Square before they stop for another conference.

FREDDY I had no idea the police were so devilishly prudish.

LIZA It's their business to hunt girls off the streets.

FREDDY We must go somewhere. We cant wander about the streets all night.

LIZA Cant we? I think it'd be lovely to wander about for ever.

FREDDY Oh, darling.

[*They embrace again, oblivious of the arrival of a crawling taxi. It stops.*]

TAXIMAN   Can I drive you and the lady anywhere, sir?
[*They start asunder.*]

LIZA   Oh, Freddy, a taxi. The very thing.

FREDDY   But, damn it, Ive no money.

LIZA   I have plenty. The Colonel thinks you should never go out without ten pounds in your pocket. Listen. We'll drive about all night; and in the morning I'll call on old Mrs Higgins and ask her what I ought to do. I'll tell you all about it in the cab. And the police wont touch us there.

FREDDY   Righto! Ripping. [*To the* TAXIMAN.] Wimbledon Common. [*They drive off.*]

ACT V

SCENE: MRS HIGGINS's *drawing room. She is at her writing table as before. The parlormaid comes in.*

THE PARLORMAID [*At the door.*]   Mr Henry, maam, is downstairs with Colonel Pickering.

MRS HIGGINS   Well, show them up.

THE PARLORMAID   Theyre using the telephone, maam. Telephoning to the police, I think.

MRS HIGGINS   What!

THE PARLORMAID [*Coming further in and lowering her voice.*] Mr Henry is in a state, maam. I thought I'd better tell you.

MRS HIGGINS   If you had told me that Mr Henry was not in a state it would have been more surprising. Tell them to come up when theyve finished with the police. I suppose he's lost something.

THE PARLORMAID   Yes, maam. [*Going.*]

MRS HIGGINS   Go upstairs and tell Miss Doolittle that Mr Henry and the Colonel are here. Ask her not to come down til I send for her.

THE PARLORMAID Yes, maam.

[HIGGINS *bursts in. He is, as the parlormaid has said, in a state.*]

HIGGINS Look here, mother: heres a confounded thing!

MRS HIGGINS Yes, dear. Good morning. [*He checks his impatience and kisses her, whilst the parlormaid goes out.*] What is it?

HIGGINS Eliza's bolted.

MRS HIGGINS [*Calmly continuing her writing.*] You must have frightened her.

HIGGINS Frightened her! nonsense! She was left last night, as usual, to turn out the lights and all that; and instead of going to bed she changed her clothes and went right off: her bed wasnt slept in. She came in a cab for her things before seven this morning; and that fool Mrs Pearce let her have them without telling me a word about it. What am I to do?

MRS HIGGINS Do without, I'm afraid, Henry. The girl has a perfect right to leave if she chooses.

HIGGINS [*Wandering distractedly across the room.*] But I cant find anything. I dont know what appointments Ive got. I'm . . . [PICKERING *comes in.* MRS HIGGINS *puts down her pen and turns away from the writing table.*]

PICKERING [*Shaking hands.*] Good morning, Mrs Higgins. Has Henry told you? [*He sits down on the ottoman.*]

HIGGINS What does that ass of an inspector say? Have you offered a reward?

MRS HIGGINS [*Rising in indignant amazement.*] You dont mean to say you have set the police after Eliza?

HIGGINS Of course. What are the police for? What else could we do? [*He sits in the Elizabethan chair.*]

PICKERING The inspector made a lot of difficulties. I really think he suspected us of some improper purpose.

MRS HIGGINS Well, of course he did. What right have you to go to the police and give the girl's name as if she were a thief, or a lost umbrella, or something? Really! [*She sits down again, deeply vexed.*]

HIGGINS   But we want to find her.

PICKERING   We cant let her go like this, you know, Mrs Higgins. What were we to do?

MRS HIGGINS   You have no more sense, either of you, than two children. Why . . .

[*The parlormaid comes in and breaks off the conversation.*]

THE PARLORMAID   Mr. Henry: a gentleman wants to see you very particular. He's been sent on from Wimpole Street.

HIGGINS   Oh, bother! I cant see anyone now. Who is it?

THE PARLORMAID   A Mr Doolittle, sir.

PICKERING   Doolittle! Do you mean the dustman?

THE PARLORMAID   Dustman! Oh no, sir: a gentleman.

HIGGINS   [*Springing up excitedly.*]   By George, Pick, it's some relative of hers that she's gone to. Somebody we know nothing about. [*To the parlormaid.*]   Send him up, quick.

THE PARLORMAID   Yes, sir. [*She goes.*]

HIGGINS   [*Eagerly, going to his mother.*]   Genteel relatives! now we shall hear something. [*He sits down in the Chippendale chair.*]

MRS HIGGINS   Do you know any of her people?

PICKERING   Only her father: the fellow we told you about.

THE PARLORMAID   [*Announcing.*]   Mr Doolittle. [*She withdraws.*]

[*DOOLITTLE enters. He is resplendently dressed as for a fashionable wedding, and might, in fact, be the bridegroom. A flower in his buttonhole, a dazzling silk hat, and patent leather shoes complete the effect. He is too concerned with the business he has come on to notice MRS HIGGINS. He walks straight to HIGGINS, and accosts him with vehement reproach.*]

DOOLITTLE   [*Indicating his own person.*]   See here! Do you see this? You done this.

HIGGINS   Done what, man?

DOOLITTLE   This, I tell you. Look at it. Look at this hat. Look at this coat.

PICKERING   Has Eliza been buying you clothes?

DOOLITTLE   Eliza! not she. Why would she buy me clothes?

MRS HIGGINS   Good morning, Mr Doolittle. Wont you sit down?

DOOLITTLE [*Taken aback as he becomes conscious that he has forgotten his hostess.*] Asking your pardon, maam. [*He approaches her and shakes her proffered hand.*] Thank you. [*He sits down on the ottoman, on* PICKERING's *right.*] I am that full of what has happened to me that I cant think of anything else.

HIGGINS   What the dickens has happened to you?

DOOLITTLE   I shouldnt mind if it had only happened to me: anything might happen to anybody and nobody to blame but Providence, as you might say. But this is something that you done to me: yes, you, Enry Iggins.

HIGGINS   Have you found Eliza?

DOOLITTLE   Have you lost her?

HIGGINS   Yes.

DOOLITTLE   You have all the luck, you have. I aint found her; but she'll find me quick enough now after what you done to me.

MRS HIGGINS   But what has my son done to you, Mr. Doolittle?

DOOLITTLE   Done to me! Ruined me. Destroyed my happiness. Tied me up and delivered me into the hands of middle-class morality.

HIGGINS [*Rising intolerantly and standing over* DOOLITTLE.] Youre raving. Youre drunk. Youre mad. I gave you five pounds. After that I had two conversations with you, at half-a-crown an hour. Ive never seen you since.

DOOLITTLE   Oh! Drunk am I? Mad am I? Tell me this. Did you or did you not write a letter to an old blighter in America that was giving five millions to found Moral Reform Societies all over the world, and that wanted you to invent a universal language for him?

HIGGINS   What! Ezra D. Wannafeller! He's dead. [*He sits down again carelessly.*]

DOOLITTLE   Yes: he's dead; and I'm done for. Now did you or did you not write a letter to him to say that the most original moralist at present in England, to the best of your knowledge, was Alfred Doolittle, a common dustman?

HIGGINS   Oh, after your first visit I remember making some silly joke of the kind.

DOOLITTLE   Ah! you may well call it a silly joke. It put the lid on me right enough. Just give him the chance he wanted to show that Americans is not like us: that they reckonize and respect merit in every class of life, however humble. Them words is in his blooming will, in which, Enry Iggins, thanks to your silly joking, he leaves me a share in his Pre-digested Cheese Trust worth four thousand a year on condition that I lecture for his Wannafeller Moral Reform World League as often as they ask me up to six times a year.

HIGGINS   The devil he does! Whew! [*Brightening suddenly.*] What a lark!

PICKERING   A safe thing for you, Doolittle. They wont ask you twice.

DOOLITTLE   It aint the lecturing I mind. I'll lecture them blue in the face, I will, and not turn a hair. It's making a gentleman of me that I object to. Who asked him to make a gentleman of me? I was happy. I was free. I touched pretty nigh everybody for money when I wanted it, same as I touched you, Enry Iggins. Now I am worrited; tied neck and heels; and everybody touches me for money. It's a fine thing for you, says my solicitor. Is it? says I. You mean it's a good thing for you, I says. When I was a poor man and had a solicitor once when they found a pram in the dust cart, he got me off, and got shut of me and got me shut of him as quick as he could. Same with the doctors: used to shove me out of the hospital before I could hardly stand on my legs, and nothing to pay. Now they finds out that I'm not a healthy man and cant live unless they looks after me twice a day. In the house I'm not let do a hand's turn for myself: somebody else must do it and touch me for it. A year ago I hadnt a relative in the world except two or three that wouldnt speak to me. Now Ive fifty, and not a decent week's wages among the lot of them. I have to live for others and not for myself: that middle-class morality. You talk of losing Eliza. Dont you be anxious: I bet she's on my doorstep by this: she that could support herself easy by selling flowers if I wasnt respectable. And the next one to touch me will

be you, Enry Iggins. I'll have to learn to speak middle-class language from you, instead of speaking proper English. Thats where
youll come in; and I daresay thats what you done it for.

MRS HIGGINS But, my dear Mr Doolittle, you need not suffer
all this if you are really in earnest. Nobody can force you to accept
this bequest. You can repudiate it. Isnt that so, Colonel Pickering?

PICKERING I believe so.

DOOLITTLE [*Softening his manner in deference to her sex.*]
Thats the tragedy of it, maam. It's easy to say chuck it; but I
havnt the nerve. Which of us has? We're all intimidated. Intimidated, maam: thats what we are. What is there for me if I chuck
it but the workhouse in my old age? I have to dye my hair already
to keep my job as a dustman. If I was one of the deserving poor,
and had put by a bit, I could chuck it; but then why should I,
acause the deserving poor might as well be millionaires for all the
happiness they ever has. They dont know what happiness is. But
I, as one of the undeserving poor, have nothing between me and
the pauper's uniform but this here blasted four thousand a year
that shoves me into the middle class. (Excuse the expression,
maam; youd use it yourself if you had my provocation.) Theyve
got you every way you turn: it's a choice between the Skilly of the
workhouse and the Char Bydis of the middle class; and I havnt
the nerve for the workhouse. Intimidated: thats what I am. Broke.
Bought up. Happier men than me will call for my dust, and touch
me for their tip; and I'll look on helpless, and envy them. And
thats what your son has brought me to. [*He is overcome by emotion.*]

MRS HIGGINS Well, I'm very glad youre not going to do anything foolish, Mr Doolittle. For this solves the problem of Eliza's
future. You can provide for her now.

DOOLITTLE [*With melancholy resignation.*] Yes, maam: I'm
expected to provide for everyone now, out of four thousand a year.

HIGGINS [*Jumping up.*] Nonsense! he cant provide for her.
He shant provide for her. She doesnt belong to him. I paid him
five pounds for her. Doolittle: either youre an honest man or a
rogue.

DOOLITTLE [*Tolerantly.*] A little of both, Henry, like the rest of us: a little of both.

HIGGINS Well, you took that money for the girl; and you have no right to take her as well.

MRS HIGGINS Henry: dont be absurd. If you want to know where Eliza is, she is upstairs.

HIGGINS [*Amazed.*] Upstairs!!! Then I shall jolly soon fetch her downstairs. [*He makes resolutely for the door.*]

MRS HIGGINS [*Rising and following him.*] Be quiet, Henry. Sit down.

HIGGINS I . . .

MRS HIGGINS Sit down, dear; and listen to me.

HIGGINS Oh very well, very well, very well. [*He throws himself ungraciously on the ottoman, with his face towards the windows.*] But I think you might have told us this half an hour ago.

MRS HIGGINS Eliza came to me this morning. She told me of the brutal way you two treated her.

HIGGINS [*Bounding up again.*] What!

PICKERING [*Rising also.*] My dear Mrs Higgins, she's been telling you stories. We didnt treat her brutally. We hardly said a word to her; and we parted on particularly good terms. [*Turning on* HIGGINS.] Higgins: did you bully her after I went to bed?

HIGGINS Just the other way about. She threw my slippers in my face. She behaved in the most outrageous way. I never gave her the slightest provocation. The slippers came bang into my face the moment I entered the room—before I had uttered a word. And used perfectly awful language.

PICKERING [*Astonished.*] But why? What did we do to her?

MRS HIGGINS I think I know pretty well what you did. The girl is naturally rather affectionate, I think. Isnt she, Mr Doolittle?

DOOLITTLE Very tenderhearted, maam. Takes after me.

MRS HIGGINS Just so. She had become attached to you both. She worked very hard for you, Henry. I dont think you quite realize what anything in the nature of brain work means to a girl of her class. Well, it seems that when the great day of trial came, and she did this wonderful thing for you without making a single mistake, you two sat there and never said a word to her, but talked together of how glad you were that it was all over and how you had been bored with the whole thing. And then you were surprised because she threw your slippers at you! *I* should have thrown the fire-irons at you.

HIGGINS We said nothing except that we were tired and wanted to go to bed. Did we, Pick?

PICKERING [*Shrugging his shoulders.*] That was all.

MRS HIGGINS [*Ironically.*] Quite sure?

PICKERING Absolutely. Really, that was all.

MRS HIGGINS You didnt thank her, or pet her, or admire her, or tell her how splendid she'd been.

HIGGINS [*Impatiently.*] But she knew all about that. We didnt make speeches to her, if thats what you mean.

PICKERING [*Conscience stricken.*] Perhaps we were a little inconsiderate. Is she very angry?

MRS HIGGINS [*Returning to her place at the writing table.*] Well, I'm afraid she wont go back to Wimpole Street, especially now that Mr Doolittle is able to keep up the position you have thrust on her; but she says she is quite willing to meet you on friendly terms and to let bygones be bygones.

HIGGINS [*Furious.*] Is she, by George? Ho!

MRS HIGGINS If you promise to behave yourself, Henry, I'll ask her to come down. If not, go home; for you have taken up quite enough of my time.

HIGGINS Oh, all right. Very well. Pick: you behave yourself. Let us put on our best Sunday manners for this creature that we picked out of the mud. [*He flings himself sulkily into the Elizabethan chair.*]

DOOLITTLE [*Remonstrating.*] Now, now, Enry Iggins! Have some consideration for my feelings as a middle-class man.

MRS HIGGINS Remember your promise, Henry. [*She presses the bell button on the writing table.*] Mr Doolittle: will you be so good as to step out on the balcony for a moment. I dont want Eliza to have the shock of your news until she has made it up with these two gentlemen. Would you mind?

DOOLITTLE As you wish, lady. Anything to help Henry to keep her off my hands. [*He disappears through the window.*]

[*The parlormaid answers the bell.* PICKERING *sits down in* DOOLITTLE'S *place.*]

MRS HIGGINS Ask Miss Doolittle to come down, please.

THE PARLORMAID Yes, maam. [*She goes out.*]

MRS HIGGINS Now, Henry: be good.

HIGGINS I am behaving myself perfectly.

PICKERING He is doing his best, Mrs Higgins.

[*A pause.* HIGGINS *throws back his head; stretches out his legs; and begins to whistle.*]

MRS HIGGINS Henry, dearest, you dont look at all nice in that attitude.

HIGGINS [*Pulling himself together.*] I was not trying to look nice, mother.

MRS HIGGINS It doesnt matter, dear. I only wanted to make you speak.

HIGGINS Why?

MRS HIGGINS Because you cant speak and whistle at the same time.

[HIGGINS *groans. Another very trying pause.*]

HIGGINS [*Springing up, out of patience.*] Where the devil is that girl? Are we to wait here all day?

[ELIZA *enters, sunny, self-possessed, and giving a staggeringly convincing exhibition of ease of manner. She carries a little workbasket, and is very much at home.* PICKERING *is too much taken aback to rise.*]

LIZA How do you do, Professor Higgins? Are you quite well?

HIGGINS [*Choking.*] Am I . . . [*He can say no more.*]

LIZA But of course you are: you are never ill. So glad to see you again, Colonel Pickering. [*He rises hastily; and they shake hands.*] Quite chilly this morning, isn't it? [*She sits down on his left. He sits beside her.*]

HIGGINS Dont you dare try this game on me. I taught it to you; and it doesnt take me in. Get up and come home; and dont be a fool.

[ELIZA *takes a piece of needlework from her basket, and begins to stitch at it, without taking the least notice of this outburst.*]

MRS HIGGINS Very nicely put, indeed, Henry. No woman could resist such an invitation.

HIGGINS You let her alone, mother. Let her speak for herself. You will jolly soon see whether she has an idea that I havnt put into her head or a word that I havnt put into her mouth. I tell you I have created this thing out of the squashed cabbage leaves of Covent Garden; and now she pretends to play the fine lady with me.

MRS HIGGINS [*Placidly.*] Yes, dear; but youll sit down, wont you?

[HIGGINS *sits down again, savagely.*]

LIZA [*To* PICKERING, *taking no apparent notice of* HIGGINS, *and working away deftly.*] Will you drop me altogether now that the experiment is over, Colonel Pickering?

PICKERING Oh dont. You mustnt think of it as an experiment. It shocks me, somehow.

LIZA Oh, I'm only a squashed cabbage leaf . . .

PICKERING [*Impulsively.*] No.

LIZA [*Continuing quietly.*] . . . but I owe so much to you that I should be very unhappy if you forgot me.

PICKERING It's very kind of you to say so, Miss Doolittle.

LIZA It's not because you paid for my dresses. I know you are generous to everybody with money. But it was from you that I learnt really nice manners; and that is what makes one a lady, isnt it? You see it was so very difficult for me with the example of Professor Higgins always before me. I was brought up to be just like him, unable to control myself, and using bad language on the slightest provocation. And I should never have known that ladies and gentlemen didnt behave like that if you hadnt been there.

HIGGINS Well!!

PICKERING Oh, thats only his way, you know. He doesnt mean it.

LIZA Oh, *I* didnt mean it either, when I was a flower girl. It was only my way. But you see I did it; and thats what makes the difference after all.

PICKERING No doubt. Still, he taught you to speak; and I couldnt have done that, you know.

LIZA [*Trivially*.] Of course: that is his profession.

HIGGINS Damnation!

LIZA [*Continuing*.] It was just like learning to dance in the fashionable way: there was nothing more than that in it. But do you know what began my real education?

PICKERING What?

LIZA [*Stopping her work for a moment*.] Your calling me Miss Doolittle that day when I first came to Wimpole Street. That was the beginning of self-respect for me. [*She resumes her stitching*.] And there were a hundred little things you never noticed, because they came naturally to you. Things about standing up and taking off your hat and opening doors . . .

PICKERING Oh, that was nothing.

LIZA Yes: things that showed you thought and felt about me as if I were something better than a scullerymaid; though of course I know you would have been just the same to a scullerymaid if she had been let into the drawing room. You never took off your boots in the dining room when I was there.

PICKERING You mustnt mind that. Higgins takes off his boots all over the place.

LIZA I know. I am not blaming him. It is his way, isn't it? But it made such a difference to me that you didnt do it. You see, really and truly, apart from the things anyone can pick up (the dressing and the proper way of speaking, and so on), the difference between a lady and a flower girl is not how she behaves, but how she's treated. I shall always be a flower girl to Professor Higgins, because he always treats me as a flower girl, and always will; but I know I can be a lady to you, because you always treat me as a lady, and always will.

MRS HIGGINS Please dont grind your teeth, Henry.

PICKERING Well, this is really very nice of you, Miss Doolittle.

LIZA I should like you to call me Eliza, now, if you would.

PICKERING Thank you. Eliza, of course.

LIZA And I should like Professor Higgins to call me Miss Doolittle.

HIGGINS I'll see you damned first.

MRS HIGGINS Henry! Henry!

PICKERING [*Laughing.*] Why dont you slang back at him? Dont stand it. It would do him a lot of good.

LIZA I cant. I could have done it once; but now I cant go back to it. You told me, you know, that when a child is brought to a foreign country, it picks up the language in a few weeks, and forgets its own. Well, I am a child in your country. I have forgotten my own language, and can speak nothing but yours. Thats the real breakoff with the corner of Tottenham Court Road. Leaving Wimpole Street finishes it.

PICKERING [*Much alarmed.*] Oh! but youre coming back to Wimpole Street, arnt you? Youll forgive Higgins?

HIGGINS [*Rising.*] Forgive! Will she, by George! Let her go. Let her find out how she can get on without us. She will relapse into the gutter in three weeks without me at her elbow.

[DOOLITTLE *appears at the center window. With a look of dignified reproach at* HIGGINS, *he comes slowly and silently to his daughter, who, with her back to the window, is unconscious of his approach.*]

PICKERING He's incorrigible, Eliza. You wont relapse, will you?

LIZA No: not now. Never again. I have learnt my lesson. I dont believe I could utter one of the old sounds if I tried. [DOOLITTLE *touches her on the left shoulder. She drops her work, losing her self-possession utterly at the spectacle of her father's splendor.*] A-a-a-a-ah-ow-ooh!

HIGGINS [*With a crow of triumph.*] Aha! Just so. A-a-a-a-ahowooh! A-a-a-a-ahowooh! A-a-a-a-ahowooh! Victory! Victory! [*He throws himself on the divan, folding his arms, and spraddling arrogantly.*]

DOOLITTLE Can you blame the girl? Dont look at me like that, Eliza. It aint my fault. Ive come into some money.

LIZA You must have touched a millionaire this time, dad.

DOOLITTLE I have. But I'm dressed something special today. I'm going to St George's, Hanover Square. Your stepmother is going to marry me.

LIZA [*Angrily*.] Youre going to let yourself down to marry that low common woman!

PICKERING [*Quietly*.] He ought to, Eliza. [*To* DOOLITTLE.] Why has she changed her mind?

DOOLITTLE [*Sadly*.] Intimidated, Governor. Intimidated. Middle-class morality claims its victim. Wont you put on your hat, Liza, and come and see me turned off?

LIZA If the Colonel says I must, I—I'll [*almost sobbing*] I'll demean myself. And get insulted for my pains, like enough.

DOOLITTLE Dont be afraid: she never comes to words with anyone now, poor woman! respectability has broke all the spirit out of her.

PICKERING [*Squeezing* ELIZA's *elbow gently*.] Be kind to them, Eliza. Make the best of it.

LIZA [*Forcing a little smile for him through her vexation*.] Oh well, just to show theres no ill feeling. I'll be back in a moment. [*She goes out*.]

DOOLITTLE [*Sitting down beside* PICKERING.] I feel uncommon nervous about the ceremony, Colonel. I wish youd come and see me through it.

PICKERING But youve been through it before, man. You were married to Eliza's mother.

DOOLITTLE Who told you that, Colonel?

PICKERING Well, nobody told me. But I concluded—naturally . . .

DOOLITTLE No: that aint the natural way, Colonel: it's only the middle-class way. My way was always the undeserving way. But dont say nothing to Eliza. She dont know: I always had a delicacy about telling her.

PICKERING Quite right. We'll leave it so, if you dont mind.

DOOLITTLE And youll come to the church, Colonel, and put me through straight?

PICKERING With pleasure. As far as a bachelor can.

MRS HIGGINS May I come, Mr Doolittle? I should be very sorry to miss your wedding.

DOOLITTLE I should indeed be honored by your condescension,

maam; and my poor old woman would take it as a tremenjous compliment. She's been very low, thinking of the happy days that are no more.

MRS HIGGINS [*Rising.*] I'll order the carriage and get ready. [*The men rise, except* HIGGINS.] I shant be more than fifteen minutes. [*As she goes to the door* ELIZA *comes in, hatted and buttoning her gloves.*] I'm going to the church to see your father married, Eliza. You had better come in the brougham with me. Colonel Pickering can go on with the bridegroom.

[MRS HIGGINS *goes out.* ELIZA *comes to the middle of the room between the center window and the ottoman.* PICKERING *joins her.*]

DOOLITTLE Bridegroom. What a word! It makes a man realize his position, somehow. [*He takes up his hat and goes towards the door.*]

PICKERING Before I go, Eliza, do forgive Higgins and come back to us.

LIZA I dont think dad would allow me. Would you, dad?

DOOLITTLE [*Sad but magnanimous.*] They played you off very cunning, Eliza, them two sportsmen. If it had been only one of them, you could have nailed him. But you see, there was two; and one of them chaperoned the other, as you might say. [*To* PICKERING.] It was artful of you, Colonel; but I bear no malice: I should have done the same myself. I been the victim of one woman after another all my life, and I dont grudge you two getting the better of Liza. I shant interfere. It's time for us to go, Colonel. So long, Henry. See you in St George's, Eliza. [*He goes out.*]

PICKERING [*Coaxing.*] Do stay with us, Eliza. [*He follows* DOOLITTLE.]

[ELIZA *goes out on the balcony to avoid being alone with* HIGGINS. *He rises and joins her there. She immediately comes back into the room and makes for the door; but he goes along the balcony and gets his back to the door before she reaches it.*]

HIGGINS Well, Eliza, youve had a bit of your own back, as you call it. Have you had enough? and are you going to be reasonable? Or do you want any more?

LIZA You want me back only to pick up your slippers and put up with your tempers and fetch and carry for you.

HIGGINS I havnt said I wanted you back at all.

LIZA Oh, indeed. Then what are we talking about?

HIGGINS About you, not about me. If you come back I shall treat you just as I have always treated you. I cant change my nature; and I dont intend to change my manners. My manners are exactly the same as Colonel Pickering's.

LIZA Thats not true. He treats a flower girl as if she was a duchess.

HIGGINS And I treat a duchess as if she was a flower girl.

LIZA I see. [*She turns away composedly, and sits on the ottoman, facing the window.*] The same to everybody.

HIGGINS Just so.

LIZA Like father.

HIGGINS [*Grinning, a little taken down.*] Without accepting the comparison at all points, Eliza, it's quite true that your father is not a snob, and that he will be quite at home in any station of life to which his eccentric destiny may call him. [*Seriously.*] The great secret, Eliza, is not having bad manners or good manners or any other particular sort of manners, but having the same manner for all human souls: in short, behaving as if you were in Heaven, where there are no third-class carriages, and one soul is as good as another.

LIZA Amen. You are a born preacher.

HIGGINS [*Irritated.*] The question is not whether I treat you rudely, but whether you ever heard me treat anyone else better.

LIZA [*With sudden sincerity.*] I dont care how you treat me. I dont mind your swearing at me. I shouldnt mind a black eye: Ive had one before this. But [*standing up and facing him*] I wont be passed over.

HIGGINS Then get out of my way; for I wont stop for you. You talk about me as if I were a motor bus.

LIZA So you are a motor bus: all bounce and go, and no consideration for anyone. But I can do without you: dont think I cant.

HIGGINS I know you can. I told you you could.

LIZA [*Wounded, getting away from him to the other side of the ottoman with her face to the hearth.*] I know you did, you brute. You wanted to get rid of me.

HIGGINS   Liar.

LIZA   Thank you. [*She sits down with dignity.*]

HIGGINS   You never asked yourself, I suppose, whether I could do without you.

LIZA   [*Earnestly.*]   Dont you try to get round me. Youll have to do without me.

HIGGINS   [*Arrogant.*]   I can do without anybody. I have my own soul: my own spark of divine fire. But [*with sudden humility*] I shall miss you, Eliza. [*He sits down near her on the ottoman.*]   I have learnt something from your idiotic notions: I confess that humbly and gratefully. And I have grown accustomed to your voice and appearance. I like them, rather.

LIZA   Well, you have both of them on your gramophone and in your book of photographs. When you feel lonely without me, you can turn the machine on. It's got no feelings to hurt.

HIGGINS   I cant turn your soul on. Leave me those feelings; and you can take away the voice and the face. They are not you.

LIZA   Oh, you are a devil. You can twist the heart in a girl as easy as some could twist her arms to hurt her. Mrs Pearce warned me. Time and again she has wanted to leave you; and you always got round her at the last minute. And you dont care a bit for her. And you dont care a bit for me.

HIGGINS   I care for life, for humanity; and you are a part of it that has come my way and been built into my house. What more can you or anyone ask?

LIZA   I wont care for anybody that doesnt care for me.

HIGGINS   Commercial principles, Eliza. Like [*reproducing her Covent Garden pronunciation with professional exactness*] s'yollin voylets [*selling violets*], isnt it?

LIZA   Dont sneer at me. It's mean to sneer at me.

HIGGINS   I have never sneered in my life. Sneering doesnt become either the human face or the human soul. I am expressing my righteous contempt for Commercialism. I dont and wont trade in affection. You call me a brute because you couldnt buy a claim on me by fetching my slippers and finding my spectacles. You were a fool: I think a woman fetching a man's slippers is a disgusting sight: did I ever fetch your slippers? I think a good deal more of you for throwing them in my face. No use slaving for me and then saying you want to be cared for: who cares for a slave? If you come back, come back for the sake of good fellowship; for youll get nothing else. Youve had a thousand times as much out of me as I have out of you; and if you dare to set up your little dog's tricks of fetching and carrying slippers against my creation of a Duchess Eliza, I'll slam the door in your silly face.

LIZA   What did you do it for if you didnt care for me?

HIGGINS [*Heartily.*]   Why, because it was my job.

LIZA   You never thought of the trouble it would make for me.

HIGGINS   Would the world ever have been made if its maker had been afraid of making trouble? Making life means making trouble. Theres only one way of escaping trouble; and thats killing things. Cowards, you notice, are always shrieking to have troublesome people killed.

LIZA   I'm no preacher: I dont notice things like that. I notice that you dont notice me.

HIGGINS [*Jumping up and walking about intolerantly.*]   Eliza: youre an idiot. I waste the treasures of my Miltonic mind by spreading them before you. Once for all, understand that I go my way and do my work without caring twopence what happens to either of us. I am not intimidated, like your father and your stepmother. So you can come back or go to the devil: which you please.

LIZA   What am I to come back for?

HIGGINS [*Bouncing up on his knees on the ottoman and leaning over it to her.*]   For the fun of it. Thats why I took you on.

LIZA [*With averted face.*]   And you may throw me out tomorrow if I dont do everything you want me to?

HIGGINS   Yes; and you may walk out tomorrow if I dont do everything you want me to.

LIZA   And live with my stepmother?

HIGGINS   Yes, or sell flowers.

LIZA   Oh! if I only could go back to my flower basket! I should be independent of both you and father and all the world! Why did you take my independence from me? Why did I give it up? I'm a slave now, for all my fine clothes.

HIGGINS   Not a bit. I'll adopt you as my daughter and settle money on you if you like. Or would you rather marry Pickering?

LIZA [*Looking fiercely round at him.*] I wouldnt marry you if you asked me; and youre nearer my age than what he is.

HIGGINS [*Gently.*] Than he is: not "than what he is."

LIZA [*Losing her temper and rising.*] I'll talk as I like. Youre not my teacher now.

HIGGINS [*Reflectively.*] I dont suppose Pickering would, though. He's as confirmed an old bachelor as I am.

LIZA Thats not what I want; and dont you think it. Ive always had chaps enough wanting me that way. Freddy Hill writes to me twice and three times a day, sheets and sheets.

HIGGINS [*Disagreeably surprised.*] Damn his impudence! [*He recoils and finds himself sitting on his heels.*]

LIZA He has a right to if he likes, poor lad. And he does love me.

HIGGINS [*Getting off the ottoman.*] You have no right to encourage him.

LIZA Every girl has a right to be loved.

HIGGINS What! By fools like that?

LIZA Freddy's not a fool. And if he's weak and poor and wants me, may be he'd make me happier than my betters that bully me and dont want me.

HIGGINS Can he make anything of you? Thats the point.

LIZA Perhaps I could make something of him. But I never thought of us making anything of one another; and you never think of anything else. I only want to be natural.

HIGGINS In short, you want me to be as infatuated about you as Freddy? Is that it?

LIZA No I dont. Thats not the sort of feeling I want from you. And dont you be too sure of yourself or of me. I could have been a bad girl if I'd liked. Ive seen more of some things than you, for all your learning. Girls like me can drag gentlemen down to make love to them easy enough. And they wish each other dead the next minute.

HIGGINS Of course they do. Then what in thunder are we quarrelling about?

LIZA [*Much troubled.*] I want a little kindness. I know I'm a common ignorant girl, and you a book-learned gentleman; but I'm not dirt under your feet. What I done [*correcting herself*] what I did was not for the dresses and the taxis: I did it because we were pleasant together and I come—came—to care for you; not to want you to make love to me, and not forgetting the difference between us, but more friendly like.

HIGGINS Well, of course. Thats just how I feel. And how Pickering feels. Eliza: youre a fool.

LIZA Thats not a proper answer to give me. [*She sinks on the chair at the writing table in tears.*]

HIGGINS It's all youll get until you stop being a common idiot. If youre going to be a lady, youll have to give up feeling neglected if the men you know dont spend half their time snivelling over you and the other half giving you black eyes. If you cant stand the coldness of my sort of life, and the strain of it, go back to the gutter. Work til youre more a brute than a human being; and then cuddle and squabble and drink til you fall asleep. Oh, it's a fine life, the life of the gutter. It's real: it's warm: it's violent: you can feel it through the thickest skin: you can taste it and smell it without any training or any work. Not like Science and Literature and Classical Music and Philosophy and Art. You find me cold, unfeeling, selfish, dont you? Very well: be off with you to the sort of people you like. Marry some sentimental hog or other with lots of money, and a thick pair of lips to kiss you with and a thick pair of boots to kick you with. If you cant appreciate what youve got, youd better get what you can appreciate.

LIZA [*Desperate.*] Oh, you are a cruel tyrant. I cant talk to you: you turn everything against me: I'm always in the wrong. But you know very well all the time that youre nothing but a bully. You know I cant go back to the gutter, as you call it, and that I have no real friends in the world but you and the Colonel. You know well I couldnt bear to live with a low common man after you two; and it's wicked and cruel of you to insult me by pretending I could. You think I must go back to Wimpole Street because I have nowhere else to go but father's. But dont you be too sure that you have me under your feet to be trampled on and talked down. I'll marry Freddy, I will, as soon as I'm able to support him.

HIGGINS [*Thunderstruck.*] Freddy!!! that young fool! That poor devil who couldnt get a job as an errand boy even if he had the guts to try for it! Woman: do you not understand that I have made you a consort for a king?

LIZA Freddy loves me: that makes him king enough for me. I dont want him to work: he wasnt brought up to it as I was. I'll go and be a teacher.

HIGGINS Whatll you teach, in heaven's name?

LIZA What you taught me. I'll teach phonetics.

HIGGINS Ha! ha! ha!

LIZA I'll offer myself as an assistant to that hairyfaced Hungarian.

HIGGINS [*Rising in a fury.*] What! That impostor! that humbug! that toadying ignoramus! Teach him my methods! my discoveries! You take one step in his direction and I'll wring your neck. [*He lays hands on her.*] Do you hear?

LIZA [*Defiantly nonresistant.*] Wring away. What do I care? I knew youd strike me some day. [*He lets her go, stamping with rage at having forgotten himself, and recoils so hastily that he stumbles back into his seat on the ottoman.*] Aha! Now I know how to deal with you. What a fool I was not to think of it before! You cant take away the knowledge you gave me. You said I had a finer ear than you. And I can be civil and kind to people, which is more than you can. Aha! [*Purposely dropping her aitches to annoy him.*] Thats done you, Enry Iggins, it az. Now I dont care that [*snapping her fingers*] for your bullying and your big talk. I'll advertise it in the papers that your duchess is only a flower girl that you taught, and that she'll teach anybody to be a duchess just the same in six months for a thousand guineas. Oh, when I think of myself crawling under your feet and being trampled on and called names, when all the time I had only to lift up my finger to be as good as you, I could just kick myself.

HIGGINS [*Wondering at her.*] You damned impudent slut, you! But it's better than snivelling; better than fetching slippers and finding spectacles, isnt it? [*Rising.*] By George, Eliza, I said I'd make a woman of you; and I have. I like you like this.

LIZA   Yes: you turn round and make up to me now that I'm not afraid of you, and can do without you.

HIGGINS   Of course I do, you little fool. Five minutes ago you were like a millstone round my neck. Now youre a tower of strength: a consort battleship. You and I and Pickering will be three old bachelors instead of only two men and a silly girl.

[MRS HIGGINS *returns, dressed for the wedding.* ELIZA *instantly becomes cool and elegant.*]

MRS HIGGINS   The carriage is waiting, Eliza. Are you ready?

LIZA   Quite. Is the Professor coming?

MRS HIGGINS   Certainly not. He cant behave himself in church. He makes remarks out loud all the time on the clergyman's pronunciation.

LIZA   Then I shall not see you again, Professor. Goodbye. [*She goes to the door.*]

MRS HIGGINS   [*Coming to* HIGGINS.]   Goodbye, dear.

HIGGINS   Goodbye, mother. [*He is about to kiss her, when he recollects something.*] Oh, by the way, Eliza, order a ham and a Stilton cheese, will you? And buy me a pair of reindeer gloves, number eights, and a tie to match that new suit of mine. You can choose the color.   [*His cheerful, careless, vigorous voice shows that he is incorrigible.*]

LIZA   [*Disdainfully.*]   Number eights are too small for you if you want them lined with lamb's wool. You have three new ties that you have forgotten in the drawer of your washstand. Colonel Pickering prefers double Gloucester to Stilton; and you dont notice the difference. I telephoned Mrs Pearce this morning not to forget the ham. What you are to do without me I cannot imagine. [*She sweeps out.*]

MRS HIGGINS   I'm afraid youve spoilt that girl, Henry. I should be uneasy about you and her if she were less fond of Colonel Pickering.

HIGGINS   Pickering! Nonsense: she's going to marry Freddy. Ha ha! Freddy! Freddy!! Ha ha ha ha ha!!!!! [*He roars with laughter as the play ends.*]

The rest of the story need not be shown in action, and indeed, would hardly need telling if our imaginations were not so enfeebled by their lazy dependence on the ready-mades and reach-me-downs of the ragshop in which Romance keeps its stock of "happy endings" to misfit all stories. Now, the history of Eliza Doolittle, though called a romance because the transfiguration it records seems exceedingly improbable, is common enough. Such transfigurations have been achieved by hundreds of resolutely ambitious young women since Nell Gwynne set them the example by playing queens and fascinating kings in the theatre in which she began by selling oranges. Nevertheless, people in all directions have assumed, for no other reason than that she became the heroine of a romance, that she must have married the hero of it. This is unbearable, not only because her little drama, if acted on such a thoughtless assumption, must be spoiled, but because the true sequel is patent to anyone with a sense of human nature in general, and of feminine instinct in particular.

Eliza, in telling Higgins she would not marry him if he asked her, was not coquetting: she was announcing a well-considered decision. When a bachelor interests, and dominates, and teaches, and becomes important to a spinster, as Higgins with Eliza, she always, if she has character enough to be capable of it, considers very seriously indeed whether she will play for becoming that bachelor's wife, especially if he is so little interested in marriage that a determined and devoted woman might capture him if she set herself resolutely to do it. Her decision will depend a good deal on whether she is really free to choose; and that, again, will depend on her age and income. If she is at the end of her youth, and has no security for her livelihood, she will marry him because she must marry anybody who will provide for her. But at Eliza's age a good-looking girl does not feel that pressure: she feels free to pick and choose. She is therefore guided by her instinct in the matter.

Eliza's instinct tells her not to marry Higgins. It does not tell her to give him up. It is not in the slightest doubt as to his remaining one of the strongest personal interests in her life. It would be very sorely strained if there was another woman likely to supplant her with him. But as she feels sure of him on that last point, she has no doubt at all as to her course, and would not have any, even if the difference of twenty years in age, which seems so great to youth, did not exist between them.

As our own instincts are not appealed to by her conclusion, let us see whether we cannot discover some reason in it. When Higgins excused his indifference to young women on the ground that they had an irresistible rival in his mother, he gave the clue to his inveterate old-bachelordom. The case is uncommon only to the extent that remarkable mothers are uncommon. If an imaginative boy has a sufficiently rich mother who has intelligence, personal grace, dignity of character without harshness, and a cultivated sense of the best art of her time to enable her to make her house beautiful, she sets a standard for him against which very few women can struggle, besides effecting for him a disengagement of his affections, his sense of beauty, and his idealism from his specifically sexual impulses. This makes him a standing puzzle to the huge number of uncultivated people who have been brought up in tasteless homes by commonplace or disagreeable parents, and to whom, consequently, literature, painting, sculpture, music, and affectionate personal relations come as modes of sex if they come at all. The word passion means nothing else to them; and that Higgins could have a passion for phonetics and idealize his mother instead of Eliza, would seem to them absurd and unnatural. Nevertheless, when we look round and see that hardly anyone is too ugly or disagreeable to find a wife or a husband if he or she wants one, whilst many old maids and bachelors are above the average in quality and culture, we cannot help suspecting that the disentanglement of sex from the associations with which it is so commonly confused, a disentanglement which persons of genius achieve by sheer intellectual analysis, is sometimes produced or aided by parental fascination.

Now, though Eliza was incapable of thus explaining to herself

Higgins's formidable powers of resistance to the charm that prostrated Freddy at the first glance, she was instinctively aware that she could never obtain a complete grip of him, or come between him and his mother (the first necessity of the married woman). To put it shortly, she knew that for some mysterious reason he had not the makings of a married man in him, according to her conception of a husband as one to whom she would be his nearest and fondest and warmest interest. Even had there been no mother-rival, she would still have refused to accept an interest in herself that was secondary to philosophic interests. Had Mrs Higgins died, there would still have been Milton and the Universal Alphabet. Landor's remark that to those who have the greatest power of loving, love is a secondary affair, would not have recommended Landor to Eliza. Put that along with her resentment of Higgins's domineering superiority, and her mistrust of his coaxing cleverness in getting round her and evading her wrath when he had gone too far with his impetuous bullying, and you will see that Eliza's instinct had good grounds for warning her not to marry her Pygmalion.

And now, whom did Eliza marry? For if Higgins was a predestinate old bachelor, she was most certainly not a predestinate old maid. Well, that can be told very shortly to those who have not guessed it from the indications she has herself given them.

Almost immediately after Eliza is stung into proclaiming her considered determination not to marry Higgins, she mentions the fact that young Mr Frederick Eynsford Hill is pouring out his love for her daily through the post. Now Freddy is young, practically twenty years younger than Higgins: he is a gentleman (or, as Eliza would qualify him, a toff), and speaks like one. He is nicely dressed, is treated by the Colonel as an equal, loves her unaffectedly, and is not her master, nor ever likely to dominate her in spite of his advantage of social standing. Eliza has no use for the foolish romantic tradition that all women love to be mastered, if not actually bullied and beaten. "When you go to women" says Nietzsche "take your whip with you." Sensible despots have never confined that precaution to women: they have taken their whips with them when they have dealt with men, and been slavishly idealized by the men over whom they have flourished the whip much more than by women. No doubt there are slavish women as well as slavish men; and women, like men, admire those that are stronger than themselves. But to admire a strong person and to live under that strong person's thumb are two different things. The weak may not be admired and hero-worshiped; but they are by no means disliked or shunned; and they never seem to have the least difficulty in marrying people who are too good for them. They may fail in emergencies; but life is not one long emergency: it is mostly a string of situations for which no exceptional strength is needed, and with which even rather weak people can cope if they have a stronger partner to help them out. Accordingly, it is a truth everywhere in evidence that strong people, masculine or feminine, not only do not marry stronger people, but do not show any preference for them in selecting their friends. When a lion meets another with a louder roar "the first lion thinks the last a bore." The man or woman who feels strong enough for two, seeks for every other quality in a partner than strength.

The converse is also true. Weak people want to marry strong people who do not frighten them too much; and this often leads them to make the mistake we describe metaphorically as "biting off more than they can chew." They want too much for too little; and when the bargain is unreasonable beyond all bearing, the union becomes impossible: it ends in the weaker party being either discarded or borne as a cross, which is worse. People who are not only weak, but silly or obtuse as well, are often in these difficulties.

This being the state of human affairs, what is Eliza fairly sure to do when she is placed between Freddy and Higgins? Will she look forward to a lifetime of fetching Higgins's slippers or to a lifetime of Freddy fetching hers? There can be no doubt about the answer. Unless Freddy is biologically repulsive to her, and Higgins biologically attractive to a degree that overwhelms all her other instincts, she will, if she marries either of them, marry Freddy.

And that is just what Eliza did.

Complications ensued; but they were economic, not romantic. Freddy had no money and no occupation. His mother's jointure, a last relic of the opulence of Largelady Park, had enabled her to struggle along in Earlscourt with an air of gentility, but not to procure any serious secondary education for her children, much less give the boy a profession. A clerkship at thirty shillings a week was beneath Freddy's dignity, and extremely distasteful to him besides. His prospects consisted of a hope that if he kept up appearances somebody would do something for him. The something appeared vaguely to his imagination as a private secretaryship or a sinecure of some sort. To his mother it perhaps appeared as a marriage to some lady of means who could not resist her boy's niceness. Fancy her feelings when he married a flower girl who had become disclassed under extraordinary circumstances which were now notorious!

It is true that Eliza's situation did not seem wholly ineligible. Her father, though formerly a dustman, and now fantastically disclassed, had become extremely popular in the smartest society by a social talent which triumphed over every prejudice and every disadvantage. Rejected by the middle class, which he loathed, he had shot up at once into the highest circles by his wit, his dustmanship (which he carried like a banner), and his Nietzschean transcendence of good and evil. At intimate ducal dinners he sat on the right hand of the Duchess; and in country houses he smoked in the pantry and was made much of by the butler when he was not feeding in the dining room and being consulted by cabinet ministers. But he found it almost as hard to do all this on four thousand a year as Mrs Eynsford Hill to live in Earlscourt on an income so pitiably smaller that I have not the heart to disclose its exact figure. He absolutely refused to add the last straw to his burden by contributing to Eliza's support.

Thus Freddy and Eliza, now Mr and Mrs Eynsford Hill, would have spent a penniless honeymoon but for a wedding present of £500 from the Colonel to Eliza. It lasted a long time because Freddy did not know how to spend money, never having had any to spend, and Eliza, socially trained by a pair of old bachelors, wore her clothes as long as they held together and looked pretty, without the least regard to their being many months out of fashion. Still, £500 will not last two young people forever;

and they both knew, and Eliza felt as well, that they must shift for themselves in the end. She could quarter herself on Wimpole Street because it had come to be her home; but she was quite aware that she ought not to quarter Freddy there, and that it would not be good for his character if she did.

Not that the Wimpole Street bachelors objected. When she consulted them, Higgins declined to be bothered about her housing problem when that solution was so simple. Eliza's desire to have Freddy in the house with her seemed of no more importance than if she had wanted an extra piece of bedroom furniture. Pleas as to Freddy's character, and the moral obligation on him to earn his own living, were lost on Higgins. He denied that Freddy had any character, and declared that if he tried to do any useful work some competent person would have the trouble of undoing it: a procedure involving a net loss to the community, and great unhappiness to Freddy himself, who was obviously intended by Nature for such light work as amusing Eliza, which, Higgins declared, was a much more useful and honorable occupation than working in the city. When Eliza referred again to her project of teaching phonetics, Higgins abated not a jot of his violent opposition to it. He said she was not within ten years of being qualified to meddle with his pet subject; and as it was evident that the Colonel agreed with him, she felt she could not go against them in this grave matter, and that she had no right, without Higgins's consent, to exploit the knowledge he had given her; for his knowledge seemed to her as much his private property as his watch: Eliza was no communist. Besides, she was superstitiously devoted to them both, more entirely and frankly after her marriage than before it.

It was the Colonel who finally solved the problem, which had cost him much perplexed cogitation. He one day asked Eliza, rather shyly, whether she had quite given up her notion of keeping a flower shop. She replied that she had thought of it, but had put it out of her head, because the Colonel had said, that day at Mrs Higgins's, that it would never do. The Colonel confessed that when he said that, he had not quite recovered from the dazzling impression of the day before. They broke the matter to Higgins that evening. The sole comment vouchsafed by him very nearly led to a serious quarrel with Eliza. It was to the effect that she would have in Freddy an ideal errand boy.

Freddy himself was next sounded on the subject. He said he had been thinking of a shop himself; though it had presented itself to his pennilessness as a small place in which Eliza should sell tobacco at one counter whilst he sold newspapers at the opposite one. But he agreed that it would be extraordinarily jolly to go early every morning with Eliza to Covent Garden and buy flowers on the scene of their first meeting: a sentiment which earned him many kisses from his wife. He added that he had always been afraid to propose anything of the sort, because Clara would make an awful row about a step that must damage her matrimonial chances, and his mother could not be expected to like it after clinging for so many years to that step of the social ladder on which retail trade is impossible.

This difficulty was removed by an event highly unexpected by Freddy's mother. Clara, in the course of her incursions into those artistic circles which were the highest within her reach, discovered that her conversational qualifications were expected to include a grounding in the novels of Mr H. G. Wells. She borrowed them in various directions so energetically that she swallowed them all within two months. The result was a conversion of a kind quite common today. A modern Acts of the Apostles would fill fifty whole Bibles if anyone were capable of writing it.

Poor Clara, who appeared to Higgins and his mother as a disagreeable and ridiculous person, and to her own mother as in some inexplicable way a social failure, had never seen herself in either light; for, though to some extent ridiculed and mimicked in West Kensington like everybody else there, she was accepted as a rational and normal—or shall we say inevitable?—sort of human being. At worst they called her The Pusher; but to them no more than to herself had it ever occurred that she was pushing the air, and pushing it in a wrong direction. Still, she was not happy. She was growing desperate. Her one asset, the fact that her mother was what the Epsom greengrocer called a carriage lady, had no exchange value, apparently. It had prevented her from getting educated, because the only education she could have afforded was education with the Earlscourt greengrocer's daughter. It had led her to seek the society of her mother's class; and that class simply would not have her, because she was much poorer than the greengrocer, and, far from being able to afford a maid, could not afford even a housemaid, and had to scrape along at home with an illiberally treated general servant. Under such circumstances nothing could give her an air of being a genuine product of Largelady Park. And yet its tradition made her regard a marriage with anyone within her reach as an unbearable humiliation. Commercial people and professional people in a small way were odious to her. She ran after painters and novelists; but she did not charm them; and her bold attempts to pick up and practice artistic and literary talk irritated them. She was, in short, an utter failure, an ignorant, incompetent, pretentious, unwelcome, penniless, useless little snob; and though she did not admit these disqualifications (for nobody ever faces unpleasant truths of this kind until the possibility of a way out dawns on them) she felt their effects too keenly to be satisfied with her position.

Clara had a startling eyeopener when, on being suddenly wakened to enthusiasm by a girl of her own age who dazzled her and produced in her a gushing desire to take her for a model, and gain her friendship, she discovered that this exquisite apparition had graduated from the gutter in a few months time. It shook her so violently, that when Mr H. G. Wells lifted her on the point of his puissant pen, and placed her at the angle of view from which the life she was leading and the society to which she clung appeared in its true relation to real human needs and worthy social structure, he effected a conversion and a conviction of sin comparable to the most sensational feats of General Booth or Gypsy Smith. Clara's snobbery went bang. Life suddenly began to move with her. Without knowing how or why, she began to make friends and enemies. Some of the acquaintances to whom she had been a tedious or indifferent or ridiculous affliction, dropped her: others became cordial. To her amazement she found that some "quite nice" people were saturated with Wells, and that this accessibility to ideas was the secret of their niceness. People she had thought deeply religious, and had tried to conciliate on that tack with disastrous results, suddenly took an interest in her, and revealed a hostility to conventional religion which she had never conceived possible except among the most desperate characters. They made her read Galsworthy; and Galsworthy exposed the vanity of Largelady Park and finished her. It exasperated her to think that the dungeon in which she had languished for so many unhappy years had been unlocked all the time, and that the impulses she had so carefully struggled with and stifled for the sake of keeping well with society, were precisely those by which alone she could have come into any sort of sincere human contact. In the radiance of these discoveries, and the tumult of their reaction, she made a fool of herself as freely and conspicuously as when she so rashly adopted Eliza's expletive in Mrs Higgins's drawing room; for the new-born Wellsian had to find her bearings almost as ridiculously as a baby; but nobody hates a baby for its ineptitudes, or thinks the worse of it for trying to eat the matches; and Clara lost no friends by her follies. They laughed at her to her face this time; and she had to defend herself and fight it out as best she could.

When Freddy paid a visit to Earlscourt (which he never did when he could possibly help it) to make the desolating announcement that he and his Eliza were thinking of blackening the Largelady scutcheon by opening a shop, he found the little household already convulsed by a prior announcement from Clara that she also was going to work in an old furniture shop in Dover Street, which had been started by a fellow Wellsian. This appointment Clara owed, after all, to her old social accomplishment of Push. She had made up her mind that, cost what it might, she would see Mr Wells in the flesh; and she had achieved her end at a garden party. She had better luck than so rash an enterprise deserved. Mr Wells came up to her expectations. Age had not withered him, nor could custom stale his infinite variety in half an hour. His pleasant neatness and compactness, his small hands and feet, his teeming ready brain, his unaffected accessibility, and a certain fine apprehensiveness which stamped him as susceptible from his topmost hair to his tipmost toe, proved irresistible. Clara talked of nothing else for weeks and weeks afterwards. And as she happened to talk to the lady of the furniture shop, and that lady also desired above all things to know Mr Wells and sell pretty things to him, she offered Clara a job on the chance of achieving that end through her.

And so it came about that Eliza's luck held, and the expected opposition to the flower shop melted away. The shop is in the arcade of a railway station not very far from the Victoria and Albert Museum; and if you live in that neighborhood you may go there any day and buy a buttonhole from Eliza.

Now here is a last opportunity for romance. Would you not like to be assured that the shop was an immense success, thanks to Eliza's charms and her early business experience in Covent Garden? Alas! the truth is the truth: the shop did not pay for a long time, simply because Eliza and her Freddy did not know how to keep it. True, Eliza had not to begin at the very beginning: she knew the names and prices of the cheaper flowers; and her elation was unbounded when she found that Freddy, like all youths educated at cheap, pretentious, and thoroughly inefficient schools, knew a little Latin. It was very little, but enough to make him appear to her a Porson or Bentley, and to put him at his ease with botanical nomenclature. Unfortunately he knew nothing else; and Eliza, though she could count money up to eighteen shillings or so, and had acquired a certain familiarity with the language of Milton from her struggles to qualify herself for winning Higgins's bet, could not write out a bill without utterly disgracing the establishment. Freddy's power of stating in Latin that Balbus built a wall and that Gaul was divided into three parts did not carry with it the slightest knowledge of accounts or business: Colonel Pickering had to explain to him what a checkbook and a bank account meant. And the pair were by no means easily teachable. Freddy backed up Eliza in her obstinate refusal to believe that they could save money by engaging a bookkeeper with some knowledge of the business. How, they argued, could you possibly save money by going to extra expense when you already could not make both ends meet? But the Colonel, after making the ends meet over and over again, at last gently insisted; and Eliza, humbled to the dust by having to beg from him so often, and stung by the uproarious derision of Higgins, to whom the notion of Freddy succeeding at anything was a joke that never palled, grasped the fact that business, like phonetics, has to be learned.

On the piteous spectacle of the pair spending their evenings in shorthand schools and polytechnic classes, learning bookkeeping and typewriting with incipient junior clerks, male and female, from the elementary schools, let me not dwell. There were even classes at the London School of Economics, and a humble personal appeal to the director of that institution to recommend a course bearing on the flower business. He, being a humorist, explained to them the method of the celebrated Dickensian essay on Chinese Metaphysics by the gentleman who read an article on China and an article on Metaphysics and combined the information. He suggested that they should combine the London School with Kew Gardens. Eliza, to whom the procedure of the Dickensian gentleman seemed perfectly correct (as in fact it was) and not in the least funny (which was only her ignorance), took the advice with entire gravity. But the effort that cost her the deepest humiliation was a request to Higgins, whose pet artistic fancy, next to Milton's verse, was calligraphy, and who himself wrote a most beautiful Italian hand, that he would teach her to write. He declared that she was congenitally incapable of forming a single letter worthy of the least of Milton's words; but she persisted; and again he suddenly threw himself into the task of teaching her with a combination of stormy intensity, concentrated patience, and occasional bursts of interesting disquisition on the beauty and nobility, the august mission and destiny, of human handwriting. Eliza ended by acquiring an extremely uncommercial script which was a positive extension of her personal beauty, and spending three times as much on stationery as anyone else because certain qualities and shapes on paper became indispensable to her. She could not even address an envelope in the usual way because it made the margins all wrong.

Their commercial schooldays were a period of disgrace and despair for the young couple. They seemed to be learning nothing about flower shops. At last they gave it up as hopeless, and shook the dust of the shorthand schools, and the polytechnics, and the

London School of Economics from their feet forever. Besides, the business was in some mysterious way beginning to take care of itself. They had somehow forgotten their objections to employing other people. They came to the conclusion that their own way was the best, and that they had really a remarkable talent for business. The Colonel, who had been compelled for some years to keep a sufficient sum on current account at his bankers to make up their deficits, found that the provision was unnecessary: the young people were prospering. It is true that there was not quite fair play between them and their competitors in trade. Their week-ends in the country cost them nothing, and saved them the price of their Sunday dinners; for the motor car was the Colonel's; and he and Higgins paid the hotel bills. Mr F. Hill, florist and greengrocer (they soon discovered that there was money in asparagus; and asparagus led to other vegetables), had an air which stamped the business as classy; and in private life he was still Frederick Eynsford Hill, Esquire. Not that there was any swank about him: nobody but Eliza knew that he had been christened Frederick Challoner. Eliza herself swanked like anything.

That is all. That is how it has turned out. It is astonishing how much Eliza still manages to meddle in the housekeeping at Wimpole Street in spite of the shop and her own family. And it is notable that though she never nags her husband, and frankly loves the Colonel as if she were his favorite daughter, she has never got out of the habit of nagging Higgins that was established on the fatal night when she won his bet for him. She snaps his head off on the faintest provocation, or on none. He no longer dares to tease her by assuming an abysmal inferiority of Freddy's mind to his own. He storms and bullies and derides; but she stands up to him so ruthlessly that the Colonel has to ask her from time to time to be kinder to Higgins; and it is the only request of his that brings a mulish expression into her face. Nothing but some emergency or calamity great enough to break down all likes and dislikes, and throw them both back on their common humanity—and may they be spared any such trial!—will ever alter this. She knows that Higgins does not need her, just as her father did not need her.

The very scrupulousness with which he told her that day that he had become used to having her there, and dependent on her for all sorts of little services, and that he should miss her if she went away (it would never have occurred to Freddy or the Colonel to say anything of the sort) deepens her inner certainty that she is "no more to him than them slippers"; yet she has a sense, too, that his indifference is deeper than the infatuation of commoner souls. She is immensely interested in him. She has even secret mischievous moments in which she wishes she could get him alone, on a desert island, away from all ties and with nobody else in the world to consider, and just drag him off his pedestal and see him making love like any common man. We all have private imaginations of that sort. But when it comes to business, to the life that she really leads as distinguished from the life of dreams and fancies, she likes Freddy and she likes the Colonel; and she does not like Higgins and Mr Doolittle. Galatea never does quite like Pygmalion: his relation to her is too godlike to be altogether agreeable.

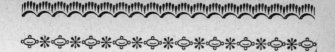

EUGENE O'NEILL

The Emperor Jones

CAST

BRUTUS JONES, *Emperor*

HENRY SMITHERS, *a Cockney Trader*

AN OLD NATIVE WOMAN

LEM, *a Native Chief*

SOLDIERS, *Adherents of Lem*

The Little Formless Fears

JEFF

The Negro Convicts

The Prison Guard

The Planters

The Auctioneer

The Slaves

The Congo Witch-Doctor

The Crocodile God

SCENE: *The action of the play takes place on an island in the West Indies as yet not self-determined by White Marines. The form of native government is, for the time being, an Empire.*

SCENE ONE

∴∴∴∴∴∴∴∴∴∴∴∴∴∴∴∴∴∴∴∴∴∴

SCENE: *The audience chamber in the palace of the Emperor—
a spacious, high-ceilinged room with bare, whitewashed walls. The
floor is of white tiles. In the rear, to the left of center, a wide archway giving out on a portico with white pillars. The palace is
evidently situated on high ground for beyond the portico nothing
can be seen but a vista of distant hills, their summits crowned
with thick groves of palm trees. In the right wall, center, a smaller
arched doorway leading to the living quarters of the palace. The
room is bare of furniture with the exception of one huge chair
made of uncut wood which stands at center, its back to rear. This
is very apparently the Emperor's throne. It is painted a dazzling,
eye-smiting scarlet. There is a brilliant orange cushion on the
seat and another smaller one is placed on the floor to serve as a
foot-stool. Strips of matting, dyed scarlet, lead from the foot of the
throne to the two entrances.*

*It is late afternoon but the sunlight still blazes yellowly beyond
the portico and there is an oppressive burden of exhausting heat in
the air.*

*As the curtain rises, a native negro woman sneaks in cautiously
from the entrance on the right. She is very old, dressed in cheap
calico, barefooted, a red bandana handkerchief covering all but a
few stray wisps of white hair. A bundle bound in colored cloth is
carried over her shoulder on the end of a stick. She hesitates beside
the doorway, peering back as if in extreme dread of being discovered. Then she begins to glide noiselessly, a step at a time,
toward the doorway in the rear. At this moment,* SMITHERS *appears
beneath the portico.*

SMITHERS *is a tall, stoop-shouldered man about forty. His bald
head, perched on a long neck with an enormous Adams apple,
looks like an egg. The tropics have tanned his naturally pasty face
with its small, sharp features to a sickly yellow, and native rum has*

painted his pointed nose to a startling red. His little, washy-blue eyes are red-rimmed and dart about him like a ferret's. His expression is one of unscrupulous meanness, cowardly and dangerous. He is dressed in a worn riding suit of dirty white drill, puttees, spurs, and wears a white cork helmet. A cartridge belt with an automatic revolver is around his waist. He carries a riding whip in his hand. He sees the woman and stops to watch her suspiciously. Then, making up his mind, he steps quickly on tiptoe into the room. The woman, looking back over her shoulder continually, does not see him until it is too late. When she does SMITHERS *springs forward and grabs her firmly by the shoulder. She struggles to get away, fiercely but silently.*

SMITHERS [*Tightening his grasp—roughly.*] Easy! None o' that, me birdie. You can't wriggle out now. I got me 'ooks on yer.

WOMAN [*Seeing the uselessness of struggling, gives way to frantic terror, and sinks to the ground, embracing his knees supplicatingly.*] No tell him! No tell him, Mister!

SMITHERS [*With great curiosity.*] Tell 'im? [*Then scornfully.*] Oh, you mean 'is bloomin' Majesty. What's the gaime, any'ow? What are you sneakin' away for? Been stealin' a bit, I s'pose. [*He taps her bundle with his riding whip significantly.*]

WOMAN [*Shaking her head vehemently.*] No, me no steal.

SMITHERS Bloody liar! But tell me what's up. There's somethin' funny goin' on. I smelled it in the air first thing I got up this mornin'. You blacks are up to some devilment. This palace of 'is is like a bleedin' tomb. Where's all the 'ands? [*The woman keeps sullenly silent.* SMITHERS *raises his whip threateningly.*] Ow, yer won't, won't yer? I'll show yer what's what.

WOMAN [*Coweringly.*] I tell, Mister. You no hit. They go— all go. [*She makes a sweeping gesture toward the hills in the distance.*]

SMITHERS Run away—to the 'ills?

WOMAN Yes, Mister. Him Emperor—Great Father. [*She touches her forehead to the floor with a quick mechanical jerk.*] Him sleep after eat. Then they go—all go. Me old woman. Me left only. Now me go too.

SMITHERS [*His astonishment giving way to an immense, mean satisfaction.*] Ow! So that's the ticket! Well, I know bloody well wot's in the air—when they runs orf to the 'ills. The tom-tom 'll be thumping out there bloomin' soon. [*With extreme vindictiveness.*] And I'm bloody glad of it, for one! Serve 'im right! Puttin' on airs, the stinkin' nigger! 'Is Majesty! Gawd blimey! I only 'opes I'm there when they takes 'im out to shoot 'im. [*Suddenly.*] 'E's still 'ere all right, ain't 'e?

WOMAN Yes. Him sleep.

SMITHERS 'E's bound to find out soon as 'e wakes up. 'E's cunnin' enough to know when 'is time's come. [*He goes to the doorway on the right and whistles shrilly with his fingers in his mouth. The old woman springs to her feet and runs out of the doorway, rear.* SMITHERS *goes after her, reaching for his revolver.*] Stop or I'll shoot! [*Then stopping—indifferently.*] Pop orf then, if yer like, yer black cow. [*He stands in the doorway, looking after her.*]

[JONES *enters from the right. He is a tall, powerfully built, full-blooded Negro of middle age. His features are typically negroid, yet there is something decidedly distinctive about his face—an underlying strength of will, a hardy, self-reliant confidence in himself that inspires respect. His eyes are alive with a keen, cunning intelligence. In manner he is shrewd, suspicious, evasive. He wears a light blue uniform coat, sprayed with brass buttons, heavy gold chevrons on his shoulders, gold braid on the collar, cuffs, etc. His pants are bright red with a light blue stripe down the side. Patent leather laced boots with brass spurs, and a belt with a long-barreled, pearl-handled revolver in a holster complete his make-up. Yet there is something not altogether ridiculous about his grandeur. He has a way of carrying it off.*]

JONES [*Not seeing anyone—greatly irritated and blinking sleepily—shouts.*] Who dare whistle dat way in my palace? Who dare wake up de Emperor? I'll git de hide frayled off some o' you niggers sho'!

SMITHERS [*Showing himself—in a manner half-afraid and half-defiant.*] It was me whistled to yer. [*As* JONES *frowns angrily.*] I got news for yer.

JONES [*Putting on his suavest manner, which fails to cover up his contempt for the white man.*] Oh, it's you, Mister Smithers. [*He sits down on his throne with easy dignity.*] What news you got to tell me?

SMITHERS [*Coming close to enjoy his discomfiture.*] Don't yer notice nothin' funny today?

JONES [*Coldly.*] Funny? No. I ain't perceived nothin' of de kind.

SMITHERS Then yer ain't so foxy as I thought yer was. Where's all your court? [*Sarcastically.*] The Generals and the Cabinet Ministers and all?

JONES [*Imperturbably.*] Where dey mostly runs to minute I closes my eyes—drinkin' rum and talkin' big down in de town. [*Sarcastically.*] How come you don't know dat? Ain't you sousin' with 'em most every day?

SMITHERS [*Smug but pretending indifference—with a wink.*] That's part of the day's work. I got ter—ain't I—in my business?

JONES [*Contemptuously.*] Yo' business!

SMITHERS [*Imprudently enraged.*] Gawd blimey, you was glad enough for me ter take yer in on it when you landed here first. You didn't 'ave no 'igh and mighty airs in them days!

JONES [*His hand going to his revolver like a flash—menacingly.*] Talk polite, white man! Talk polite, you heah me! I'm boss heah now, is you fergettin'? [*The Cockney seems about to challenge this last statement with the facts but something in the other's eyes holds and cows him.*]

SMITHERS [*In a cowardly whine.*] No 'arm meant, old top.

JONES [*Condescendingly.*] I accepts yo' apology. [*Lets his hand fall from his revolver.*] No use'n you rakin' up ole times. What I was den is one thing. What I is now's another. You didn't let me in on yo' crooked work out o' no kind feelin's dat time. I done de dirty work fo' you—and most o' de brain work, too, fo' dat matter—and I was wu'th money to you, dat's de reason.

SMITHERS Well, blimey, I give yer a start, didn't I—when no one else would. I wasn't afraid to 'ire yer like the rest was—'count of the story about your breakin' jail back in the States.

JONES No, you didn't have no s'cuse to look down on me fo'
dat. You been in jail you'self more'n once.

SMITHERS [*Furiously.*] It's a lie! [*Then trying to pass it off
by an attempt at scorn.*] Garn! Who told yer that fairy tale?

JONES Dey's some tings I ain't got to be tole. I kin see 'em in
folk's eyes. [*Then after a pause—meditatively.*] Yes, you sho'
give me a start. And it didn't take long from dat time to git dese
fool, woods' niggers right where I wanted dem. [*With pride.*]
From stowaway to Emperor in two years! Dat's goin' some!

SMITHERS [*With curiosity.*] And I bet you got yer pile o'
money 'id safe some place.

JONES [*With satisfaction.*] I sho' has! And it's in a foreign
bank where no pusson don't get it out but me no matter
what come. You didn't s'pose I was holdin' down dis Emperor
job for de glory in it, did you? Sho'! De fuss and glory part of it,
dat's only to turn de heads o' de low-flung, bush niggers dat's
here. Dey wants de big circus show for deir money. I gives it to
'em an' I gits de money. [*With a grin.*] De long green, dat's
me every time! [*Then rebukingly.*] But you ain't got no kick agin
me, Smithers. I'se paid you back all you done for me many times.
Ain't I pertected you and winked at all de crooked tradin' you
been doin' right out in de broad day. Sho' I has—and me makin'
laws to stop it at de same time! [*He chuckles.*]

SMITHERS [*Grinning.*] But, meanin' no 'arm, you been grab-
bin' right and left yourself, ain't yer? Look at the taxes you've
put on 'em! Blimey! You've squeezed 'em dry!

JONES [*Chuckling.*] No, dey ain't *all* dry yet. I'se still heah,
ain't I?

SMITHERS [*Smiling at his secret thought.*] They're dry right
now, you'll find out. [*Changing the subject abruptly.*] And as
for me breakin' laws, you've broke 'em all yerself just as fast as
yer made 'em.

JONES Ain't I de Emperor? De laws don't go for him. [*Judicially.*] You heah what I tells you, Smithers. Dere's little stealin'
like you does, and dere's big stealin' like I does. For de little
stealin' dey gits you in jail soon or late. For de big stealin' dey

makes you Emperor and puts you in de Hall o' Fame when you croaks. [*Reminiscently.*] If dey's one thing I learns in ten years on de Pullman ca's listenin' to de white quality talk, it's dat same fact. And when I gits a chance to use it I winds up Emperor in two years.

SMITHERS [*Unable to repress the genuine admiration of the small fry for the large.*] Yes, yer turned the bleedin' trick, all right. Blimey, I never seen a bloke 'as 'ad the bloomin' luck you 'as.

JONES [*Severely.*] Luck? What you mean—luck?

SMITHERS I suppose you'll say as that swank about the silver bullet ain't luck—and that was what first got the fool blacks on yer side the time of the revolution, wasn't it?

JONES [*With a laugh.*] Oh, dat silver bullet! Sho' was luck! But I makes dat luck, you heah? I loads de dice! Yessuh! When dat murderin' nigger ole Lem hired to kill me takes aim ten feet away and his gun misses fire and I shoots him dead, what you heah me say?

SMITHERS You said yer'd got a charm so's no lead bullet'd kill yer. You was so strong only a silver bullet could kill yer, you told 'em. Blimey, wasn't that swank for yer—and plain, fat-'eaded luck?

JONES [*Proudly.*] I got brains and I uses 'em quick. Dat ain't luck.

SMITHERS Yer know they wasn't 'ardly liable to get no silver bullets. And it was luck 'e didn't 'it you that time.

JONES [*Laughing.*] And dere all dem fool, bush niggers was kneelin' down and bumpin' deir heads on de ground like I was a miracle out o' de Bible. Oh Lawd, from dat time on I has dem all eatin' out of my hand. I cracks de whip and dey jumps through.

SMITHERS [*With a sniff.*] Yankee bluff done it.

JONES Ain't a man's talkin' big what makes him big—long as he makes folks believe it? Sho', I talks large when I ain't got nothin' to back it up, but I ain't talkin' wild just de same. I knows I kin fool 'em—I *knows* it—and dat's backin' enough fo' my game. And ain't I got to learn deir lingo and teach some of dem English befo' I kin talk to 'em? Ain't dat wuk? You ain't never learned ary word er it, Smithers, in de ten years you been heah, dough you knows it's money in yo' pocket tradin' wid' em if you does. But you'se too shiftless to take de trouble.

SMITHERS [*Flushing.*] Never mind about me. What's this I've 'eard about yer really 'avin' a silver bullet molded for yourself?

JONES It's playin' out my bluff. I has de silver bullet molded and I tells 'em when de time comes I kills myself wid it. I tells 'em dat's 'cause I'm de on'y man in de world big enuff to git me. No use'n deir tryin'. And dey falls down and bumps their heads. [*He laughs.*] I does dat so's I kin take a walk in peace widout no jealous nigger gunnin' at me from behind de trees.

SMITHERS [*Astonished.*] Then you 'ad it made—'onest?

JONES Sho' did. Heah she be. [*He takes out his revolver, breaks it, and takes the silver bullet out of one chamber.*] Five lead an' dis silver baby at de last. Don't she shine pretty? [*He holds it in his hand, looking at it admiringly, as if strangely fascinated.*]

SMITHERS Let me see. [*Reaches out his hand for it.*]

JONES [*Harshly.*] Keep yo' hands whar dey b'long, white man. [*He replaces it in the chamber and puts the revolver back on his hip.*]

SMITHERS [*Snarling.*] Gawd blimey! Think I'm a bleedin' thief, you would.

JONES No, 'tain't dat. I knows you'se scared to steal from me. On'y I ain't 'lowin' nary body to touch dis baby. She's my rabbit's foot.

SMITHERS [*Sneering.*] A bloomin' charm, wot? [*Venomously.*] Well, you'll need all the bloody charms you 'as before long, s' 'elp me!

JONES [*Judicially.*] Oh, I'se good for six months yit 'fore dey gits sick o' my game. Den, when I sees trouble comin', I makes my getaway.

SMITHERS Ho! You got it all planned, ain't yer?

JONES I ain't no fool. I knows dis Emperor's time is sho't. Dat why I make hay when de sun shine. Was you thinkin' I'se aimin' to hold down dis job for life? No, suh! What good is gittin' money if you stays back in dis raggedy country? I wants action when I spends. And when I sees dese niggers gettin' up deir nerve to tu'n me out, and I'se got all de money in sight, I resigns on de spot and beats it quick.

SMITHERS   Where to?

JONES   None o' yo' business.

SMITHERS   Not back to the bloody States, I'll lay my oath.

JONES   [Suspiciously.]   Why don't I? [Then with an easy laugh.]   You mean 'count of dat story 'bout me breakin' from jail back dere? Dat's all talk.

SMITHERS   [Skeptically.]   Ho, yes!

JONES   [Sharply.]   You ain't 'sinuatin' I'se a liar, is you?

SMITHERS   [Hastily.]   No, Gawd strike me! I was only thinkin' o' the bloody lies you told the blacks 'ere about killin' white men in the States.

JONES   [Angered]   How come dey're lies?

SMITHERS   You'd 'ave been in jail if you 'ad, wouldn't yer then? [With venom.]   And from what I've 'eard it ain't 'ealthy for a black to kill a white man in the States. They burns 'em in oil, don't they?

JONES   [With cool deadliness.]   You mean lynchin' 'd scare me? Well, I tells you, Smithers, maybe I does kill one white man back dere. Maybe I does. And maybe I kills another right heah 'fore long if he don't look out.

SMITHERS   [Trying to force a laugh.]   I was on'y spoofin' yer. Can't yer take a joke? And you was just sayin' you'd never been in jail.

JONES   [In the same tone—slightly boastful.]   Maybe I goes to jail dere for gettin' in an argument wid razors ovah a crap game. Maybe I gits twenty years when dat colored man die. Maybe I gits in 'nother argument wid de prison guard was overseer ovah us when we're wukin' de roads. Maybe he hits me wid a whip and I splits his head wid a shovel and runs away and files de chain off my leg and gits away safe. Maybe I does all dat an' maybe I don't. It's a story I tells you so's you knows I'se de kind of man dat if you evah repeats one word of it, I ends yo' stealin' on dis yearth mighty damn quick!

SMITHERS [*Terrified.*] Think I'd peach on yer? Not me! Ain't I always been yer friend?

JONES [*Suddenly relaxing.*] Sho' you has—and you better be.

SMITHERS [*Recovering his composure—and with it his malice.*] And just to show yer I'm yer friend, I'll tell yer that bit o' news I was goin' to.

JONES Go ahead! Shoot de piece. Must be bad news from de happy way you look.

SMITHERS [*Warningly.*] Maybe it's gettin' time for you to resign—with that bloomin' silver bullet, wot? [*He finishes with a mocking grin.*]

JONES [*Puzzled.*] What's dat you say? Talk plain.

SMITHERS Ain't noticed any of the guards or servants about the place today, I 'aven't.

JONES [*Carelessly.*] Dey're all out in de garden, sleepin' under de trees. When I sleeps, dey sneaks a sleep, too, and I pretends I never suspicions it. All I got to do is to ring de bell and dey come flyin', makin' a bluff dey was wukin' all de time.

SMITHERS [*In the same mocking tone.*] Ring the bell now an' you'll bloody well see what I means.

JONES [*Startled to alertness, but preserving the same careless tone.*] Sho' I rings. [*He reaches below the throne and pulls out a big, common dinner bell which is painted the same vivid scarlet as the throne. He rings this vigorously—then stops to listen. Then he goes to both doors, rings again, and looks out.*]

SMITHERS [*Watching him with malicious satisfaction, after a pause—mockingly.*] The bloody ship is sinkin' an' the bleedin' rats 'as slung their 'ooks.

JONES [*In a sudden fit of anger flings the bell clattering into a corner.*] Low-flung, woods' niggers! [*Then catching SMITHERS' eye on him, he controls himself and suddenly bursts into a low chuckling laugh.*] Reckon I overplays my hand dis once! A man can't take de pot on a bob-tailed flush all de time. Was I sayin' I'd sit in six months mo'? Well, I'se changed my mind den. I cashes in and resigns de job of Emperor right dis minute.

SMITHERS [*With real admiration.*] Blimey, but you're a cool bird, and no mistake.

JONES No use'n fussin'. When I knows de game's up I kisses it good-bye widout no long waits. Dey've all run off to de hills, ain't dey?

SMITHERS Yes—every bleedin' man jack of 'em.

JONES Den de revolution is at de post. And de Emperor better git his feet smokin' up de trail. [*He starts for the door in rear.*]

SMITHERS Goin' out to look for your 'orse? Yer won't find any. They steals the 'orses first thing. Mine was gone when I went for 'im this mornin'. That's wot first give me a suspicion of wot was up.

JONES [*Alarmed for a second, scratches his head, then philosophically.*] Well, den I hoofs it. Feet, do yo' duty! [*He pulls out a gold watch and looks at it.*] Three-thuty. Sundown's at six-thuty or dere-abouts. [*Puts his watch back—with cool confidence.*] I got plenty o'time to make it easy.

SMITHERS Don't be so bloomin' sure of it. They'll be after you 'ot and 'eavy. Ole Lem is at the bottom o' this business an' 'e 'ates you like 'ell. 'E'd rather do for you than eat 'is dinner, 'e would!

JONES [*Scornfully.*] Dat fool no-count nigger! Does you think I'se scared o' him? I stands him on his thick head more'n once befo' dis, and I does it again if he come in my way . . . [*Fiercely.*] And dis time I leave him a dead nigger fo' sho'!

SMITHERS You'll 'ave to cut through the big forest—an' these blacks 'ere can sniff and follow a trail in the dark like 'ounds. You'd 'ave to 'ustle to get through that forest in twelve hours even if you knew all the bloomin' trails like a native.

JONES [*With indignant scorn.*] Look-a-heah, white man! Does you think I'se a natural bo'n fool? Give me credit fo' havin' some sense, fo' Lawd's sake! Don't you s'pose I'se looked ahead and made sho' of all de chances? I'se gone out in dat big forest, pretendin' to hunt, so many times dat I knows it high an' low like a book. I could go through on dem trails wid my eyes shut. [*With great contempt.*] Think dese ign'rent bush niggers dat ain't got brains enuff to know deir own names even can catch Brutus Jones? Huh, I s'pects not! Not on yo' life! Why, man, de white men went after me wid bloodhounds where I came from an' I jes' laughs at 'em. It's a shame to fool dese black trash around heah, dey're so easy. You watch me, man. I'll make dem look sick, I will. I'll be 'cross de plain to de edge of de forest by time dark comes. Once in de woods in de night, dey got a swell chance o' findin' dis baby! Dawn tomorrow I'll be out at de oder side and on de coast whar dat French gunboat is stayin'. She picks me up, take me to Martinique when she go dar, and dere I is safe wid a mighty big bankroll in my jeans. It's easy as rollin' off a log.

SMITHERS [*Maliciously.*] But s'posin' somethin' 'appens wrong an' they do nab yer?

JONES [*Decisively.*] Dey don't—dat's de answer.

SMITHERS But, just for argyment's sake—what'd you do?

JONES [*Frowning.*] I'se got five lead bullets in dis gun good enuff fo' common bush niggers—and after dat I got de silver bullet left to cheat 'em out o' gittin' me.

SMITHERS [*Jeeringly.*] Ho, I was fergettin' that silver bullet. You'll bump yourself orf in style, won't yer? Blimey!

JONES [*Gloomily.*] You kin bet yo' whole roll on one thing, white man. Dis baby plays out his string to de end and when he quits, he quits wid a bang de way he ought. Silver bullet ain't none too good for him when he go, dat's a fac'! [*Then shaking off his nervousness—with a confident laugh.*] Sho'! What is I talkin' about? Ain't come to dat yit and I never will—not wid trash niggers like dese yere. [*Boastfully.*] Silver bullet bring me luck anyway. I kin outguess, outrun, outfight, an' outplay de whole lot o' dem all ovah de board any time o' de day er night! You watch me! [*From the distant hills comes the faint, steady thump of a tom-tom, low and vibrating. It starts at a rate exactly corresponding to normal pulse beat—72 to the minute—and continues at a gradually accelerating rate from this point uninterruptedly to the very end of the play.*]

[JONES *starts at the sound. A strange look of apprehension creeps into his face for a moment as he listens. Then he asks, with an attempt to regain his most casual manner.*] What's dat drum beatin' fo'?

SMITHERS [*With a mean grin.*] For you. That means the bleedin' ceremony 'as started. I've 'eard it before and I knows.

JONES Cer'mony? What cer'mony?

SMITHERS The blacks is 'oldin' a bloody meetin', 'avin' a war dance, gettin' their courage worked up b'fore they starts after you.

JONES Let dem! Dey'll sho' need it!

SMITHERS And they're 'oldin' their 'eathen religious service— makin' no end of devil spells and charms to 'elp 'em against your silver bullets. [*He guffaws loudly.*] Blimey, but they're balmy as 'ell!

JONES [*A tiny bit awed and shaken in spite of himself.*] Huh! Takes more'n dat to scare dis chicken!

SMITHERS [*Scenting the other's feelings—maliciously.*] Ter-night when it's pitch black in the forest, they'll 'ave their pet devils and ghosts 'oundin' after you. You'll find yer bloody 'air 'll be standin' on end before termorrow mornin'. [*Seriously.*] It's a bleedin' queer place, that stinkin' forest, even in daylight. Yer don't know what might 'appen in there, it's that rotten still. Al-ways sends the cold shivers down my back minute I gets in it.

JONES [*With a contemptuous sniff.*] I ain't no chicken-liver like you is. Trees an' me, we'se friends, and dar's a full moon comin' bring me light. And let dem po' niggers make all de fool spells dey'se a min' to. Does yo' s'pect I'se silly enuff to b'lieve in ghosts an' ha'nts an' all dat ole woman's talk? G'long, white man! You ain't talkin' to me. [*With a chuckle.*] Doesn't you know dey's got to do wid a man was member in good standin' o' de Baptist Church. Sho' I was dat when I was porter on de Pull-mans, befo' I gits into my little trouble. Let dem try deir heathen tricks. De Baptist Church done pertect me and land dem all in hell. [*Then with more confident satisfaction.*] And I'se got little silver bullet o' my own, don't forgit.

SMITHERS Ho! You 'aven't give much 'eed to your Baptist Church since you been down 'ere. I've 'eard myself you 'ad turned yer coat an' was takin' up with their blarsted witch-doctors, or whatever the 'ell yer calls the swine.

JONES [*Vehemently.*] I pretends to! Sho' I pretends! Dat's part o' my game from de fust. If I finds out dem niggers believes dat black is white, den I yells it out louder 'n deir loudest. It don't git me nothin' to do missionary work for de Baptist Church. I'se after de coin, an' I lays my Jesus on de shelf for de time bein'. [*Stops abruptly to look at his watch—alertly*.]   But I ain't got de time to waste no more fool talk wid you. I'se gwine away from heah dis secon'. [*He reaches in under the throne and pulls out an expensive Panama hat with a bright multicolored band and sets it jauntily on his head.*]   So long, white man! [*With a grin.*]   See you in jail sometime, maybe!

SMITHERS   Not me, you won't. Well, I wouldn't be in yer bloody shoes for no bloomin' money, but 'ere's wishin' yer luck just the same.

JONES [*Contemptuously.*]   You're de frightenedest man evah I see! I tells you I'se safe's 'f I was in New York City. It takes dem niggers from now to dark to git up de nerve to start somethin'. By dat time, I'se got a head start dey never kotch up wid.

SMITHERS [*Maliciously.*]   Give my regards to any ghosts yer meets up with.

JONES [*Grinning.*]   If dat ghost got money, I'll tell him never ha'nt you less'n he wants to lose it.

SMITHERS [*Flattered.*]   Garn! [*Then   curiously.*]   Ain't yer takin' no baggage with yer?

JONES   I travels light when I wants to move fast. And I got tinned grub buried on de edge o' de forest. [*Boastfully.*]   Now say dat I don't look ahead an' use my brains! [*With a wide, liberal gesture.*]   I will all dat's left in de palace to you—and you better grab all you kin sneak away wid befo' dey gits here.

SMITHERS [*Gratefully.*]   Righto—and thanks ter yer. [*As* JONES *walks toward the door in rear—cautioningly.*]   Say! Look 'ere, you ain't goin' out that way, are yer?

JONES   Does you think I'd slink out de back door like a common nigger? I'se Emperor yit, ain't I? And de Emperor Jones leaves de way he comes, and dat black trash don't dare stop him —not yit, leastways. [*He stops for a moment in the doorway, listening to the far-off but insistent beat of the tom-tom.*]   Listen to dat roll-call, will you? Must be mighty big drum carry dat far. [*Then with a laugh.*]   Well, if dey ain't no whole brass band to see me off, I sho' got de drum part of it. So long, white man.

[*He puts his hand in his pockets and with studied carelessness, whistling a tune, he saunters out of the doorway and off to the left.*]

SMITHERS [*Looks after him with a puzzled admiration.*] 'E's got 'is bloomin' nerve with 'im, s'elp me. [*Then angrily.*] Ho— the bleedin' nigger—puttin' on 'is bloody airs! I 'opes they nabs 'im an' gives 'im what's what! [*Then putting business before the pleasure of this thought, looking around him with cupidity.*] A bloke ought to find a 'ole lot in this palace that'd go for a bit of cash. Let's take a look, 'Arry, me lad. [*He starts for the doorway on right as the curtain falls.*]

SCENE TWO

SCENE: *Nightfall. The end of the plain where the Great Forest begins. The foreground is sandy, level ground dotted by a few stones and clumps of stunted bushes cowering close against the earth to escape the buffeting of the trade wind. In the rear the forest is a wall of darkness dividing the world. Only when the eye becomes accustomed to the gloom can the outlines of separate trunks of the nearest trees be made out, enormous pillars of deeper blackness. A somber monotone of wind lost in the leaves moans in the air. Yet this sound serves but to intensify the impression of the forest's relentless immobility, to form a background throwing into relief its brooding, implacable silence.*

[JONES *enters from the left, walking rapidly. He stops as he nears the edge of the forest, looks around him quickly, peering into the dark as if searching for some familiar landmark. Then, apparently satisfied that he is where he ought to be, he throws himself on the ground, dog-tired.*]

Well, heah I is. In de nick o' time, too! Little mo' an' it'd be blacker'n de ace of spades heah-abouts. [*He pulls a bandana handkerchief from his hip pocket and mops off his perspiring face.*] Sho'! Gimme air! I'se tuckered out sho' 'nuff. Dat soft Emperor job ain't no trainin' fo' a long hike ovah dat plain in de brilin'

sun. [*Then with a chuckle.*] Cheah up, nigger, de worst is yet
to come. [*He lifts his head and stares at the forest. His chuckle
peters out abruptly. In a tone of awe.*] My goodness, look at dem
woods, will you? Dat no-count Smithers said dey'd be black an'
he sho' called de turn. [*Turning away from them quickly and
looking down at his feet, he snatches at a chance to change the
subject—solicitously.*] Feet, you is holdin' up yo' end fine an' I
sutinly hopes you ain't blisterin' none. It's time you git a rest.
[*He takes off his shoes, his eyes studiously avoiding the forest. He
feels of the soles of his feet gingerly.*] You is still in de pink—
on'y a little mite feverish. Cool yo'selfs. Remember you done got
a long journey yit befo' you. [*He sits in a weary attitude, listening to the rhythmic beating of the tom-tom. He grumbles in a
loud tone to cover up a growing uneasiness.*] Bush niggers! Wonder dey wouldn' git sick o' beatin' dat drum. Sound louder, seem
like. I wonder if dey's startin' after me? [*He scrambles to his feet,
looking back across the plain.*] Couldn't see dem, nohow, if dey
was hundred feet away. [*Then shaking himself like a wet dog to
get rid of these depressing thoughts.*] Sho', dey's miles an' miles
behind. What you gittin' fidgety about? [*But he sits down and
begins to lace up his shoes in great haste, all the time muttering
reassuringly.*] You know what? Yo' belly is empty, dat's what's
de matter wid you. Come time to eat! Wid nothin' but wind on
yo' stumach, o' course you feels jiggedy. Well, we eats right heah
an' now soon's I git dese pesky shoes laced up! [*He finishes
lacing up his shoes.*] Dere! Now let's see. [*Gets on his hands
and knees and searches the ground around him with his eyes.*]
White stone, white stone, where is you? [*He sees the first white
stone and crawls to it—with satisfaction.*] Heah you is! I knowed
dis was de right place. Box of grub, come to me. [*He turns over
the stone and feels in under it—in a tone of dismay.*] Ain't heah!
Gorry, is I in de right place or isn't I? Dere's 'nother stone. Guess
dat's it. [*He scrambles to the next stone and turns it over.*] Ain't
heah, neither! Grub, whar is you? Ain't heah. Gorry, has I got
to go hungry into dem woods—all de night? [*While he is talking
he scrambles from one stone to another, turning them over in
frantic haste. Finally, he jumps to his feet excitedly.*] Is I lost

de place? Must have! But how dat happen when I was followin'
de trail across de plain in broad daylight? [*Almost plaintively.*]
I'se hungry, I is! I gotta git my feed. Whar's my strength gonna
come from if I doesn't? Gorry, I gotta find dat grub high an'
low somehow! Why it come dark so quick like dat? Can't see
nothin'. [*He scratches a match on his trousers and peers about
him. The rate of the beat of the far-off tom-tom increases perceptibly as he does so. He mutters in a bewildered voice.*]   How come
all dese white stones come heah when I only remembers one?
[*Suddenly, with a frightened gasp, he flings the match on the
ground and stamps on it.*]   Nigger, is you gone crazy mad? Is you
lightin' matches to show dem whar you is? Fo' Lawd's sake use
yo' haid. Gorry, I'se got to be careful! [*He stares at the plain behind him apprehensively, his hand on his revolver.*]   But how
come all dese white stones? And whar's dat tin box o' grub I hid
all wrapped up in oil cloth?

[*While his back is turned, the* LITTLE FORMLESS FEARS *creep
out from the deeper blackness of the forest. They are black, shape-
less, only their glittering little eyes can be seen. If they have any
describable form at all it is that of a grubworm about the size of a
creeping child. They move noiselessly, but with deliberate, painful effort, striving to raise themselves on end, failing and sinking
prone again.* JONES *turns about to face the forest. He stares up at
the tops of the trees, seeking vainly to discover his whereabouts by
their conformation.*]

Can't tell nothin' from dem trees! Gorry, nothin' 'round heah
look like I evah seed it befo'. I'se done lost de place sho' 'nuff!
[*With mournful foreboding.*]   It's mighty queer! It's mighty
queer! [*With sudden forced defiance—in an angry tone.*]
Woods, is you tryin' to put somethin' ovah on me?

[*From the formless creatures on the ground in front of him
comes a tiny gale of low mocking laughter like a rustling of leaves.
They squirm upward toward him in twisted attitudes.* JONES *looks
down, leaps backward with a yell of terror, yanking out his revolver as he does so—in a quavering voice.*]   What's dat? Who's
dar? What is you? Git away from me befo' I shoots you up! You
don't? . . .

[*He fires. There is a flash, a loud report, then silence broken only by the far-off, quickened throb of the tom-tom. The formless creatures have scurried back into the forest.* JONES *remains fixed in his position, listening intently. The sound of the shot, the reassuring feel of the revolver in his hand, have somewhat restored his shaken nerve. He addresses himself with renewed confidence.*]

Dey're gone. Dat shot fix 'em. Dey was only little animals—little wild pigs, I reckon. Dey've maybe rooted out yo' grub an' eat it. Sho' you fool nigger, what you think dey is—ha'nts? [*Excitedly.*] Gorry, you give de game away when you fire dat shot. Dem niggers heah dat fo' su'tin! Time you beat it in de woods widout no long waits. [*He starts for the forest—hesitates before the plunge—then urging himself in with manful resolution.*] Git in, nigger! What you skeered at? Ain't nothin' dere but de trees! Git in! [*He plunges boldly into the forest.*]

SCENE THREE

SCENE: *Nine o'clock. In the forest. The moon has just risen. Its beams, drifting through the canopy of leaves, make a barely perceptible, suffused, eerie glow. A dense low wall of underbrush and creepers is in the nearer foreground, fencing in a small triangular clearing. Beyond this is the massed blackness of the forest like an encompassing barrier. A path is dimly discerned leading down to the clearing from left, rear, and winding away from it again toward the right. As the scene opens nothing can be distinctly made out. Except for the beating of the tom-tom, which is a trifle louder and quicker than in the previous scene, there is silence, broken every few seconds by a queer, clicking sound. Then gradually the figure of the negro,* JEFF, *can be discerned crouching on his haunches at the rear of the triangle. He is middle-aged, thin, brown in color, is dressed in a Pullman porter's uniform, cap, etc. He is throwing a pair of dice on the ground before him, picking them up, shaking them, casting them out with the regular, rigid, mechanical movements of an automaton. The heavy, plodding footsteps of someone approaching along the trail from the left are heard and* JONES' *voice, pitched in a slightly higher key and strained in a cheering effort to overcome its own tremors.*

De moon's rizen. Does you heah that, nigger? You gits more light from dis out. No mo' buttin' yo' fool head again' de trunks an' scratchin' de hide off yo' legs in de bushes. Now you sees whar yo'se gwine. So cheer up! From now on you has a snap. [*He steps just to the rear of the triangular clearing and mops off his face on his sleeve. He has lost his Panama hat. His face is scratched, his brilliant uniform shows several large rents.*] What time's it gittin' to be, I wonder? I dassent light no match to find out. Phoo'. It's wa'm an' dat's a fac'! [*Wearily.*] How long I been makin' tracks in dese woods? Must be hours an' hours. Seems like fo'evah! Yit can't be, when de moon's jes riz. Dis am a long night fo' yo', yo' Majesty! [*With a mournful chuckle.*] Majesty! Der ain't much majesty 'bout dis baby now. [*With attempted cheerfulness.*] Never min'. It's all part o' de game. Dis night come to an end like everything else. And when you gits dar safe and has dat bankroll in yo' hands you laughs at all dis. [*He starts to whistle but checks himself abruptly.*] What yo' whistlin' for, you po' dope! Want all de worl' to heah you? [*He stops talking to listen.*] Heah dat ole drum! Sho' gits nearer from de sound. Dey're packin' it along wid'em. Time fo' me to move. [*He takes a step forward, then stops —worriedly.*] What's dat odder queer clickety sound I heah? Dere it is! Sound close! Sound like—sound like—Fo' God sake, sound like some nigger was shootin' crap! [*Frightenedly.*] I better beat it quick when I gits dem notions. [*He walks quickly into the clear space—then stands transfixed as he sees* JEFF—*in a terrified gasp.*] Who dar? Who dat? Is dat you, Jeff? [*Starting toward the other, forgetful for a moment of his surroundings and really believing it is a living man that he sees—in a tone of happy relief.*] Jeff! I'se sho' mighty glad to see you! Dey tol' me you done died from dat razor cut I gives you. [*Stopping suddenly, bewilderedly.*] But how you come to be heah, nigger? [*He stares fascinatedly at the other who continues his mechanical play with the dice.* JONES' *eyes begin to roll wildly. He stutters.*] Ain't you gwine—look up—can't you speak to me? Is you—is you—a ha'nt?

[*He jerks out his revolver in a frenzy of terrified rage.*] Nigger, I kills you dead once. Has I got to kill you again? You take it den. [*He fires. When the smoke clears away* JEFF *has disappeared.* JONES *stands trembling—then with a certain reassurance.*] He's gone, anyway. Ha'nt or no ha'nt, dat shot fix him. [*The beat of the far-off tom-tom is perceptibly louder and more rapid.* JONES *becomes conscious of it—with a start, looking back over his shoulder.*] Dey's gittin' near! Dey'se comin' fast! And heah I is shootin' shots to let 'em know jus' whar I is. Oh, Gorry, I'se got to run. [*Forgetting the path he plunges wildly into the underbrush in the rear and disappears in the shadow.*]

SCENE FOUR

SCENE: *Eleven o'clock. In the forest. A wide dirt road runs diagonally from right, front, to left, rear. Rising sheer on both sides the forest walls it in. The moon is now up. Under its light the road glimmers ghastly and unreal. It is as if the forest had stood aside momentarily to let the road pass through and accomplish its veiled purpose. This done, the forest will fold in upon itself again and the road will be no more.* JONES *stumbles in from the forest on the right. His uniform is ragged and torn. He looks about him with numbed surprise when he sees the road, his eyes blinking in the bright moonlight. He flops down exhaustedly and pants heavily for a while. Then with sudden anger.*

I'm meltin' wid heat! Runnin' an' runnin' an' runnin'! Damn dis heah coat! Like a strait jacket! [*He tears off his coat and flings it away from him, revealing himself stripped to the waist.*] Dere! Dat's better! Now I kin breathe! [*Looking down at his feet, the spurs catch his eye.*] And to hell wid dese high-fangled spurs. Dey're what's been a-trippin' me up an' breakin' my neck. [*He unstraps them and flings them away disgustedly.*] Dere! I gits rid o' dem frippety Emperor trappin's an' I travels lighter. Lawd! I'se tired! [*After a pause, listening to the insistent beat of the tom-tom in the distance.*] I must'a put some distance between myself an' dem—runnin' like dat—and yit—dat damn drum sound jes' de same—nearer, even. Well, I guess I a'most holds my lead anyhow. Dey won't never catch up. [*With a sigh.*] If on'y my fool legs stands up. Oh, I'se sorry I evah went in for dis. Dat Emperor job is sho' hard to shake. [*He looks around him supiciously.*] How'd dis road evah git heah? Good level road, too. I never remembers seein' it befo'. [*Shaking his head apprehensively.*] Dese woods is sho' full o' de queerest things at night. [*With a sudden terror.*] Lawd God, don't let me see no more o' dem ha'nts! Dey gits my goat! [*Then trying to talk himself into confidence.*] Ha'nts! You fool nigger, dey ain't no such things! Don't de Baptist parson tell you dat many time? Is you civilized, or is you like dese ign'rent black niggers heah? Sho'! Dat was all in yo' own head. Wasn't nothin' dere. Wasn't no Jeff! Know what? You jus' get seein' dem things 'cause yo' belly's empty and you's sick wid hunger inside. Hunger 'fects yo' head and yo' eyes. Any fool knows dat. [*Then pleading fervently.*] But bless God, I don't come across no more o' dem, whatever dey is! [*Then cautiously.*] Rest! Don't talk! Rest! You needs it. Den you gits on yo' way again. [*Looking at the moon.*] Night's half gone a'most. You hits de coast in de mawning! Den you'se all safe.

[*From the right forward a small gang of Negroes enter. They are dressed in striped convict suits, their heads are shaven, one leg drags limpingly, shackled to a heavy ball and chain. Some carry picks, the others shovels. They are followed by a white man dressed in the uniform of a prison guard. A Winchester rifle is slung across his shoulders and he carries a heavy whip. At a signal from the* GUARD *they stop on the road opposite where* JONES *is sitting.* JONES, *who has been staring up at the sky, unmindful of their noiseless approach, suddenly looks down and sees them. His eyes pop out, he tries to get to his feet and fly, but sinks back, too numbed by fright to move. His voice catches in a choking prayer.*]

Lawd Jesus!

[*The* PRISON GUARD *cracks his whip—noiselessly—and at that signal all the convicts start to work on the road. They swing their picks, they shovel, but not a sound comes from their labor. Their movements, like those of* JEFF *in the preceding scene, are those of*

automatons—rigid, slow, and mechanical. The PRISON GUARD
points sternly at JONES *with his whip, motions him to take his
place among the other shovelers.* JONES *gets to his feet in a hypnotized stupor. He mumbles subserviently.*]

Yes, suh! Yes, suh! I'se comin'.

[*As he shuffles, dragging one foot, over to his place, he curses
under his breath with rage and hatred.*]

God damn yo' soul, I gits even wid you yit, sometime.

[*As if there were a shovel in his hands he goes through weary,
mechanical gestures of digging up dirt, and throwing it to the road-
side. Suddenly the* GUARD *approaches him angrily, threateningly.
He raises his whip and lashes* JONES *viciously across the shoulders
with it.* JONES *winces with pain and cowers abjectly. The* GUARD
*turns his back on him and walks away contemptuously. With
arms upraised as if his shovel were a club in his hands he springs
murderously at the unsuspecting* GUARD. *In the act of crashing
down his shovel on the white man's skull,* JONES *suddenly becomes
aware that his hands are empty. He cries despairingly.*]

Whar's my shovel? Gimme my shovel 'till I splits his damn head!
[*Appealing to his fellow convicts.*]   Gimme a shovel, one o' you,
fo' God's sake!

[*They stand fixed in motionless attitudes, their eyes on the
ground. The* GUARD *seems to wait expectantly, his back turned
to the attacker.* JONES *bellows with baffled, terrified rage, tugging
frantically at his revolver.*]

I kills you, you white debil, if it's de last thing I evah does!
Ghost or debil, I kill you agin!

[*He frees the revolver and fires point blank at the* GUARD'S *back.
Instantly the walls of the forest close in from both sides, the road
and the figures of the convict gang are blotted out in an enshroud-
ing darkness. The only sounds are a crashing in the underbrush as
*JONES *leaps away in mad flight and the throbbing of the tom-tom,
still far distant, but increased in volume of sound and rapidity of
beat.*]

SCENE FIVE

scene: *One o'clock. A large circular clearing, enclosed by the serried ranks of gigantic trunks of tall trees whose tops are lost to view. In the center is a big dead stump worn by time into a curious resemblance to an auction block. The moon floods the clearing with a clear light.* jones *forces his way in through the forest on the left. He looks wildly about the clearing with hunted, fearful glances. His pants are in tatters, his shoes cut and mis-shapen, flapping about his feet. He slinks cautiously to the stump in the center and sits down in a tense position, ready for instant flight. Then he holds his head in his hands and rocks back and forth, moaning to himself miserably.*

Oh Lawd, Lawd! Oh Lawd, Lawd! [*Suddenly he throws him-self on his knees and raises his clasped hands to the sky—in a voice of agonized pleading.*]   Lawd Jesus, heah my prayer! I'se a po' sinner, a po' sinner! I knows I done wrong. I knows it! When I cotches Jeff cheatin' wid loaded dice my anger overcomes me and I kills him dead! Lawd, I done wrong! When dat guard hits me wid de whip, my anger overcomes me, and I kills him dead. Lawd, I done wrong! And down heah whar dese fool bush niggers raises me up to the seat o' de mighty, I steals all I could grab. Lawd, I done wrong! I knows it! I'se sorry! Forgive me, Lawd! For-give dis po' sinner! [*Then beseeching terrifiedly.*]   And keep dem away, Lawd! Keep dem away from me! And stop dat drum soundin' in my ears! Dat begin to sound ha'nted, too. [*He gets to his feet, evidently slightly reassured by his prayer—with at-tempted confidence.*]   De Lawd'll preserve me from dem ha'nts after dis. [*Sits down on the stump again.*]   I ain't skeered o' real men. Let dem come. But dem odders . . . [*He shudders—then looks down at his feet, working his toes inside the shoes—with a groan.*]   Oh, my po' feet! Dem shoes ain't no use no more 'ceptin' to hurt. I'se better off widout dem. [*He unlaces them and pulls them off—holds the wrecks of the shoes in his hands and regards them mournfully.*]   You was real, A-one patin' leather, too. Look at you now. Emperor, yu'se gettin' mighty low!

[*He sits dejectedly and remains with bowed shoulders, staring down at the shoes in his hands as if reluctant to throw them away. While his attention is thus occupied, a crowd of figures silently enter the clearing from all sides. All are dressed in Southern costumes of the period of the fifties of the last century. There are middle-aged men who are evidently well-to-do planters. There is one spruce, authoritative individual—the* AUCTIONEER. *There is a crowd of curious spectators, chiefly young belles and dandies who have come to the slave market for diversion. All exchange courtly greetings in dumb show and chat silently together. There is some-thing stiff, rigid, unreal, marionettish about their movements. They group themselves about the stump. Finally a batch of slaves are led in from the left by an attendant—three men of different ages, two women, one with a baby in her arms, nursing. They are placed to the left of the stump, beside* JONES.

The white planters look them over appraisingly as if they were cattle, and exchange judgments on each. The dandies point with their fingers and make witty remarks. The belles titter bewitch-ingly. All this in silence save for the ominous throb of the tom-tom. The* AUCTIONEER *holds up his hand, taking his place at the stump. The groups strain forward attentively. He touches* JONES *on the shoulder peremptorily, motioning for him to stand on the stump—the auction block.

JONES *looks up, sees the figures on all sides, looks wildly for some opening to escape, sees none, screams and leaps madly to the top of the stump to get as far away from them as possible. He stands there, cowering, paralyzed with horror. The* AUCTIONEER *begins his silent spiel. He points to* JONES, *appeals to the planters to see for themselves. Here is a good field hand, sound in wind and limb as they can see. Very strong still in spite of his being middle-aged. Look at that back. Look at those shoulders. Look at the muscles in his arms and his sturdy legs. Capable of any amount of hard labor. Moreover, of a good disposition, intelligent and tractable. Will any gentleman start the bidding? The* PLANTERS *raise their fingers, make their bids. They are apparently all eager to possess* JONES.

The bidding is lively, the crowd interested. While this has been going on, JONES *has been seized by the courage of desperation. He dares to look down and around him. Over his face abject terror gives way to mystification, to gradual realization—stutteringly.*]

What you all doin', white folks? What's all dis? What you all lookin' at me fo'? What you doin' wid me, anyhow? [*Suddenly convulsed with raging hatred and fear.*] Is dis a auction? Is you sellin' me like dey uster befo' de war? [*Jerking out his revolver just as the* AUCTIONEER *knocks him down to one of the planters— glaring from him to the purchaser.*] And you sells me? And you buys me? I shows you I'se a free nigger, damn yo' souls! [*He fires at the* AUCTIONEER *and at the* PLANTER *with such rapidity that the two shots are almost simultaneous. As if this were a signal the walls of the forest fold in. Only blackness remains and silence broken by* JONES *as he rushes off, crying with fear—and by the quickened, ever louder beat of the tom-tom.*]

SCENE SIX

SCENE: *Three o'clock. A cleared space in the forest. The limbs of the trees meet over it forming a low ceiling about five feet from the ground. The interlocked ropes of creepers reaching upward to entwine the tree trunks give an arched appearance to the sides. The space thus enclosed is like the dark noisome hold of some ancient vessel. The moonlight is almost completely shut out and only a vague, wan light filters through. There is the noise of some-one approaching from the left, stumbling and crawling through the undergrowth.* JONES' *voice is heard between chattering moans.*

Oh, Lawd, what I gwine do now? Aint got no bullet left on'y de silver one. If mo' o' dem ha'nts come after me, how I gwine skeer dem away? Oh, Lawd, on'y de silver one left—an' I gotta save dat fo' luck. If I shoots dat one I'm a goner sho'! Lawd, it's black heah! Whar's de moon? Oh, Lawd, don't dis night evah come to an end? [*By the sounds, he is feeling his way cautiously forward.*] Dere! Dis feels like a clear space. I gotta lie down an' rest. I don't care if dem niggers does cotch me. I gotta rest. [*He is well forward now where his figure can be dimly made out. His pants have been so torn away that what is left of them is no better than a breech cloth. He flings himself full length, face downward on the ground, panting with exhaustion. Gradually it seems to grow lighter in the enclosed space and two rows of seated figures can be seen behind* JONES. *They are sitting in crumpled, despairing attitudes, hunched, facing one another with their backs touching the forest walls as if they were shackled to them. All Negroes, naked save for loin cloths. At first they are silent and motionless. Then they begin to sway slowly forward toward each other and back again in unison, as if they were laxly letting themselves follow the long roll of a ship at sea. At the same time, a low, melancholy murmur rises among them, increasing gradually by rhythmic degrees which seem to be directed and controlled by the throb of the tom-tom in the distance, to a long, tremulous wail of despair that reaches a certain pitch, unbearably acute, then falls by slow gradations of tone into silence and is taken up again.* JONES *starts, looks up, sees the figures, and throws himself down again to shut out the sight. A shudder of terror shakes his whole body as the wail rises up about him again. But the next time, his voice, as if under some uncanny compulsion, starts with the others. As their chorus lifts he rises to a sitting posture similar to the others, swaying back and forth. His voice reaches the highest pitch of sorrow, of desolation. The light fades out, the other voices cease, and only darkness is left.* JONES *can be heard scrambling to his feet and running off, his voice sinking down the scale and receding as he moves farther and farther away in the forest. The tom-tom beats louder, quicker, with a more insistent, triumphant pulsation.*]

SCENE SEVEN

SCENE: *Five o'clock. The foot of a gigantic tree by the edge of a great river. A rough structure of boulders, like an altar, is by the tree. The raised river bank is in the nearer background. Beyond this the surface of the river spreads out, brilliant and unruffled in the moonlight, blotted out and merged into a veil of bluish mist in the distance.* JONES' *voice is heard from the left rising and falling in the long, despairing wail of the chained slaves, to the rhythmic beat of the tom-tom. As his voice sinks into silence, he enters the open space. The expression of his face is fixed and stony, his eyes have an obsessed glare, he moves with a strange deliberation like a sleepwalker or one in a trance. He looks around at the tree, the rough stone altar, the moonlit surface of the river beyond, and passes his hand over his head with a vague gesture of puzzled bewilderment. Then, as if in obedience to some obscure impulse, he sinks into a kneeling, devotional posture before the altar. Then he seems to come to himself partly, to have an uncertain realization of what he is doing, for he straightens up and stares about him horrifiedly—in an incoherent mumble.*

What—what is I doin'? What is—dis place? Seems like—seems like I know dat tree—an' dem stones—an' de river. I remember—seems like I been heah befo'. [*Tremblingly.*] Oh, Gorry, I'se skeered in dis place! I'se skeered! Oh, Lawd, pertect dis sinner!

[*Crawling away from the altar, he cowers close to the ground, his face hidden, his shoulders heaving with sobs of hysterical fright. From behind the trunk of the tree, as if he had sprung out of it, the figure of the* CONGO WITCH-DOCTOR *appears. He is wizened and old, naked except for the fur of some small animal tied about his waist, its bushy tail hanging down in front. His body is stained all over a bright red. Antelope horns are on each side of his head, branching upward. In one hand he carries a bone rattle, in the other a charm stick with a bunch of white cockatoo feathers tied to the end. A great number of glass beads and bone ornaments are about his neck, ears, wrists, and ankles. He struts noiselessly with a queer prancing step to a position in the clear ground between* JONES *and the altar. Then with a preliminary, summoning stamp of his foot on the earth, he begins to dance and to chant. As if in response to his summons the beating of the tom-tom grows to a fierce, exultant boom whose throbs seem to fill the air with vibrating rhythm.* JONES *looks up, starts to spring to his feet, reaches a half-kneeling, half-squatting position and remains rigidly fixed there, paralyzed with awed fascination by this new apparition. The* WITCH-DOCTOR *sways, stamping with his foot, his bone rattle clicking the time. His voice rises and falls in a weird, monotonous croon, without articulate word divisions. Gradually his dance becomes clearly one of a narrative in pantomime, his croon is an incantation, a charm to allay the fierceness of some implacable deity demanding sacrifice. He flees, he is pursued by devils, he hides, he flees again. Ever wilder and wilder becomes his flight, nearer and nearer draws the pursuing evil, more and more the spirit of terror gains possession of him. His croon, rising to intensity, is punctuated by shrill cries.* JONES *has become completely hypnotized. His voice joins in the incantation, in the cries, he beats time with his hands and sways his body to and fro from the waist. The whole spirit and meaning of the dance has entered into him, has become his spirit. Finally the theme to the pantomime halts on a howl of despair, and is taken up again in a note of savage hope. There is a salvation. The forces of evil demand sacrifice. They must be appeased. The* WITCH-DOCTOR *points with his wand to the sacred tree, to the river beyond, to the altar, and finally to* JONES *with a ferocious command.* JONES *seems to sense the meaning of this. It is he who must offer himself for sacrifice. He beats his forehead abjectly to the ground, moaning hysterically.*]

Mercy, Oh Lawd! Mercy! Mercy on dis po' sinner.

[*The* WITCH-DOCTOR *springs to the river bank. He stretches out his arms and calls to some God within its depths. Then he starts backward slowly, his arms remaining out. A huge head of a crocodile appears over the bank and its eyes, glittering greenly, fasten upon* JONES. *He stares into them fascinatedly. The* WITCH-DOCTOR *prances up to him, touches him with his wand, motions him with his hideous command toward the waiting monster.* JONES *squirms on his belly nearer and nearer, moaning continually.*]

Mercy, Lawd! Mercy!

[*The crocodile heaves more of his enormous hulk onto the land.* JONES *squirms toward him. The* WITCH-DOCTOR'S *voice shrills out in furious exultation, the tom-tom beats madly.* JONES *cries out in fierce, exhausted spasm of anguished pleading.*]

Lawd, save me! Lawd Jesus, heah my prayer!

[*Immediately in answer to his prayer, comes the thought of the one bullet left him. He snatches at his hip, shouting defiantly.*]

De silver bullet! You don't git me yit!

[*He fires at the green eyes in front of him. The head of the crocodile sinks back behind the river bank, the* WITCH-DOCTOR *springs behind the sacred tree and disappears.* JONES *lies with his face to the ground, his arms outstretched, whimpering with fear as the throb of the tom-tom fills the silence about him with a somber pulsation, a baffled but revengeful power.*]

SCENE EIGHT

SCENE: *Dawn. Same as Scene Two, the dividing line of forest and plain. The nearest tree trunks are dimly revealed but the forest behind them is still a mass of glooming shadow. The tom-tom seems on the very spot, so loud and continuously vibrating are its beats.* LEM *enters from the left, followed by a small squad of his soldiers, and by the Cockney trader,* SMITHERS. LEM *is a heavy-set, ape-faced old savage of the extreme African type, dressed only in a loin cloth. A revolver and cartridge belt are about his waist. His soldiers are in different degrees of rag-concealed nakedness. All wear broad palm-leaf hats. Each one carries a rifle.* SMITHERS *is the same as in Scene One. One of the soldiers, evidently a tracker, is peering about keenly on the ground. He grunts and points to the spot where* JONES *entered the forest.* LEM *and* SMITHERS *come to look.*

SMITHERS [*After a glance, turns away in disgust.*] That's where 'e went in right enough. Much good it'll do yer. 'E's miles orf by this an' safe to the Coast, damn 'is 'ide! I tole yer yer'd lose 'im, didn't I?—wastin' the 'ole bloomin' night beatin' yer bloody drum an' castin' yer silly spells! Gawd blimey, wot a pack!

LEM [*Gutturally.*] We cotch him. You see. [*He makes a motion to his soldiers who squat down on their haunches in a semicircle.*]

SMITHERS [*Exasperatedly.*]   Well, ain't yer goin' in an' 'unt 'im in the woods? What the 'ell's the good of waitin'?

LEM [*Imperturbably—squatting down himself.*]   We cotch him.

SMITHERS [*Turning away from him comtemptuously.*]   Aw! Garn! 'E's a better man than the lot o' you put together. I 'ates the sight o' 'im but I'll say that for 'im. [*A sound of snapping twigs comes from the forest. The soldiers jump to their feet, cocking their rifles alertly.* LEM *remains sitting with an imperturbable expression, but listening intently. The sound from the woods is repeated.* LEM *makes a quick signal with his hand. His followers creep quietly but noiselessly into the forest, scattering so that each enters at a different spot.*]

SMITHERS [*In the silence that follows—in a contemptuous whisper.*]   You ain't thinkin' that would be 'im, I 'ope?

LEM [*Calmly.*]   We cotch him.

SMITHERS   Blarsted fat 'eads! [*Then after a second's thought —wonderingly.*]   Still an' all, it might 'appen. If 'e lost 'is bloody way in these stinkin' woods 'e'd likely turn in a circle without 'is knowin' it. They all does.

LEM [*Peremptorily.*]   Sssh! [*The reports of several rifles sound from the forest, followed a second later by savage, exultant yells. The beating of the tom-tom abruptly ceases.* LEM *looks up at the white man with a grin of satisfaction.*]   We cotch him. Him dead.

SMITHERS [*With a snarl.*]   'Ow d'yer know it's 'im an' 'ow d'yer know 'e's dead?

LEM   My mens dey got'um silver bullets. Dey kill him shore.

SMITHERS [*Astonished.*]   They got silver bullets?

LEM   Lead bullet no kill him. He got um strong charm. I cook um money, make um silver bullet, make um strong charm, too.

SMITHERS [*Light breaking upon him.*]   So that's wot you was up to all night, wot? You was scared to put after 'im till you'd molded silver bullets, eh?

LEM [*Simply stating a fact.*]   Yes. Him got strong charm. Lead no good.

SMITHERS [*Slapping his thigh and guffawing.*] Haw-haw! If yer don't beat all 'ell![*Then recovering himself—scornfully.*] I'll bet yer it ain't 'im they shot at all, yer bleedin' looney!

LEM [*Calmly.*] Dey come bring him now. [*The soldiers come out of the forest, carrying* JONES' *limp body. There is a little reddish-purple hole under his left breast. He is dead. They carry him to* LEM, *who examines his body with great satisfaction.* SMITHERS *leans over his shoulder—in a tone of frightened awe.*] Well, they did for yer right enough, Jonesey, me lad! Dead as a 'erring! [*Mockingly.*] Where's yer 'igh an' mighty airs now, yer bloomin' Majesty? [*Then with a grin.*] Silver bullets! Gawd blimey, but yer died in the 'eighth o' style, any'ow! [LEM *makes a motion to the soldiers to carry the body out left.* SMITHERS *speaks to him sneeringly.*]

SMITHERS And I s'pose you think it's yer bleedin' charms and yer silly beatin' the drum that made 'im run in a circle when 'e'd lost 'imself, don't yer? [*But* LEM *makes no reply, does not seem to hear the question, walks out left after his men.* SMITHERS *looks after him with contemptuous scorn.*] Stupid as 'ogs, the lot of 'em! Blarsted niggers!

[*Curtain falls.*]

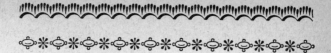

ARTHUR MILLER

Death of a Salesman

CERTAIN PRIVATE CONVERSATIONS IN TWO
ACTS AND A REQUIEM

CAST

WILLY LOMAN

LINDA

BIFF

HAPPY

BERNARD

THE WOMAN

CHARLEY

UNCLE BEN

HOWARD WAGNER

JENNY

STANLEY

MISS FORSYTHE

LETTA

SCENE: *The action takes place in Willy Loman's house and yard and in various places he visits in the New York and Boston of today.*

ACT I

{wavy decorative border}

SCENE: *A melody is heard, played upon a flute. It is small and fine, telling of grass and trees and the horizon. The curtain rises.*

Before us is the Salesman's house. We are aware of towering, angular shapes behind it, surrounding it on all sides. Only the blue light of the sky falls upon the house and forestage; the surrounding area shows an angry glow of orange. As more light appears, we see a solid vault of apartment houses around the small, fragile-seeming home. An air of the dream clings to the place, a dream rising out of reality. The kitchen at center seems actual enough, for there is a kitchen table with three chairs, and a refrigerator. But no other fixtures are seen. At the back of the kitchen there is a draped entrance, which leads to the living room. To the right of the kitchen, on a level raised two feet, is a bedroom furnished only with a brass bedstead and a straight chair. On a shelf over the bed a silver athletic trophy stands. A window opens onto the apartment house at the side.

Behind the kitchen, on a level raised six and a half feet, is the boys' bedroom, at present barely visible. Two beds are dimly seen, and at the back of the room a dormer window. (This bedroom is above the unseen living room.) At the left a stairway curves up to it from the kitchen.

The entire setting is wholly or, in some places, partially transparent. The roof-line of the house is one-dimensional; under and over it we see the apartment buildings. Before the house lies an apron, curving beyond the forestage into the orchestra. This forward area serves as the back yard as well as the locale of all WILLY'S *imaginings and of his city scenes. Whenever the action is in the present the actors observe the imaginary wall-lines, entering the house only through its door at the left. But in the scenes of the past these boundaries are broken, and characters enter or leave a room by stepping "through" a wall onto the forestage.*

From the right, WILLY LOMAN, *the Salesman, enters, carrying two large sample cases. The flute plays on. He hears but is not aware of it. He is past sixty years of age, dressed quietly. Even as he crosses the stage to the doorway of the house, his exhaustion is apparent. He unlocks the door, comes into the kitchen, and thankfully lets his burden down, feeling the soreness of his palms. A word-sigh escapes his lips—it might be "Oh, boy, oh, boy." He closes the door, then carries his cases out into the living room, through the draped kitchen doorway.*

LINDA, *his wife, has stirred in her bed at the right. She gets out and puts on a robe, listening. Most often jovial, she has developed an iron repression of her exceptions to* WILLY's *behavior—she more than loves him, she admires him, as though his mercurial nature, his temper, his massive dreams and little cruelties, served her only as sharp reminders of the turbulent longings within him, longings which she shares but lacks the temperament to utter and follow to their end.*

LINDA [*Hearing* WILLY *outside the bedroom, calls with some trepidation.*] Willy!

WILLY   It's all right. I came back.

LINDA   Why? What happened? [*Slight pause.*] Did something happen, Willy?

WILLY   No, nothing happened.

LINDA   You didn't smash the car, did you?

WILLY [*With casual irritation.*] I said nothing happened. Didn't you hear me?

LINDA   Don't you feel well?

WILLY   I'm tired to the death. [*The flute has faded away. He sits on the bed beside her, a little numb.*] I couldn't make it. I just couldn't make it, Linda.

LINDA [*Very carefully, delicately.*] Where were you all day? You look terrible.

WILLY   I got as far as a little above Yonkers. I stopped for a cup of coffee. Maybe it was the coffee.

LINDA   What?

WILLY [*After a pause.*] I suddenly couldn't drive any more. The car kept going off onto the shoulder, y'know?

LINDA [*Helpfully.*] Oh. Maybe it was the steering again. I don't think Angelo knows the Studebaker.

WILLY No, it's me, it's me. Suddenly I realize I'm goin' sixty miles an hour and I don't remember the last five minutes. I'm— I can't seem to—keep my mind to it.

LINDA Maybe it's your glasses. You never went for your new glasses.

WILLY No, I see everything. I came back ten miles an hour. It took me nearly four hours from Yonkers.

LINDA [*Resigned.*] Well, you'll just have to take a rest, Willy, you can't continue this way.

WILLY I just got back from Florida.

LINDA But you didn't rest your mind. Your mind is overactive, and the mind is what counts, dear.

WILLY I'll start out in the morning. Maybe I'll feel better in the morning. [*She is taking off his shoes.*] These goddam arch supports are killing me.

LINDA Take an aspirin. Should I get you an aspirin? It'll soothe you.

WILLY [*With wonder.*] I was driving along, you understand? And I was fine. I was even observing the scenery. You can imagine, me looking at scenery, on the road every week of my life. But it's so beautiful up there, Linda, the trees are so thick, and the sun is warm. I opened the windshield and just let the warm air bathe over me. And then all of a sudden I'm goin' off the road! I'm tellin' ya, I absolutely forgot I was driving. If I'd've gone the other way over the white line I might've killed somebody. So I went on again—and five minutes later I'm dreamin' again, and I nearly . . . [*He presses two fingers against his eyes.*] I have such thoughts, I have such strange thoughts.

LINDA Willy, dear. Talk to them again. There's no reason why you can't work in New York.

WILLY They don't need me in New York. I'm the New England man. I'm vital in New England.

LINDA   But you're sixty years old. They can't expect you to keep traveling every week.

WILLY   I'll have to send a wire to Portland. I'm supposed to see Brown and Morrison tomorrow morning at ten o'clock to show the line. Goddammit, I could sell them! [*He starts putting on his jacket.*]

LINDA   [*Taking the jacket from him.*]   Why don't you go down to the place tomorrow and tell Howard you've simply got to work in New York? You're too accommodating, dear.

WILLY   If old man Wagner was alive I'd a been in charge of New York now! That man was a prince, he was a masterful man. But that boy of his, that Howard, he don't appreciate. When I went north the first time, the Wagner Company didn't know where New England was!

LINDA   Why don't you tell those things to Howard, dear?

WILLY   [*Encouraged.*]   I will, I definitely will. Is there any cheese?

LINDA   I'll make you a sandwich.

WILLY   No, go to sleep. I'll take some milk. I'll be up right away. The boys in?

LINDA   They're sleeping. Happy took Biff on a date tonight.

WILLY   [*Interested.*]   That so?

LINDA   It was so nice to see them shaving together, one behind the other, in the bathroom. And going out together. You notice? The whole house smells of shaving lotion.

WILLY   Figure it out. Work a lifetime to pay off a house. You finally own it, and there's nobody to live in it.

LINDA   Well, dear, life is a casting off. It's always that way.

WILLY   No, no, some people—some people accomplish something. Did Biff say anything after I went this morning?

LINDA   You shouldn't have criticized him, Willy, especially after he just got off the train. You mustn't lose your temper with him.

WILLY   When the hell did I lose my temper? I simply asked him if he was making any money. Is that a criticism?

LINDA   But, dear, how could he make any money?

WILLY [*Worried and angered.*] There's such an undercurrent in him. He became a moody man. Did he apologize when I left this morning?

LINDA He was crestfallen, Willy. You know how he admires you. I think if he finds himself, then you'll both be happier and not fight any more.

WILLY How can he find himself on a farm? Is that a life? A farmhand? In the beginning, when he was young, I thought, well, a young man, it's good for him to tramp around, take a lot of different jobs. But it's more than ten years now and he has yet to make thirty-five dollars a week!

LINDA He's finding himself, Willy.

WILLY Not finding yourself at the age of thirty-four is a disgrace!

LINDA Shh!

WILLY The trouble is he's lazy, goddammit!

LINDA Willy, please!

WILLY Biff is a lazy bum!

LINDA They're sleeping. Get something to eat. Go on down.

WILLY Why did he come home? I would like to know what brought him home.

LINDA I don't know. I think he's still lost, Willy. I think he's very lost.

WILLY Biff Loman is lost. In the greatest country in the world a young man with such—personal attractiveness, gets lost. And such a hard worker. There's one thing about Biff—he's not lazy.

LINDA Never.

WILLY [*With pity and resolve.*] I'll see him in the morning; I'll have a nice talk with him. I'll get him a job selling. He could be big in no time. My God! Remember how they used to follow him around in high school? When he smiled at one of them their faces lit up. When he walked down the street . . . [*He loses himself in reminiscences.*]

LINDA [*Trying to bring him out of it.*] Willy, dear, I got a new kind of American-type cheese today. It's whipped.

WILLY Why do you get American when I like Swiss?

LINDA I just thought you'd like a change . . .

WILLY I don't want a change! I want Swiss cheese. Why am I always being contradicted?

LINDA [*With a covering laugh.*] I thought it would be a surprise.

WILLY Why don't you open a window in here, for God's sake?

LINDA [*With infinite patience.*] They're all open, dear.

WILLY The way they boxed us in here. Bricks and windows, windows and bricks.

LINDA We should've bought the land next door.

WILLY The street is lined with cars. There's not a breath of fresh air in the neighborhood. The grass don't grow any more, you can't raise a carrot in the back yard. They should've had a law against apartment houses. Remember those two beautiful elm trees out there? When I and Biff hung the swing between them?

LINDA Yeah, like being a million miles from the city.

WILLY They should've arrested the builder for cutting those down. They massacred the neighborhood. [*Lost.*] More and more I think of those days, Linda. This time of year it was lilac and wisteria. And then the peonies would come out, and the daffodils. What fragrance in this room!

LINDA Well, after all, people had to move somewhere.

WILLY No, there's more people now.

LINDA I don't think there's more people. I think . . .

WILLY There's more people! That's what ruining this country! Population is getting out of control. The competition is maddening! Smell the stink from that apartment house! And another one on the other side . . . How can they whip cheese?

[*On Willy's last line, Biff and Happy raise themselves up in their beds, listening.*]

LINDA Go down, try it. And be quiet.

WILLY [*Turning to* LINDA, *guiltily.*] You're not worried about me, are you, sweetheart?

BIFF What's the matter?

HAPPY Listen!

LINDA You've got too much on the ball to worry about.

WILLY You're my foundation and my support, Linda.

LINDA Just try to relax, dear. You make mountains out of molehills.

WILLY I won't fight with him any more. If he wants to go back to Texas, let him go.

LINDA He'll find his way.

WILLY Sure. Certain men just don't get started till later in life. Like Thomas Edison, I think. Or B. F. Goodrich. One of them was deaf. [*He starts for the bedroom doorway.*] I'll put my money on Biff.

LINDA And Willy—if it's warm Sunday we'll drive in the country. And we'll open the windshield, and take lunch.

WILLY No, the windshields don't open on the new cars.

LINDA But you opened it today.

WILLY Me? I didn't. [*He stops.*] Now isn't that peculiar! Isn't that a remarkable . . . [*He breaks off in amazement and fright as the flute is heard distantly.*]

LINDA What, darling?

WILLY That is the most remarkable thing.

LINDA What, dear?

WILLY I was thinking of the Chevvy. [*Slight pause.*] Nineteen twenty-eight . . . when I had that red Chevvy . . . [*Breaks off.*] That funny? I coulda sworn I was driving that Chevvy today.

LINDA Well, that's nothing. Something must've reminded you.

WILLY Remarkable. Ts. Remember those days? The way Biff used to simonize that car? The dealer refused to believe there was eighty thousand miles on it. [*He shakes his head.*] Heh! [*To* LINDA.] Close your eyes, I'll be right up. [*He walks out of the bedroom.*]

HAPPY [*To* BIFF.] Jesus, maybe he smashed up the car again!

LINDA [*Calling after* WILLY.] Be careful on the stairs, dear! The cheese is on the middle shelf. [*She turns, goes over to the bed, takes his jacket, and goes out of the bedroom.*]

[*Light has risen on the boys' room. Unseen,* WILLY *is heard talking to himself, "Eighty thousand miles," and a little laugh.* BIFF *gets out of bed, comes downstage a bit, and stands atten-*

tively. BIFF *is two years older than his brother* HAPPY, *well built, but in these days bears a worn air and seems less self-assured. He has succeeded less, and his dreams are stronger and less acceptable than* HAPPY'S. HAPPY *is tall, powerfully made. Sexuality is like a visible color on him, or a scent that many women have discovered. He, like his brother, is lost, but in a different way, for he has never allowed himself to turn his face toward defeat and is thus more confused and hard-skinned, although seemingly more content.*]

HAPPY [*Getting out of bed.*]   He's going to get his license taken away if he keeps that up. I'm getting nervous about him, y'know, Biff?

BIFF   His eyes are going.

HAPPY   No, I've driven with him. He sees all right. He just doesn't keep his mind on it. I drove into the city with him last week. He stops at a green light and then it turns red and he goes. [*He laughs.*]

BIFF   Maybe he's color-blind.

HAPPY   Pop? Why he's got the finest eye for color in the business. You know that.

BIFF [*Sitting down on his bed.*]   I'm going to sleep.

HAPPY   You're not still sour on Dad, are you, Biff?

BIFF   He's all right, I guess.

WILLY [*Underneath them, in the living room.*]   Yes, sir, eighty thousand miles—eighty-two thousand!

BIFF   You smoking?

HAPPY [*Holding out a pack of cigarettes.*]   Want one?

BIFF [*Taking a cigarette.*]   I can never sleep when I smell it.

WILLY   What a simonizing job, heh!

HAPPY [*With deep sentiment.*]   Funny, Biff, y'know? Us sleeping in here again? The old beds. [*He pats his bed affectionately.*]   All the talk that went across those two beds, huh? Our whole lives.

BIFF   Yeah. Lotta dreams and plans.

HAPPY [*With a deep and masculine laugh.*]   About five hundred women would like to know what was said in this room.

[*They share a soft laugh.*]

BIFF   Remember that big Betsy something—what the hell was her name—over on Bushwick Avenue?

HAPPY [*Combing his hair.*]   With the collie dog!

BIFF   That's the one. I got you in there, remember?

HAPPY   Yeah, that was my first time—I think. Boy, there was a pig. [*They laugh, almost crudely.*]   You taught me everything I know about women. Don't forget that.

BIFF   I bet you forgot how bashful you used to be. Especially with girls.

HAPPY   Oh, I still am, Biff.

BIFF   Oh, go on.

HAPPY   I just control it, that's all. I think I got less bashful and you got more so. What happened, Biff? Where's the old humor, the old confidence? [*He shakes* BIFF's *knee.* BIFF *gets up and moves restlessly about the room.*]   What's the matter?

BIFF   Why does Dad mock me all the time?

HAPPY   He's not mocking you, he . . .

BIFF   Everything I say there's a twist of mockery on his face. I can't get near him.

HAPPY   He just wants you to make good, that's all. I wanted to talk to you about Dad for a long time, Biff. Something's—happening to him. He—talks to himself.

BIFF   I noticed that this morning. But he always mumbled.

HAPPY   But not so noticeable. It got so embarrassing I sent him to Florida. And you know something? Most of the time he's talking to you.

BIFF   What's he say about me?

HAPPY   I can't make it out.

BIFF   What's he say about me?

HAPPY   I think the fact that you're not settled, that you're still kind of up in the air . . .

BIFF   There's one or two other things depressing him, Happy.

HAPPY   What do you mean?

BIFF   Never mind. Just don't lay it all to me.

HAPPY   But I think if you just got started—I mean—is there any future for you out there?

BIFF   I tell ya, Hap, I don't know what the future is. I don't know—what I'm supposed to want.

HAPPY   What do you mean?

BIFF   Well, I spent six or seven years after high school trying to work myself up. Shipping clerk, salesman, business of one kind or another. And it's a measly manner of existence. To get on that subway on the hot mornings in summer. To devote your whole life to keeping stock, or making phone calls, or selling or buying. To suffer fifty weeks of the year for the sake of a two-week vacation, when all you really desire is to be outdoors, with your shirt off. And always to have to get ahead of the next fella. And still—that's how you build a future.

HAPPY   Well, you really enjoy it on a farm? Are you content out there?

BIFF   [*With rising agitation.*]   Hap, I've had twenty or thirty different kinds of jobs since I left home before the war, and it always turns out the same. I just realized it lately. In Nebraska when I herded cattle, and the Dakotas, and Arizona, and now in Texas. It's why I came home now, I guess, because I realized it. This farm I work on, it's spring there now, see? And they've got about fifteen new colts. There's nothing more inspiring or—beautiful than the sight of a mare and a new colt. And it's cool there now, see? Texas is cool now, and it's spring. And whenever spring comes to where I am, I suddenly get the feeling, my God, I'm not gettin' anywhere! What the hell am I doing, playing around with horses, twenty-eight dollars a week! I'm thirty-four years old, I oughta be makin' my future. That's when I come running home. And now, I get here, and I don't know what to do with myself. [*After a pause.*]   I've always made a point of not wasting my life, and everytime I come back here I know that all I've done is to waste my life.

HAPPY   You're a poet, you know that, Biff? You're a—you're an idealist!

BIFF   No, I'm mixed up very bad. Maybe I oughta get married. Maybe I oughta get stuck into something. Maybe that's my trouble. I'm like a boy. I'm not married, I'm not in business, I just—I'm like a boy. Are you content, Hap? You're a success, aren't you? Are you content?

HAPPY Hell, no!

BIFF Why? You're making money, aren't you?

HAPPY [*Moving about with energy, expressiveness.*] All I can do now is wait for the merchandise manager to die. And suppose I get to be merchandise manager? He's a good friend of mine, and he just built a terrific estate on Long Island. And he lived there about two months and sold it, and now he's building another one. He can't enjoy it once it's finished. And I know that's just what I would do. I don't know what the hell I'm workin' for. Sometimes I sit in my apartment—all alone. And I think of the rent I'm paying. And it's crazy. But then, it's what I always wanted. My own apartment, a car, and plenty of women. And still, goddammit, I'm lonely.

BIFF [*With enthusiasm.*] Listen, why don't you come out West with me?

HAPPY You and I, heh?

BIFF Sure, maybe we could buy a ranch. Raise cattle, use our muscles. Men built like we are should be working out in the open.

HAPPY [*Avidly.*] The Loman Brothers, heh?

BIFF [*With vast affection.*] Sure, we'd be known all over the counties!

HAPPY [*Enthralled.*] That's what I dream about, Biff. Sometimes I want to just rip my clothes off in the middle of the store and outbox that goddam merchandise manager. I mean I can outbox, outrun, and outlift anybody in that store, and I have to take orders from those common, petty sons-of-bitches till I can't stand it any more.

BIFF I'm tellin' you, kid, if you were with me I'd be happy out there.

HAPPY [*Enthused.*] See, Biff, everybody around me is so false that I'm constantly lowering my ideals . . .

BIFF Baby, together we'd stand up for one another, we'd have someone to trust.

HAPPY If I were around you . . .

BIFF Hap, the trouble is we weren't brought up to grub for money. I don't know how to do it.

HAPPY Neither can I!

BIFF Then let's go!

HAPPY The only thing is—what can you make out there?

BIFF But look at your friend. Builds an estate and then hasn't the peace of mind to live in it.

HAPPY Yeah, but when he walks into the store the waves part in front of him. That's fifty-two thousand dollars a year coming through the revolving door, and I got more in my pinky finger than he's got in his head.

BIFF Yeah, but you just said . . .

HAPPY I gotta show some of those pompous, self-important executives over there that Hap Loman can make the grade. I want to walk into the store the way he walks in. Then I'll go with you, Biff. We'll be together yet, I swear. But take those two we had tonight. Now weren't they gorgeous creatures?

BIFF Yeah, yeah, most gorgeous I've had in years.

HAPPY I get that any time I want, Biff. Whenever I feel disgusted. The only trouble is, it gets like bowling or something. I just keep knockin' them over and it doesn't mean anything. You still run around a lot?

BIFF Naa. I'd like to find a girl—steady, somebody with substance.

HAPPY That's what I long for.

BIFF Go on! You'd never come home.

HAPPY I would! Somebody with character, with resistance! Like Mom, y'know? You're gonna call me a bastard when I tell you this. That girl Charlotte I was with tonight is engaged to be married in five weeks. [*He tries on his new hat.*]

BIFF No kiddin'!

HAPPY Sure, the guy's in line for the vice-presidency of the store. I don't know what gets into me, maybe I just have an overdeveloped sense of competition or something, but I went and ruined her, and furthermore I can't get rid of her. And he's the third executive I've done that to. Isn't that a crummy characteristic? And to top it all, I go to their weddings! [*Indignantly, but laughing.*] Like I'm not supposed to take bribes. Manufacturers offer me a hundred-dollar bill now and then to throw an order their way. You know how honest I am, but it's like this girl, see. I hate myself for it. Because I don't want the girl, and, still, I take it and—I love it!

BIFF Let's go to sleep.

HAPPY I guess we didn't settle anything, heh?

BIFF I just got one idea that I think I'm going to try.

HAPPY What's that?

BIFF Remember Bill Oliver?

HAPPY Sure, Oliver is very big now. You want to work for him again?

BIFF No, but when I quit he said something to me. He put his arm on my shoulder, and he said, "Biff, if you ever need anything, come to me."

HAPPY I remember that. That sounds good.

BIFF I think I'll go to see him. If I could get ten thousand or even seven or eight thousand dollars I could buy a beautiful ranch.

HAPPY I bet he'd back you. 'Cause he thought highly of you, Biff. I mean, they all do. You're well liked, Biff. That's why I say to come back here, and we both have the apartment. And I'm tellin' you, Biff, any babe you want . . .

BIFF No, with a ranch I could do the work I like and still be something. I just wonder though. I wonder if Oliver still thinks I stole that carton of basketballs.

HAPPY Oh, he probably forgot that long ago. It's almost ten years. You're too sensitive. Anyway, he didn't really fire you.

BIFF Well, I think he was going to. I think that's why I quit. I was never sure whether he knew or not. I know he thought the world of me, though. I was the only one he'd let lock up the place.

WILLY [*Below.*] You gonna wash the engine, Biff?

HAPPY Shh!

[BIFF *looks at* HAPPY, *who is gazing down, listening.* WILLY *is mumbling in the parlor.*]

HAPPY You hear that?

[*They listen.* WILLY *laughs warmly.*]

BIFF [*Growing angry.*]   Doesn't he know Mom can hear that?

WILLY   Don't get your sweater dirty, Biff!

[*A look of pain crosses* BIFF's *face.*]

HAPPY   Isn't that terrible? Don't leave again, will you? You'll find a job here. You gotta stick around. I don't know what to do about him, it's getting embarrassing.

WILLY   What a simonizing job!

BIFF   Mom's hearing that!

WILLY   No kiddin', Biff, you got a date? Wonderful!

HAPPY   Go on to sleep. But talk to him in the morning, will you?

BIFF [*Reluctantly getting into bed.*]   With her in the house. Brother!

HAPPY [*Getting into bed.*]   I wish you'd have a good talk with him.

[*The light on their room begins to fade.*]

BIFF [*To himself in bed.*]   That selfish, stupid . . .

HAPPY   Sh . . . Sleep, Biff.

[*Their light is out. Well before they have finished speaking,* WILLY's *form is dimly seen below in the darkened kitchen. He opens the refrigerator, searches in there, and takes out a bottle of milk. The apartment houses are fading out, and the entire house and surroundings become covered with leaves. Music insinuates itself as the leaves appear.*]

WILLY   Just wanna be careful with those girls, Biff, that's all. Don't make any promises. No promises of any kind. Because a girl, y'know, they always believe what you tell 'em, and you're very young, Biff, you're too young to be talking seriously to girls.

[*Light rises on the kitchen.* WILLY, *talking, shuts the refrigerator door and comes downstage to the kitchen table. He pours milk into a glass. He is totally immersed in himself, smiling faintly.*]

WILLY   Too young entirely, Biff. You want to watch your schooling first. Then when you're all set, there'll be plenty of girls for a boy like you. [*He smiles broadly at a kitchen chair.*]

That so? The girls pay for you? [*He laughs.*] Boy, you must really be makin' a hit.

[WILLY *is gradually addressing—physically—a point offstage, speaking through the wall of the kitchen, and his voice has been rising in volume to that of a normal conversation.*]

WILLY I been wondering why you polish the car so careful. Ha! Don't leave the hubcaps, boys. Get the chamois to the hubcaps. Happy, use newspaper on the windows, it's the easiest thing. Show him how to do it, Biff! You see, Happy? Pad it up, use it like a pad. That's it, that's it, good work. You're doin' all right, Hap. [*He pauses, then nods in approbation for a few seconds, then looks upward.*] Biff, first thing we gotta do when we get time is clip that big branch over the house. Afraid it's gonna fall in a storm and hit the roof. Tell you what. We get a rope and sling her around, and then we climb up there with a couple of saws and take her down. Soon as you finish the car, boys, I wanna see ya. I got a surprise for you, boys.

BIFF [*Offstage.*] Whatta ya got, Dad?

WILLY No, you finish first. Never leave a job till you're finished—remember that. [*Looking toward the "big trees."*] Biff, up in Albany I saw a beautiful hammock. I think I'll buy it next trip, and we'll hang it right between those two elms. Wouldn't that be something? Just swingin' there under those branches. Boy, that would be . . .

[YOUNG BIFF *and* YOUNG HAPPY *appear from the direction* WILLY *was addressing.* HAPPY *carries rags and a pail of water.* BIFF, *wearing a sweater with a block "S," carries a football.*]

BIFF [*Pointing in the direction of the car offstage.*] How's that, Pop, professional?

WILLY Terrific. Terrific job, boys. Good work, Biff.

HAPPY Where's the surprise, Pop?

WILLY In the back seat of the car.

HAPPY Boy! [*He runs off.*]

BIFF What is it, Dad? Tell me, what'd you buy?

WILLY [*Laughing, cuffs him.*] Never mind, something I want you to have.

BIFF [*Turns and starts off.*] What is it, Hap?

HAPPY [*Offstage.*] It's a punching bag!

BIFF Oh, Pop!

WILLY It's got Gene Tunney's signature on it!

[HAPPY *runs onstage with a punching bag.*]

BIFF Gee, how'd you know we wanted a punching bag?

WILLY Well, it's the finest thing for the timing.

HAPPY [*Lies down on his back and pedals with his feet.*] **I'm** losing weight, you notice, Pop?

WILLY [*To* HAPPY.] Jumping rope is good too.

BIFF Did you see the new football I got?

WILLY [*Examining the ball.*] Where'd you get a new ball?

BIFF The coach told me to practice my passing.

WILLY That so? And he gave you the ball, heh?

BIFF Well, I borrowed it from the locker room. [*He laughs confidentially.*]

WILLY [*Laughing with him at the theft.*] I want you to return that.

HAPPY I told you he wouldn't like it!

BIFF [*Angrily.*] Well, I'm bringing it back!

WILLY [*Stopping the incipient argument, to* HAPPY.] Sure, he's gotta practice with a regulation ball, doesn't he? [*To* BIFF.] Coach'll probably congratulate you on your initiative!

BIFF Oh, he keeps congratulating my initiative all the time, Pop.

WILLY That's because he likes you. If somebody else took that ball there'd be an uproar. So what's the report, boys, what's the report?

BIFF Where'd you go this time, Dad? Gee we were lonesome for you.

WILLY [*Pleased, puts an arm around each boy and they come down to the apron.*] Lonesome, heh?

BIFF Missed you every minute.

WILLY Don't say? Tell you a secret, boys. Don't breathe it to a soul. Someday I'll have my own business, and I'll never have to leave home any more.

HAPPY Like Uncle Charley, heh?

WILLY   Bigger than Uncle Charley! Because Charley is not—liked. He's liked, but he's not—well liked.

BIFF   Where'd you go this time, Dad?

WILLY   Well, I got on the road, and I went north to Providence. Met the Mayor.

BIFF   The Mayor of Providence!

WILLY   He was sitting in the hotel lobby.

BIFF   What'd he say?

WILLY   He said, "Morning!" And I said, "You got a fine city here, Mayor." And then he had coffee with me. And then I went to Waterbury. Waterbury is a fine city. Big clock city, the famous Waterbury clock. Sold a nice bill there. And then Boston—Boston is the cradle of the Revolution. A fine city. And a couple of other towns in Mass., and on to Portland and Bangor and straight home!

BIFF   Gee, I'd love to go with you sometime, Dad.

WILLY   Soon as summer comes.

HAPPY   Promise?

WILLY   You and Hap and I, and I'll show you all the towns. America is full of beautiful towns and fine, upstanding people. And they know me, boys, they know me up and down New England. The finest people. And when I bring you fellas up, there'll be open sesame for all of us, 'cause one thing, boys: I have friends. I can park my car in any street in New England, and the cops protect it like their own. This summer, heh?

BIFF and HAPPY [*Together.*]   Yeah! You bet!

WILLY   We'll take our bathing suits.

HAPPY   We'll carry your bags, Pop!

WILLY   Oh, won't that be something! Me comin' into the Boston stores with you boys carryin' my bags. What a sensation!

[BIFF *is prancing around, practicing passing the ball.*]

WILLY   You nervous, Biff, about the game?

BIFF   Not if you're gonna be there.

WILLY   What do they say about you in school, now that they made you captain?

HAPPY   There's a crowd of girls behind him everytime the classes change.

BIFF [*Taking* WILLY'S *hand.*]   This Saturday, Pop, this Saturday—just for you, I'm going to break through for a touchdown.

HAPPY You're supposed to pass.

BIFF I'm takin' one play for Pop. You watch me, Pop, and when I take off my helmet, that means I'm breakin' out. Then you watch me crash through that line!

WILLY [*Kisses* BIFF.] Oh, wait'll I tell this in Boston!

[BERNARD *enters in knickers. He is younger than* BIFF, *earnest and loyal, a worried boy.*]

BERNARD Biff, where are you? You're supposed to study with me today.

WILLY Hey, looka Bernard. What're you lookin' so anemic about, Bernard?

BERNARD He's gotta study, Uncle Willy. He's got Regents next week.

HAPPY [*Tauntingly, spinning* BERNARD *around.*] Let's box, Bernard!

BERNARD Biff! [*He gets away from* HAPPY.] Listen, Biff, I heard Mr. Birnbaum say that if you don't start studyin' math he's gonna flunk you, and you won't graduate. I heard him!

WILLY You better study with him, Biff. Go ahead now.

BERNARD I heard him!

BIFF Oh, Pop, you didn't see my sneakers! [*He holds up a foot for* WILLY *to look at.*]

WILLY Hey, that's a beautiful job of printing!

BERNARD [*Wiping his glasses.*] Just because he printed University of Virginia on his sneakers doesn't mean they've got to graduate him, Uncle Willy!

WILLY [*Angrily.*] What're you talking about? With scholarships to three universities they're gonna flunk him?

BERNARD But I heard Mr. Birnbaum say . . .

WILLY Don't be a pest, Bernard! [*To his boys.*] What an anemic!

BERNARD Okay, I'm waiting for you in my house, Biff.

[BERNARD *goes off.* THE LOMANS *laugh.*]

WILLY Bernard is not well liked, is he?

BIFF He's liked, but he's not well liked.

HAPPY That's right, Pop.

WILLY That's just what I mean. Bernard can get the best marks in school, y'understand, but when he gets out in the business world, y'understand, you are going to be five times ahead of him. That's why I thank Almighty God you're both built like Adonises. Because the man who makes an appearance in the business world, the man who creates personal interest, is the man who gets ahead. Be liked and you will never want. You take me, for instance. I never have to wait in line to see a buyer. "Willy Loman is here!" That's all they have to know, and I go right through.

BIFF Did you knock them dead, Pop?

WILLY Knocked 'em cold in Providence, slaughtered 'em in Boston.

HAPPY [On his back, pedaling again.] I'm losing weight, you notice, Pop?

[LINDA enters, as of old, a ribbon in her hair, carrying a basket of washing.]

LINDA [With youthful energy.] Hello, dear!

WILLY Sweetheart!

LINDA How'd the Chevvy run?

WILLY Chevrolet, Linda, is the greatest car ever built. [To the boys.] Since when do you let your mother carry wash up the stairs?

BIFF Grab hold there, boy!

HAPPY Where to, Mom?

LINDA Hang them up on the line. And you better go down to your friends, Biff. The cellar is full of boys. They don't know what to do with themselves.

BIFF Ah, when Pop comes home they can wait!

WILLY [Laughs appreciatively.] You better go down and tell them what to do, Biff.

BIFF I think I'll have them sweep out the furnace room.

WILLY Good work, Biff.

BIFF [Goes through wall-line of kitchen to doorway at back and calls down.] Fellas! Everybody sweep out the furnace room! I'll be right down!

VOICES All right! Okay, Biff.

BIFF George and Sam and Frank, come out back! We're hangin' up the wash! Come on, Hap, on the double! [*He and* HAPPY *carry out the basket.*]

LINDA The way they obey him!

WILLY Well, that's training, the training. I'm tellin' you, I was sellin' thousands and thousands, but I had to come home.

LINDA Oh, the whole block'll be at that game. Did you sell anything?

WILLY I did five hundred gross in Providence and seven hundred gross in Boston.

LINDA No! Wait a minute, I've got a pencil. [*She pulls pencil and paper out of her apron pocket.*] That makes your commission . . . Two hundred—my God! Two hundred and twelve dollars!

WILLY Well, I didn't figure it yet, but . . .

LINDA How much did you do?

WILLY Well, I—I did—about a hundred and eighty gross in Providence. Well, no—it came to—roughly two hundred gross on the whole trip.

LINDA [*Without hesitation.*] Two hundred gross. That's . . . [*She figures.*]

WILLY The trouble was that three of the stores were half-closed for inventory in Boston. Otherwise I woulda broke records.

LINDA Well, it makes seventy dollars and some pennies. That's very good.

WILLY What do we owe?

LINDA Well, on the first there's sixteen dollars on the refrigerator . . .

WILLY Why sixteen?

LINDA Well, the fan belt broke, so it was a dollar eighty.

WILLY But it's brand new.

LINDA Well, the man said that's the way it is. Till they work themselves in, y'know.

[*They move through the wall-line into the kitchen.*]

WILLY I hope we didn't get stuck on that machine.

LINDA They got the biggest ads of any of them!

WILLY I know, it's a fine machine. What else?

LINDA Well, there's nine-sixty for the washing machine. And for the vacuum cleaner there's three and a half due on the fifteenth. Then the roof, you got twenty-one dollars remaining.

WILLY It don't leak, does it?

LINDA No, they did a wonderful job. Then you owe Frank for the carburetor.

WILLY I'm not going to pay that man! That goddam Chevrolet, they ought to prohibit the manufacture of that car!

LINDA Well, you owe him three and a half. And odds and ends, comes to around a hundred and twenty dollars by the fifteenth.

WILLY A hundred and twenty dollars! My God, if business don't pick up I don't know what I'm gonna do!

LINDA Well, next week you'll do better.

WILLY Oh, I'll knock 'em dead next week. I'll go to Hartford. I'm very well liked in Hartford. You know, the trouble is, Linda, people don't seem to take to me.

[*They move onto the forestage.*]

LINDA Oh, don't be foolish.

WILLY I know it when I walk in. They seem to laugh at me.

LINDA Why? Why would they laugh at you? Don't talk that way, Willy.

[WILLY *moves to the edge of the stage.* LINDA *goes into the kitchen and starts to darn stockings.*]

WILLY I don't know the reason for it, but they just pass me by. I'm not noticed.

LINDA But you're doing wonderful, dear. You're making seventy to a hundred dollars a week.

WILLY But I gotta be at it ten, twelve hours a day. Other men —I don't know—they do it easier. I don't know why—I can't stop myself—I talk too much. A man oughta come in with a few words. One thing about Charley. He's a man of few words, and they respect him.

LINDA You don't talk too much, you're just lively.

WILLY [*Smiling.*] Well, I figure, what the hell, life is short, a couple of jokes. [*To himself.*] I joke too much! [*The smile goes.*]

LINDA Why? You're . . .

WILLY I'm fat. I'm very—foolish to look at, Linda. I didn't tell you, but Christmas time I happened to be calling on F. H. Stewarts, and a salesman I know, as I was going in to see the buyer I heard him say something about—walrus. And I—I cracked him right across the face. I won't take that. I simply will not take that. But they do laugh at me. I know that.

LINDA Darling . . .

WILLY I gotta overcome it. I know I gotta overcome it. I'm not dressing to advantage, maybe.

LINDA Willy, darling, you're the handsomest man in the world . . .

WILLY Oh, no, Linda.

LINDA To me you are. [*Slight pause.*] The handsomest.

[*From the darkness is heard the laughter of a woman.* WILLY *doesn't turn to it, but it continues through* LINDA'S *lines.*]

LINDA And the boys, Willy. Few men are idolized by their children the way you are.

[*Music is heard as behind a scrim, to the left of the house;* THE WOMAN, *dimly seen, is dressing.*]

WILLY [*With great feeling.*] You're the best there is, Linda, you're a pal, you know that? On the road—on the road I want to grab you sometimes and just kiss the life outa you.

[*The laughter is loud now, and he moves into a brightening area at the left, where* THE WOMAN *has come from behind the scrim and is standing, putting on her hat, looking into a "mirror" and laughing.*]

WILLY 'Cause I get so lonely—especially when business is bad and there's nobody to talk to. I get the feeling that I'll never sell anything again, that I won't make a living for you, or a business, a business for the boys. [*He talks through* THE WOMAN's *subsiding laughter;* THE WOMAN *primps at the "mirror."*] There's so much I want to make for . . .

THE WOMAN Me? You didn't make me, Willy. I picked you.

WILLY [*Pleased.*] You picked me?

THE WOMAN [*Who is quite proper-looking,* WILLY's *age.*] I did. I've been sitting at that desk watching all the salesmen go by, day in, day out. But you've got such a sense of humor, and we do have such a good time together, don't we?

WILLY Sure, sure. [*He takes her in his arms.*] Why do you have to go now?

THE WOMAN It's two o'clock . . .

WILLY No, come on in! [*He pulls her.*]

THE WOMAN . . . my sisters'll be scandalized. When'll you be back?

WILLY Oh, two weeks about. Will you come up again?

THE WOMAN Sure thing. You do make me laugh. It's good for me. [*She squeezes his arm, kisses him.*] And I think you're a wonderful man.

WILLY You picked me, heh?

THE WOMAN Sure. Because you're so sweet. And such a kidder.

WILLY Well, I'll see you next time I'm in Boston.

THE WOMAN I'll put you right through to the buyers.

WILLY [*Slapping her bottom.*] Right. Well, bottoms up!

THE WOMAN [*Slaps him gently and laughs.*] You just kill me, Willy. [*He suddenly grabs her and kisses her roughly.*] You kill me. And thanks for the stockings. I love a lot of stockings. Well, good night.

WILLY Good night. And keep your pores open!

THE WOMAN Oh, Willy!

[THE WOMAN *bursts out laughing, and* LINDA's *laughter blends in.* THE WOMAN *disappears into the dark. Now the area at the kitchen table brightens.* LINDA *is sitting where she was at the kitchen table, but now is mending a pair of her silk stockings.*]

LINDA You are, Willy. The handsomest man. You've got no reason to feel that . . .

WILLY [*Coming out of* THE WOMAN's *dimming area and going over to* LINDA.] I'll make it all up to you, Linda, I'll . . .

LINDA There's nothing to make up, dear. You're doing fine, better than . . .

WILLY [*Noticing her mending.*] What's that?

262 / ARTHUR MILLER

LINDA   Just mending my stockings. They're so expensive . . .

WILLY   [*Angrily, taking them from her.*]   I won't have you mending stockings in this house! Now throw them out!

[LINDA *puts the stockings in her pocket.*]

BERNARD   [*Entering on the run.*]   Where is he? If he doesn't study!

WILLY   [*Moving to the forestage, with great agitation.*]   You'll give him the answers!

BERNARD   I do, but I can't on a Regents! That's a state exam! They're liable to arrest me!

WILLY   Where is he? I'll whip him, I'll whip him!

LINDA   And he'd better give back that football, Willy, it's not nice.

WILLY   Biff! Where is he? Why is he taking everything?

LINDA   He's too rough with the girls, Willy. All the mothers are afraid of him!

WILLY   I'll whip him!

BERNARD   He's driving the car without a license!

[THE WOMAN's *laugh is heard.*]

WILLY   Shut up!

LINDA   All the mothers . . .

WILLY   Shut up!

BERNARD   [*Backing quietly away and out.*]   Mr. Birnbaum says he's stuck up.

WILLY   Get outa here!

BERNARD   If he doesn't buckle down he'll flunk math! [*He goes off.*]

LINDA   He's right, Willy, you've gotta . . .

WILLY   [*Exploding at her.*]   There's nothing the matter with him! You want him to be a worm like Bernard? He's got spirit, personality . . .

[*As he speaks,* LINDA, *almost in tears, exits into the living room.* WILLY *is alone in the kitchen, wilting and staring. The leaves are gone. It is night again, and the apartment houses look down from behind.*]

WILLY Loaded with it. Loaded! What is he stealing? He's giving it back, isn't he? Why is he stealing? What did I tell him? I never in my life told him anything but decent things.

[HAPPY *in pajamas has come down the stairs;* WILLY *suddenly becomes aware of* HAPPY'S *presence.*]

HAPPY Let's go now, come on.

WILLY [*Sitting down at the kitchen table.*] Huh! Why did she have to wax the floors herself? Everytime she waxes the floors she keels over. She knows that!

HAPPY Shh! Take it easy. What brought you back tonight?

WILLY I got an awful scare. Nearly hit a kid in Yonkers. God! Why didn't I go to Alaska with my brother Ben that time! Ben! That man was a genius, that man was success incarnate! What a mistake! He begged me to go.

HAPPY Well, there's no use in . . .

WILLY You guys! There was a man started with the clothes on his back and ended up with diamond mines!

HAPPY Boy, someday I'd like to know how he did it.

WILLY What's the mystery? The man knew what he wanted and went out and got it! Walked into a jungle, and comes out, the age of twenty-one, and he's rich! The world is an oyster, but you don't crack it open on a mattress!

HAPPY Pop, I told you I'm gonna retire you for life.

WILLY You'll retire me for life on seventy goddam dollars a week? And your women and your car and your apartment, and you'll retire me for life! Christ's sake, I couldn't get past Yonkers today! Where are you guys, where are you? The woods are burning! I can't drive a car!

[CHARLEY *has appeared in the doorway. He is a large man, slow of speech, laconic, immovable. In all he says, despite what he says, there is pity, and, now, trepidation. He has a robe over pajamas, slippers on his feet. He enters the kitchen.*]

CHARLEY Everything all right?

HAPPY Yeah, Charley, everything's . . .

WILLY What's the matter?

CHARLEY I heard some noise. I thought something happened.

Can't we do something about the walls? You sneeze in here, and in my house hats blow off.

HAPPY   Let's go to bed, Dad. Come on.

[CHARLEY *signals to* HAPPY *to go.*]

WILLY   You go ahead, I'm not tired at the moment.

HAPPY   [*To* WILLY]   Take it easy, huh? [*He exits.*]

WILLY   What're you doin' up?

CHARLEY   [*Sitting down at the kitchen table opposite* WILLY.] Couldn't sleep good. I had a heartburn.

WILLY   Well, you don't know how to eat.

CHARLEY   I eat with my mouth.

WILLY   No, you're ignorant. You gotta know about vitamins and things like that.

CHARLEY   Come on, let's shoot. Tire you out a little.

WILLY   [*Hesitantly.*]   All right. You got cards?

CHARLEY   [*Taking a deck from his pocket.*]   Yeah, I got them. Someplace. What is it with those vitamins?

WILLY   [*Dealing.*]   They build up your bones. Chemistry.

CHARLEY   Yeah, but there's no bones in a heartburn.

WILLY   What are you talkin' about? Do you know the first thing about it?

CHARLEY   Don't get insulted.

WILLY   Don't talk about something you don't know anything about.

[*They are playing. Pause.*]

CHARLEY   What're you doin' home?

WILLY   A little trouble with the car.

CHARLEY   Oh. [*Pause.*]   I'd like to take a trip to California.

WILLY   Don't say.

CHARLEY   You want a job?

WILLY   I got a job, I told you that. [*After a slight pause.*] What the hell are you offering me a job for?

CHARLEY   Don't get insulted.

WILLY   Don't insult me.

CHARLEY   I don't see no sense in it. You don't have to go on this way.

WILLY I got a good job. [*Slight pause.*] What do you keep comin' in here for?

CHARLEY You want me to go?

WILLY [*After a pause, withering.*] I can't understand it. He's going back to Texas again. What the hell is that?

CHARLEY Let him go.

WILLY I got nothin' to give him, Charley, I'm clean, I'm clean.

CHARLEY He won't starve. None a them starve. Forget about him.

WILLY Then what have I got to remember?

CHARLEY You take it too hard. To hell with it. When a deposit bottle is broken you don't get your nickel back.

WILLY That's easy enough for you to say.

CHARLEY That ain't easy for me to say.

WILLY Did you see the ceiling I put up in the living room?

CHARLEY Yeah, that's a piece of work. To put up a ceiling is a mystery to me. How do you do it?

WILLY What's the difference?

CHARLEY Well, talk about it.

WILLY You gonna put up a ceiling?

CHARLEY How could I put up a ceiling?

WILLY Then what the hell are you bothering me for?

CHARLEY You're insulted again.

WILLY A man who can't handle tools is not a man. You're disgusting.

CHARLEY Don't call me disgusting, Willy.

[UNCLE BEN, *carrying a valise and an umbrella, enters the forestage from around the right corner of the house. He is a stolid man, in his sixties, with a mustache and an authoritative air. He is utterly certain of his destiny, and there is an aura of far places about him. He enters exactly as* WILLY *speaks.*]

WILLY I'm getting awfully tired, Ben.

[BEN'S *music is heard.* BEN *looks around at everything.*]

CHARLEY Good, keep playing; you'll sleep better. Did you call me Ben?

[BEN *looks at his watch.*]

WILLY   That's funny. For a second there you reminded me of my brother Ben.

BEN   I only have a few minutes. [*He strolls, inspecting the place.* WILLY *and* CHARLEY *continue playing.*]

CHARLEY   You never heard from him again, heh? Since that time?

WILLY   Didn't Linda tell you? Couple of weeks ago we got a letter from his wife in Africa. He died.

CHARLEY   That so.

BEN   [*Chuckling.*]   So this is Brooklyn, eh?

CHARLEY   Maybe you're in for some of his money.

WILLY   Naa, he had seven sons. There's just one opportunity I had with that man . . .

BEN   I must make a train, William. There are several properties I'm looking at in Alaska.

WILLY   Sure, sure! If I'd gone with him to Alaska that time, everything would've been totally different.

CHARLEY   Go on, you'd froze to death up there.

WILLY   What're you talking about?

BEN   Opportunity is tremendous in Alaska, William. Surprised you're not up there.

WILLY   Sure, tremendous.

CHARLEY   Heh?

WILLY   There was the only man I ever met who knew the answers.

CHARLEY   Who?

BEN   How are you all?

WILLY   [*Taking a pot, smiling.*]   Fine, fine.

CHARLEY   Pretty sharp tonight.

BEN   Is Mother living with you?

WILLY   No, she died a long time ago.

CHARLEY   Who?

BEN   That's too bad. Fine specimen of a lady, Mother.

WILLY   [*To* CHARLEY.]   Heh?

BEN   I'd hoped to see the old girl.

CHARLEY   Who died?

BEN   Heard anything from Father, have you?

WILLY [*Unnerved.*] What do you mean, who died?

CHARLEY [*Taking a pot.*] What're you talkin' about?

BEN [*Looking at his watch.*] William, it's half-past eight!

WILLY [*As though to dispel his confusion he angrily stops* CHARLEY'S *hand.*] That's my build!

CHARLEY I put the ace . . .

WILLY If you don't know how to play the game I'm not gonna throw my money away on you!

CHARLEY [*Rising.*] It was my ace, for God's sake!

WILLY I'm through, I'm through!

BEN When did Mother die?

WILLY Long ago. Since the beginning you never knew how to play cards.

CHARLEY [*Picks up the cards and goes to the door.*] All right! Next time I'll bring a deck with five aces.

WILLY I don't play that kind of game!

CHARLEY [*Turning to him.*] You ought to be ashamed of yourself!

WILLY Yeah?

CHARLEY Yeah! [*He goes out.*]

WILLY [*Slamming the door after him.*] Ignoramus!

BEN [*As* WILLY *comes toward him through the wall-line of the kitchen.*] So you're William.

WILLY [*Shaking* BEN'S *hand.*] Ben! I've been waiting for you so long! What's the answer? How did you do it?

BEN Oh, there's a story in that.

[LINDA *enters the forestage, as of old, carrying the wash basket.*]

LINDA Is this Ben?

BEN [*Gallantly.*] How do you do, my dear.

LINDA Where've you been all these years? Willy's always wondered why you . . .

WILLY [*Pulling* BEN *away from her impatiently.*] Where is Dad? Didn't you follow him? How did you get started?

BEN Well, I don't know how much you remember.

WILLY Well, I was just a baby, of course, only three or four years old . . .

BEN Three years and eleven months.

WILLY What a memory, Ben!

BEN I have many enterprises, William, and I have never kept books.

WILLY I remember I was sitting under the wagon in—was it Nebraska?

BEN It was South Dakota, and I gave you a bunch of wild flowers.

WILLY I remember you walking away down some open road.

BEN [Laughing.] I was going to find Father in Alaska.

WILLY Where is he?

BEN At that age I had a very faulty view of geography, William. I discovered after a few days that I was heading due south, so instead of Alaska, I ended up in Africa.

LINDA Africa!

WILLY The Gold Coast!

BEN Principally diamond mines.

LINDA Diamond mines!

BEN Yes, my dear. But I've only a few minutes . . .

WILLY No! Boys! Boys! [YOUNG BIFF and HAPPY appear.] Listen to this. This is your Uncle Ben, a great man! Tell my boys, Ben!

BEN Why, boys, when I was seventeen I walked into the jungle, and when I was twenty-one I walked out. [He laughs.] And by God I was rich.

WILLY [To the boys.] You see what I been talking about? The greatest things can happen!

BEN [Glancing at his watch.] I have an appointment in Ketchikan Tuesday week.

WILLY No, Ben! Please tell about Dad. I want my boys to hear. I want them to know the kind of stock they spring from. All I remember is a man with a big beard, and I was in Mamma's lap, sitting around a fire, and some kind of high music.

BEN His flute. He played the flute.

WILLY Sure, the flute, that's right!

[New music is heard, a high, rollicking tune.]

BEN Father was a very great and a very wild-hearted man. We would start in Boston, and he'd toss the whole family into the wagon, and then he'd drive the team right across the country; through Ohio, and Indiana, Michigan, Illinois, and all the Western states. And we'd stop in the towns and sell the flutes that he'd made on the way. Great inventor, Father. With one gadget he made more in a week than a man like you could make in a lifetime.

WILLY   That's just the way I'm bringing them up, Ben—rugged, well liked, all-around.

BEN   Yeah? [*To* BIFF.]   Hit that, boy—hard as you can. [*He pounds his stomach.*]

BIFF   Oh, no, sir!

BEN [*Taking boxing stance.*]   Come on, get to me! [*He laughs.*]

WILLY   Go to it, Biff! Go ahead, show him!

BIFF   Okay! [*He cocks his fists and starts in.*]

LINDA [*To* WILLY.]   Why must he fight, dear?

BEN [*Sparring with* BIFF.]   Good boy! Good boy!

WILLY   How's that, Ben, heh?

HAPPY   Give him the left, Biff!

LINDA   Why are you fighting?

BEN   Good boy! [*Suddenly comes in, trips* BIFF, *and stands over him, the point of his umbrella poised over* BIFF's *eye.*]

LINDA   Look out, Biff!

BIFF   Gee!

BEN [*Patting* BIFF's *knee.*]   Never fight fair with a stranger, boy. You'll never get out of the jungle that way. [*Taking* LINDA's *hand and bowing.*]   It was an honor and a pleasure to meet you, Linda.

LINDA [*Withdrawing her hand coldly, frightened.*]   Have a nice—trip.

BEN [*To* WILLY.]   And good luck with your—what do you do?

WILLY   Selling.

BEN   Yes. Well . . . [*He raises his hand in farewell to all.*]

WILLY   No, Ben, I don't want you to think . . . [*He takes* BEN's *arm to show him.*]   It's Brooklyn, I know, but we hunt too.

BEN   Really, now.

WILLY   Oh, sure, there's snakes and rabbits and—that's why I moved out here. Why, Biff can fell any one of these trees in no time! Boys! Go right over to where they're building the apartment house and get some sand. We're gonna rebuild the entire front stoop right now! Watch this, Ben!

BIFF   Yes, sir! On the double, Hap!

HAPPY [*As he and* BIFF *run off.*]   I lost weight, Pop, you notice?

[CHARLEY *enters in knickers, even before the boys are gone.*]

CHARLEY   Listen, if they steal any more from that building the watchman'll put the cops on them!

LINDA [*To* WILLY.]   Don't let Biff . . .

[BEN *laughs lustily.*]

WILLY   You shoulda seen the lumber they brought home last week. At least a dozen six-by-tens worth all kinds a money.

CHARLEY   Listen, if that watchman . . .

WILLY   I gave them hell, understand. But I got a couple of fearless characters there.

CHARLEY   Willy, the jails are full of fearless characters.

BEN [*Clapping* WILLY *on the back, with a laugh at* CHARLEY.] And the stock exchange, friend!

WILLY [*Joining in* BEN'S *laughter.*]   Where are the rest of your pants?

CHARLEY   My wife bought them.

WILLY   Now all you need is a golf club and you can go upstairs and go to sleep. [*To* BEN.]   Great athlete! Between him and his son Bernard they can't hammer a nail!

BERNARD [*Rushing in.*]   The watchman's chasing Biff!

WILLY [*Angrily.*]   Shut up! He's not stealing anything!

LINDA [*Alarmed, hurrying off left.*]   Where is he? Biff, dear! [*She exits.*]

WILLY [*Moving toward the left, away from* BEN.]   There's nothing wrong. What's the matter with you?

BEN   Nervy boy. Good!

WILLY [*Laughing.*]   Oh, nerves of iron, that Biff!

CHARLEY   Don't know what it is. My New England man comes back and he's bleedin', they murdered him up there.

WILLY   It's contacts, Charley, I got important contacts!

CHARLEY [*Sarcastically.*]   Glad to hear it, Willy. Come in later, we'll shoot a little casino. I'll take some of your Portland money. [*He laughs at* WILLY *and exits.*]

WILLY [*Turning to* BEN.] Business is bad, it's murderous. But not for me, of course.

BEN I'll stop by on my way back to Africa.

WILLY [*Longingly.*] Can't you stay a few days? You're just what I need, Ben, because I—I have a fine position here, but I—well, Dad left when I was such a baby and I never had a chance to talk to him and I still feel—kind of temporary about myself.

BEN I'll be late for my train.

[*They are at opposite ends of the stage.*]

WILLY Ben, my boys—can't we talk? They'd go into the jaws of hell for me, see, but I . . .

BEN William, you're being first-rate with your boys. Outstanding, manly chaps!

WILLY [*Hanging on to his words.*] Oh, Ben, that's good to hear! Because sometimes I'm afraid that I'm not teaching them the right kind of—Ben, how should I teach them?

BEN [*Giving great weight to each word, and with a certain vicious audacity.*] William, when I walked into the jungle, I was seventeen. When I walked out I was twenty-one. And, by God, I was rich! [*He goes off into darkness around the right corner of the house.*]

WILLY . . . was rich! That's just the spirit I want to imbue them with! To walk into a jungle! I was right! I was right! I was right!

[BEN *is gone, but* WILLY *is still speaking to him as* LINDA, *in nightgown and robe, enters the kitchen, glances around for* WILLY, *then goes to the door of the house, looks out and sees him. Comes down to his left. He looks at her.*]

LINDA Willy, dear? Willy?

WILLY I was right!

LINDA Did you have some cheese? [*He can't answer.*] It's very late, darling. Come to bed, heh?

WILLY [*Looking straight up.*] Gotta break your neck to see a star in this yard.

LINDA   You coming in?

WILLY   Whatever happened to that diamond watch fob? Remember? When Ben came from Africa that time? Didn't he give me a watch fob with a diamond in it?

LINDA   You pawned it, dear. Twelve, thirteen years ago. For Biff's radio correspondence course.

WILLY   Gee, that was a beautiful thing. I'll take a walk.

LINDA   But you're in your slippers.

WILLY   [Starting to go around the house at the left.]   I was right! I was! [Half to LINDA, as he goes, shaking his head.]   What a man! There was a man worth talking to. I was right!

LINDA   [Calling after WILLY.]   But in your slippers, Willy!

[WILLY is almost gone when BIFF, in his pajamas, comes down the stairs and enters the kitchen.]

BIFF   What is he doing out there?

LINDA   Sh!

BIFF   God Almighty, Mom, how long has he been doing this?

LINDA   Don't, he'll hear you.

BIFF   What the hell is the matter with him?

LINDA   It'll pass by morning.

BIFF   Shouldn't we do anything?

LINDA   Oh, my dear, you should do a lot of things, but there's nothing to do, so go to sleep.

[HAPPY comes down the stair and sits on the steps.]

HAPPY   I never heard him so loud, Mom.

LINDA   Well, come around more often; you'll hear him. [She sits down at the table and mends the lining of WILLY's jacket.]

BIFF   Why didn't you ever write me about this, Mom?

LINDA   How would I write to you? For over three months you had no address.

BIFF   I was on the move. But you know I thought of you all the time. You know that, don't you, pal?

LINDA   I know, dear, I know. But he likes to have a letter. Just to know that there's still a possibility for better things.

BIFF   He's not like this all the time, is he?

LINDA   It's when you come home he's always the worst.

BIFF   When I come home?

LINDA   When you write you're coming, he's all smiles, and talks about the future, and—he's just wonderful. And then the closer you seem to come, the more shaky he gets, and then, by the time you get here, he's arguing, and he seems angry at you. I think it's just that maybe he can't bring himself to—to open up to you. Why are you so hateful to each other? Why is that?

BIFF   [*Evasively.*]   I'm not hateful, Mom.

LINDA   But you no sooner come in the door than you're fighting!

BIFF   I don't know why. I mean to change. I'm tryin', Mom, you understand?

LINDA   Are you home to stay now?

BIFF   I don't know. I want to look around, see what's doin'.

LINDA   Biff, you can't look around all your life, can you?

BIFF   I just can't take hold, Mom. I can't take hold of some kind of a life.

LINDA   Biff, a man is not a bird, to come and go with the springtime.

BIFF   Your hair . . . [*He touches her hair.*]   Your hair got so gray.

LINDA   Oh, it's been gray since you were in high school. I just stopped dyeing it, that's all.

BIFF   Dye it again, will ya? I don't want my pal looking old. [*He smiles.*]

LINDA   You're such a boy! You think you can go away for a year and . . . You've got to get it into your head now that one day you'll knock on this door and there'll be strange people here . . .

BIFF   What are you talking about? You're not even sixty, Mom.

LINDA   But what about your father?

BIFF   [*Lamely.*]   Well, I meant him too.

HAPPY   He admires Pop.

LINDA   Biff, dear, if you don't have any feeling for him, then you can't have any feeling for me.

BIFF   Sure I can, Mom.

LINDA   No. You can't just come to see me, because I love him. [*With a threat, but only a threat, of tears.*]   He's the dearest man in the world to me, and I won't have anyone making him feel unwanted and low and blue. You've got to make up your mind now, darling, there's no leeway any more. Either he's your father and you pay him that respect, or else you're not to come here. I know he's not easy to get along with—nobody knows that better than me—but . . .

WILLY [*From the left, with a laugh.*] Hey, hey, Biffo!

BIFF [*Starting to go out after* WILLY.] What the hell is the matter with him? [*Happy stops him.*]

LINDA Don't—don't go near him!

BIFF Stop making excuses for him! He always, always wiped the floor with you. Never had an ounce of respect for you.

HAPPY He's always had respect for . . .

BIFF What the hell do you know about it?

HAPPY [*Surlily.*] Just don't call him crazy!

BIFF He's got no character—Charley wouldn't do this. Not in his own house—spewing out that vomit from his mind.

HAPPY Charley never had to cope with what he's got to.

BIFF People are worse off than Willy Loman. Believe me, I've seen them!

LINDA Then make Charley your father, Biff. You can't do that, can you? I don't say he's a great man. Willy Loman never made a lot of money. His name was never in the paper. He's not the finest character that ever lived. But he's a human being, and a terrible thing is happening to him. So attention must be paid. He's not to be allowed to fall into his grave like an old dog. Attention, attention must be finally paid to such a person. You called him crazy . . .

BIFF I didn't mean . . .

LINDA No, a lot of people think he's lost his—balance. But you don't have to be very smart to know what his trouble is. The man is exhausted.

HAPPY Sure!

LINDA A small man can be just as exhausted as a great man. He works for a company thirty-six years this March, opens up unheard-of territories to their trademark, and now in his old age they take his salary away.

HAPPY [*Indignantly.*] I didn't know that, Mom.

LINDA You never asked, my dear! Now that you get your spending money someplace else you don't trouble your mind with him.

HAPPY But I gave you money last . . .

LINDA Christmas time, fifty dollars! To fix the hot water it cost ninety-seven fifty! For five weeks he's been on straight commission, like a beginner, an unknown!

BIFF Those ungrateful bastards!

LINDA Are they any worse than his sons? When he brought them business, when he was young, they were glad to see him. But now his old friends, the old buyers that loved him so and always found some order to hand him in a pinch—they're all dead, retired. He used to be able to make six, seven calls a day in Boston. Now he takes his valises out of the car and puts them back and takes them out again and he's exhausted. Instead of walking he talks now. He drives seven hundred miles, and when he gets there no one knows him any more, no one welcomes him. And what goes through a man's mind, driving seven hundred miles home without having earned a cent? Why shouldn't he talk to himself? Why? When he has to go to Charley and borrow fifty dollars a week and pretend to me that it's his pay? How long can that go on? How long? You see what I'm sitting here and waiting for? And you tell me he has no character? The man who never worked a day but for your benefit? When does he get the medal for that? Is this his reward—to turn around at the age of sixty-three and find his sons, who he loved better than his life, one a philandering bum . . .

HAPPY Mom!

LINDA That's all you are, my baby! [*To* BIFF.] And you! What happened to the love you had for him? You were such pals! How you used to talk to him on the phone every night! How lonely he was till he could come home to you!

BIFF All right, Mom. I'll live here in my room, and I'll get a job. I'll keep away from him, that's all.

LINDA No, Biff. You can't stay here and fight all the time.

BIFF He threw me out of this house, remember that.

LINDA   Why did he do that? I never knew why.

BIFF   Because I know he's a fake and he doesn't like anybody around who knows!

LINDA   Why a fake? In what way? What do you mean?

BIFF   Just don't lay it all at my feet. It's between me and him —that's all I have to say. I'll chip in from now on. He'll settle for half my pay check. He'll be all right. I'm going to bed. [*He starts for the stairs.*]

LINDA   He won't be all right.

BIFF   [*Turning on the stairs, furiously.*]   I hate this city and I'll stay here. Now what do you want?

LINDA   He's dying, Biff.

[HAPPY *turns quickly to her, shocked.*]

BIFF   [*After a pause.*]   Why is he dying?

LINDA   He's been trying to kill himself.

BIFF   [*With great horror.*]   How?

LINDA   I live from day to day.

BIFF   What're you talking about?

LINDA   Remember I wrote you that he smashed up the car again? In February?

BIFF   Well?

LINDA   The insurance inspector came. He said that they have evidence. That all these accidents in the last year—weren't—weren't—accidents.

HAPPY   How can they tell that? That's a lie.

LINDA   It seems there's a woman . . . [*She takes a breath as*

⎰ BIFF   [*Sharply but contained.*]   What woman?

⎱ LINDA   [*Simultaneously.*]   . . . and this woman . . .

LINDA   What?

BIFF   Nothing. Go ahead.

LINDA   What did you say?

BIFF   Nothing. I just said what woman?

HAPPY   What about her?

LINDA   Well, it seems she was walking down the road and saw his car. She says that he wasn't driving fast at all, and that he didn't skid. She says he came to that little bridge, and then de-

liberately smashed into the railing, and it was only the shallow-
ness of the water that saved him.

BIFF   Oh, no, he probably just fell asleep again.

LINDA   I don't think he fell asleep.

BIFF   Why not?

LINDA   Last month . . . [*With great difficulty.*]   Oh, boys,
it's so hard to say a thing like this! He's just a big stupid man to
you, but I tell you there's more good in him than in many other
people. [*She chokes, wipes her eyes.*]   I was looking for a fuse.
The lights blew out, and I went down the cellar. And behind the
fuse box—it happened to fall out—was a length of rubber pipe—
just short.

HAPPY   No kidding?

LINDA   There's a little attachment on the end of it. I knew
right away. And sure enough, on the bottom of the water heater
there's a new little nipple on the gas pipe.

HAPPY [*Angrily.*]   That—jerk.

BIFF   Did you have it taken off?

LINDA   I'm—I'm ashamed to. How can I mention it to him?
Every day I go down and take away that little rubber pipe. But,
when he comes home, I put it back where it was. How can I
insult him that way? I don't know what to do. I live from day to
day, boys. I tell you, I know every thought in his mind. It sounds
so old-fashioned and silly, but I tell you he put his whole life
into you and you've turned your backs on him. [*She is bent over
in the chair, weeping, her face in her hands.*]   Biff, I swear to
God! Biff, his life is in your hands!

HAPPY [*To* BIFF.]   How do you like that damned fool!

BIFF [*Kissing her.*]   All right, pal, all right. It's all settled now.
I've been remiss. I know that, Mom. But now I'll stay, and I swear
to you, I'll apply myself. [*Kneeling in front of her, in a fever of
self-reproach.*]   It's just—you see, Mom, I don't fit in business.
Not that I won't try. I'll try, and I'll make good.

HAPPY   Sure you will. The trouble with you in business was
you never tried to please people.

BIFF   I know, I . . .

HAPPY Like when you worked for Harrison's. Bob Harrison said you were tops, and then you go and do some damn fool thing like whistling whole songs in the elevator like a comedian.

BIFF [*Against* HAPPY.] So what? I like to whistle sometimes.

HAPPY You don't raise a guy to a responsible job who whistles in the elevator!

LINDA Well, don't argue about it now.

HAPPY Like when you'd go off and swim in the middle of the day instead of taking the line around.

BIFF [*His resentment rising.*] Well, don't you run off? You take off sometimes, don't you? On a nice summer day?

HAPPY Yeah, but I cover myself!

LINDA Boys!

HAPPY If I'm going to take a fade the boss can call any number where I'm supposed to be and they'll swear to him that I just left. I'll tell you something that I hate to say, Biff, but in the business world some of them think you're crazy.

BIFF [*Angered.*] Screw the business world!

HAPPY All right, screw it! Great, but cover yourself!

LINDA Hap, Hap!

BIFF I don't care what they think! They've laughed at Dad for years, and you know why? Because we don't belong in this nuthouse of a city! We should be mixing cement on some open plain, or—or carpenters. A carpenter is allowed to whistle!

[WILLY *walks in from the entrance of the house, at left.*]

WILLY Even your grandfather was better than a carpenter. [*Pause. They watch him.*] You never grew up. Bernard does not whistle in the elevator, I assure you.

BIFF [*As though to laugh* WILLY *out of it.*] Yeah, but you do, Pop.

WILLY I never in my life whistled in an elevator! And who in the business world thinks I'm crazy?

BIFF I didn't mean it like that, Pop. Now don't make a whole thing out of it, will ya?

WILLY Go back to the West! Be a carpenter, a cowboy, enjoy yourself!

LINDA Willy, he was just saying . . .

WILLY I heard what he said!

HAPPY [*Trying to quiet* WILLY.] Hey, Pop, come on now . . .

WILLY [*Continuing over* HAPPY's *line.*] They laugh at me, heh? Go to Filene's, go to the Hub, go to Slattery's, Boston. Call out the name Willy Loman and see what happens! Big shot!

BIFF All right, Pop.

WILLY Big!

BIFF All right!

WILLY Why do you always insult me?

BIFF I didn't say a word. [*To* LINDA.] Did I say a word?

LINDA He didn't say anything, Willy.

WILLY [*Going to the doorway of the living room.*] All right, good night, good night.

LINDA Willy, dear, he just decided . . .

WILLY [*To* BIFF.] If you get tired hanging around tomorrow, paint the ceiling I put up in the living room.

BIFF I'm leaving early tomorrow.

HAPPY He's going to see Bill Oliver, Pop.

WILLY [*Interestedly.*] Oliver? For what?

BIFF [*With reserve, but trying, trying.*] He always said he'd stake me. I'd like to go into business, so maybe I can take him up on it.

LINDA Isn't that wonderful?

WILLY Don't interrupt. What's wonderful about it? There's fifty men in the City of New York who'd stake him. [*To* BIFF.] Sporting goods?

BIFF I guess so. I know something about it and . . .

WILLY He knows something about it! You know sporting goods better than Spalding, for God's sake! How much is he giving you?

BIFF I don't know, I didn't even see him yet, but . . .

WILLY Then what're you talkin' about?

BIFF [*Getting angry.*] Well, all I said was I'm gonna see him, that's all!

WILLY [*Turning away.*] Ah, you're counting your chickens again.

BIFF [*Starting left for the stairs.*] Oh, Jesus, I'm going to sleep!

WILLY [*Calling after him.*]   Don't curse in this house!

BIFF [*Turning.*]   Since when did you get so clean?

HAPPY [*Trying to stop them.*]   Wait a . . .

WILLY   Don't use that language to me! I won't have it!

HAPPY [*Grabbing* BIFF, *shouts.*]   Wait a minute! I got an idea. I got a feasible idea. Come here, Biff, let's talk this over now, let's talk some sense here. When I was down in Florida last time, I thought of a great idea to sell sporting goods. It just came back to me. You and I, Biff—we have a line, the Loman Line. We train a couple of weeks, and put on a couple of exhibitions, see?

WILLY   That's an idea!

HAPPY   Wait! We form two basketball teams, see? Two water-polo teams. We play each other. It's a million dollars' worth of publicity. Two brothers, see? The Loman Brothers. Displays in the Royal Palms—all the hotels. And banners over the ring and the basketball court: "Loman Brothers." Baby, we could sell sporting goods!

WILLY   That is a one-million-dollar idea!

LINDA   Marvelous!

BIFF   I'm in great shape as far as that's concerned.

HAPPY   And the beauty of it is, Biff, it wouldn't be like a business. We'd be out playin' ball again . . .

BIFF [*Enthused.*]   Yeah, that's . . .

WILLY   Million-dollar . . .

HAPPY   And you wouldn't get fed up with it, Biff. It'd be the family again. There'd be the old honor, and comradeship, and if you wanted to go off for a swim or somethin'—well, you'd do it! Without some smart cooky gettin' up ahead of you!

WILLY   Lick the world! You guys together could absolutely lick the civilized world.

BIFF   I'll see Oliver tomorrow. Hap, if we could work that out . . .

LINDA   Maybe things are beginning to . . .

WILLY [*Wildly enthused, to* LINDA.]   Stop interrupting! [*To* BIFF.]   But don't wear sport jacket and slacks when you see Oliver.

BIFF No, I'll . . .

WILLY A business suit, and talk as little as possible, and don't crack any jokes.

BIFF He did like me. Always liked me.

LINDA He loved you!

WILLY [*To* LINDA.] Will you stop! [*To* BIFF.] Walk in very serious. You are not applying for a boy's job. Money is to pass. Be quiet, fine, and serious. Everybody likes a kidder, but nobody lends him money.

HAPPY I'll try to get some myself, Biff. I'm sure I can.

WILLY I see great things for you kids, I think your troubles are over. But remember, start big and you'll end big. Ask for fifteen. How much you gonna ask for?

BIFF Gee, I don't know . . .

WILLY And don't say "Gee." "Gee" is a boy's word. A man walking in for fifteen thousand dollars does not say "Gee!"

BIFF Ten, I think, would be top though.

WILLY Don't be so modest. You always started too low. Walk in with a big laugh. Don't look worried. Start off with a couple of your good stories to lighten things up. It's not what you say, it's how you say it—because personality always wins the day.

LINDA Oliver always thought the highest of him . . .

WILLY Will you let me talk?

BIFF Don't yell at her, Pop, will ya?

WILLY [*Angrily.*] I was talking, wasn't I?

BIFF I don't like you yelling at her all the time, and I'm tellin' you, that's all.

WILLY What're you, takin' over this house?

LINDA Willy . . .

WILLY [*Turning to her.*] Don't take his side all the time, god-dammit!

BIFF [*Furiously.*] Stop yelling at her!

WILLY [*Suddenly pulling on his cheek, beaten down, guilt ridden.*] Give my best to Bill Oliver—he may remember me. [*He exits through the living room doorway.*]

LINDA [*Her voice subdued.*] What'd you have to start that for?

[BIFF *turns away.*] You see how sweet he was as soon as you talked hopefully? [*She goes over to* BIFF.] Come up and say good night to him. Don't let him go to bed that way.

HAPPY Come on, Biff, let's buck him up.

LINDA Please, dear. Just say good night. It takes so little to make him happy. Come. [*She goes through the living room doorway, calling upstairs from within the living room.*] Your pajamas are hanging in the bathroom, Willy!

HAPPY [*Looking toward where* LINDA *went out.*] What a woman! They broke the mold when they made her. You know that, Biff?

BIFF He's off salary. My God, working on commission!

HAPPY Well, let's face it: he's no hot-shot selling man. Except that sometimes, you have to admit, he's a sweet personality.

BIFF [*Deciding.*] Lend me ten bucks, will ya? I want to buy some new ties.

HAPPY I'll take you to a place I know. Beautiful stuff. Wear one of my striped shirts tomorrow.

BIFF She got gray. Mom got awful old. Gee, I'm gonna go in to Oliver tomorrow and knock him for a . . .

HAPPY Come on up. Tell that to Dad. Let's give him a whirl. Come on.

BIFF [*Steamed up.*] You know, with ten thousand bucks, boy!

HAPPY [*As they go into the living room.*] That's the talk, Biff, that's the first time I've heard the old confidence out of you! [*From within the living room, fading off.*] You're gonna live with me, kid, and any babe you want just say the word . . . [*The last lines are hardly heard. They are mounting the stairs to their parents' bedroom.*]

LINDA [*Entering her bedroom and addressing* WILLY, *who is in the bathroom. She is straightening the bed for him.*] Can you do anything about the shower? It drips.

WILLY [*From the bathroom.*] All of a sudden everything falls to pieces! Goddam plumbing, oughta be sued, those people. I hardly finished putting it in and the thing . . . [*His words rumble off.*]

LINDA I'm just wondering if Oliver will remember him. You think he might?

WILLY [*Coming out of the bathroom in his pajamas.*] Remember him? What's the matter with you, you crazy? If he'd've stayed with Oliver he'd be on top by now! Wait'll Oliver gets a look at him. You don't know the average caliber any more. The average young man today—[*he is getting into bed*]—is got a caliber of zero. Greatest thing in the world for him was to bum around.

[BIFF *and* HAPPY *enter the bedroom. Slight pause.*]

WILLY [*Stops short, looking at* BIFF.] Glad to hear it, boy.

HAPPY He wanted to say good night to you, sport.

WILLY [*To* BIFF.] Yeah. Knock him dead, boy. What'd you want to tell me?

BIFF Just take it easy, Pop. Good night. [*He turns to go.*]

WILLY [*Unable to resist.*] And if anything falls off the desk while you're talking to him—like a package or something—don't you pick it up. They have office boys for that.

LINDA I'll make a big breakfast . . .

WILLY Will you let me finish? [*To* BIFF.] Tell him you were in the business in the West. Not farm work.

BIFF All right, Dad.

LINDA I think everything . . .

WILLY [*Going right through her speech.*] And don't undersell yourself. No less than fifteen thousand dollars.

BIFF [*Unable to bear him.*] Okay. Good night, Mom. [*He starts moving.*]

WILLY Because you got a greatness in you, Biff, remember that. You got all kinds a greatness . . . [*He lies back, exhausted.* BIFF *walks out.*]

LINDA [*Calling after* BIFF.] Sleep well, darling!

HAPPY I'm gonna get married, Mom. I wanted to tell you.

LINDA Go to sleep, dear.

HAPPY [*Going.*] I just wanted to tell you.

WILLY Keep up the good work. [HAPPY *exits.*] God . . . remember that Ebbets Field game? The championship of the city?

LINDA Just rest. Should I sing to you?

WILLY   Yeah. Sing to me. [LINDA *hums a soft lullaby.*]   When that team came out—he was the tallest, remember?

LINDA   Oh, yes. And in gold.

[BIFF *enters the darkened kitchen, takes a cigarette, and leaves the house. He comes downstage into a golden pool of light. He smokes, staring at the night.*]

WILLY   Like a young god. Hercules—something like that. And the sun, the sun all around him. Remember how he waved to me? Right up from the field, with the representatives of three colleges standing by? And the buyers I brought, and the cheers when he came out—Loman, Loman, Loman! God Almighty, he'll be great yet. A star like that, magnificent, can never really fade away!

[*The light on* WILLY *is fading. The gas heater begins to glow through the kitchen wall, near the stairs, a blue flame beneath red coils.*]

LINDA   [*Timidly.*]   Willy dear, what has he got against you?

WILLY   I'm so tired. Don't talk any more.

[BIFF *slowly returns to the kitchen. He stops, stares toward the heater.*]

LINDA   Will you ask Howard to let you work in New York?

WILLY   First thing in the morning. Everything'll be all right.

[BIFF *reaches behind the heater and draws out a length of rubber tubing. He is horrified and turns his head toward* WILLY'S *room, still dimly lit, from which the strains of* LINDA'S *desperate but monotonous humming rise.*]

WILLY   [*Staring through the window into the moonlight.*]   Gee, look at the moon moving between the buildings!

[BIFF *wraps the tubing around his hand and quickly goes up the stairs.*]

ACT II

ʒʒʒʒʒʒʒʒʒʒʒʒʒʒʒʒʒʒʒʒʒʒʒʒʒʒʒ

SCENE: *Music is heard, gay and bright. The curtain rises as the music fades away.* WILLY, *in shirt sleeves, is sitting at the kitchen table, sipping coffee, his hat in his lap.* LINDA *is filling his cup when she can.*

WILLY   Wonderful coffee. Meal in itself.

LINDA   Can I make you some eggs?

WILLY   No. Take a breath.

LINDA   You look so rested, dear.

WILLY   I slept like a dead one. First time in months. Imagine, sleeping till ten on a Tuesday morning. Boys left nice and early, heh?

LINDA   They were out of here by eight o'clock.

WILLY   Good work!

LINDA   It was so thrilling to see them leaving together. I can't get over the shaving lotion in this house!

WILLY   [*Smiling.*] Mmm . . .

LINDA   Biff was very changed this morning. His whole attitude seemed to be hopeful. He couldn't wait to get downtown to see Oliver.

WILLY   He's heading for a change. There's no question, there simply are certain men that take longer to get—solidified. How did he dress?

LINDA   His blue suit. He's so handsome in that suit. He could be a—anything in that suit!

[WILLY *gets up from the table.* LINDA *holds his jacket for him.*]

WILLY   There's no question, no question at all. Gee, on the way home tonight I'd like to buy some seeds.

LINDA   [*Laughing.*] That'd be wonderful. But not enough sun gets back there. Nothing'll grow any more.

WILLY You wait, kid, before it's all over we're gonna get a little place out in the country, and I'll raise some vegetables, a couple of chickens . . .

LINDA You'll do it yet, dear.

[WILLY *walks out of his jacket.* LINDA *follows him.*]

WILLY And they'll get married, and come for a weekend. I'd build a little guest house. 'Cause I got so many fine tools, all I'd need would be a little lumber and some peace of mind.

LINDA [*Joyfully.*] I sewed the lining . . .

WILLY I could build two guest houses, so they'd both come. Did he decide how much he's going to ask Oliver for?

LINDA [*Getting him into the jacket.*] He didn't mention it, but I imagine ten or fifteen thousand. You going to talk to Howard today?

WILLY Yeah. I'll put it to him straight and simple. He'll just have to take me off the road.

LINDA And Willy, don't forget to ask for a little advance, because we've got the insurance premium. It's the grace period now.

WILLY That's a hundred . . . ?

LINDA A hundred and eight, sixty-eight. Because we're a little short again.

WILLY Why are we short?

LINDA Well, you had the motor job on the car . . .

WILLY That goddam Studebaker!

LINDA And you got one more payment on the refrigerator . . .

WILLY But it just broke again!

LINDA Well, it's old, dear.

WILLY I told you we should've bought a well-advertised machine. Charley bought a General Electric and it's twenty years old and it's still good, that son-of-a-bitch.

LINDA But, Willy . . .

WILLY Whoever heard of a Hastings refrigerator? Once in my life I would like to own something outright before it's broken! I'm always in a race with the junkyard! I just finished paying for the car and it's on its last legs. The refrigerator consumes belts like a goddam maniac. They time those things. They time them so when you finally paid for them, they're used up.

LINDA [*Buttoning up his jacket as he unbuttons it.*]   All told, about two hundred dollars would carry us, dear. But that includes the last payment on the mortgage. After this payment, Willy, the house belongs to us.

WILLY   It's twenty-five years!

LINDA   Biff was nine years old when we bought it.

WILLY   Well, that's a great thing. To weather a twenty-five year mortgage is . . .

LINDA   It's an accomplishment.

WILLY   All the cement, the lumber, the reconstruction I put in this house! There ain't a crack to be found in it any more.

LINDA   Well, it served its purpose.

WILLY   What purpose? Some stranger'll come along, move in, and that's that. If only Biff would take this house, and raise a family . . . [*He starts to go.*]   Good-by, I'm late.

LINDA [*Suddenly remembering.*]   Oh, I forgot! You're supposed to meet them for dinner.

WILLY   Me?

LINDA   At Frank's Chop House on Forty-eighth near Sixth Avenue.

WILLY   Is that so! How about you?

LINDA   No, just the three of you. They're gonna blow you to a big meal!

WILLY   Don't say! Who thought of that?

LINDA   Biff came to me this morning, Willy, and he said, "Tell Dad, we want to blow him to a big meal." Be there six o'clock. You and your two boys are going to have dinner.

WILLY   Gee whiz! That's really somethin'. I'm gonna knock Howard for a loop, kid. I'll get an advance, and I'll come home with a New York job. Goddammit, now I'm gonna do it!

LINDA   Oh, that's the spirit, Willy!

WILLY   I will never get behind a wheel the rest of my life!

LINDA   It's changing, Willy, I can feel it changing!

WILLY   Beyond a question. G'by, I'm late. [*He starts to go again.*]

LINDA [*Calling after him as she runs to the kitchen table for a handkerchief.*]   You got your glasses?

WILLY [*Feels for them, then comes back in.*]   Yeah, yeah, got my glasses.

LINDA [*Giving him the handkerchief.*]   And a handkerchief.

WILLY   Yeah, handkerchief.

LINDA   And your saccharine?

WILLY   Yeah, my saccharine.

LINDA   Be careful on the subway stairs.

[*She kisses him, and a silk stocking is seen hanging from her hand. Willy notices it.*]

WILLY   Will you stop mending stockings? At least while I'm in the house. It gets me nervous. I can't tell you. Please.

[LINDA *hides the stocking in her hand as she follows* WILLY *across the forestage in front of the house.*]

LINDA   Remember, Frank's Chop House.

WILLY [*Passing the apron.*]   Maybe beets would grow out there.

LINDA [*Laughing.*]   But you tried so many times.

WILLY   Yeah. Well, don't work hard today. [*He disappears around the right corner of the house.*]

LINDA   Be careful!

[*As* WILLY *vanishes,* LINDA *waves to him. Suddenly the phone rings. She runs across the stage and into the kitchen and lifts it.*]

LINDA   Hello? Oh, Biff! I'm so glad you called, I just . . . Yes, sure, I just told him. Yes, he'll be there for dinner at six o'clock, I didn't forget. Listen, I was just dying to tell you. You know that little rubber pipe I told you about? That he connected to the gas heater? I finally decided to go down the cellar this morning and take it away and destroy it. But it's gone! Imagine? He took it away himself, it isn't there! [*She listens.*]   When? Oh, then you took it. Oh—nothing, it's just that I'd hoped he'd taken it away himself. Oh, I'm not worried, darling, because this morning he left in such high spirits, it was like the old days! I'm not afraid any more. Did Mr. Oliver see you? . . . Well, you wait there then. And make a nice impression on him, darling. Just don't perspire too much before you see him. And have a nice time with Dad. He may have big news too! . . . That's right, a New

York job. And be sweet to him tonight, dear. Be loving to him. Because he's only a little boat looking for a harbor. [*She is trembling with sorrow and joy.*] Oh, that's wonderful, Biff, you'll save his life. Thanks, darling. Just put your arm around him when he comes into the restaurant. Give him a smile. That's the boy . . . Good-by, dear. . . . You got your comb? . . . That's fine. Good-by, Biff dear.

[*In the middle of her speech,* HOWARD WAGNER, *thirty-six, wheels on a small typewriter table on which is a wire-recording machine and proceeds to plug it in. This is on the left forestage. Light slowly fades on* LINDA *as it rises on* HOWARD. HOWARD *is intent on threading the machine and only glances over his shoulder as* WILLY *appears.*]

WILLY   Pst! Pst!

HOWARD   Hello, Willy, come in.

WILLY   Like to have a little talk with you, Howard.

HOWARD   Sorry to keep you waiting. I'll be with you in a minute.

WILLY   What's that, Howard?

HOWARD   Didn't you ever see one of these? Wire recorder.

WILLY   Oh. Can we talk a minute?

HOWARD   Records things. Just got delivery yesterday. Been driving me crazy, the most terrific machine I ever saw in my life. I was up all night with it.

WILLY   What do you do with it?

HOWARD   I bought it for dictation, but you can do anything with it. Listen to this. I had it home last night. Listen to what I picked up. The first one is my daughter. Get this. [*He flicks the switch and "Roll out the Barrel" is heard being whistled.*] Listen to that kid whistle.

WILLY   That is lifelike, isn't it?

HOWARD   Seven years old. Get that tone.

WILLY   Ts, ts. Like to ask a little favor if you . . .

[*The whistling breaks off, and the voice of* HOWARD's *daughter is heard.*]

HIS DAUGHTER "Now you, Daddy."

HOWARD She's crazy for me! [*Again the same song is whistled.*] That's me! Ha! [*He winks.*]

WILLY You're very good!

[*The whistling breaks off again. The machine runs silent for a moment.*]

HOWARD Sh! Get this now, this is my son.

HIS SON "The capital of Alabama is Montgomery; the capital of Arizona is Phoenix; the capital of Arkansas is Little Rock; the capital of California is Sacramento . . ." [*and on, and on.*]

HOWARD [*Holding up five fingers.*] Five years old, Willy!

WILLY He'll make an announcer some day!

HIS SON [*Continuing.*] "The capital . . ."

HOWARD Get that—alphabetical order! [*The machine breaks off suddenly.*] Wait a minute. The maid kicked the plug out.

WILLY It certainly is a . . .

HOWARD Sh, for God's sake!

HIS SON "It's nine o'clock, Bulova watch time. So I have to go to sleep."

WILLY That really is . . .

HOWARD Wait a minute! The next is my wife.

[*They wait.*]

HOWARD'S VOICE "Go on, say something." [*Pause.*] "Well, you gonna talk?"

HIS WIFE "I can't think of anything."

HOWARD'S VOICE "Well, talk—it's turning."

HIS WIFE [*Shyly, beaten.*] "Hello." [*Silence.*] "Oh, Howard, I can't talk into this . . ."

HOWARD [*Snapping the machine off.*] That was my wife.

WILLY That is a wonderful machine. Can we . . .

HOWARD I tell you, Willy, I'm gonna take my camera, and my bandsaw, and all my hobbies, and out they go. This is the most fascinating relaxation I ever found.

WILLY I think I'll get one myself.

HOWARD Sure, they're only a hundred and a half. You can't do without it. Supposing you wanna hear Jack Benny, see? But you can't be at home at that hour. So you tell the maid to turn the radio on when Jack Benny comes on, and this automatically goes on with the radio . . .

WILLY And when you come home you . . .

HOWARD You can come home twelve o'clock, one o'clock, any time you like, and you get yourself a Coke and sit yourself down, throw the switch, and there's Jack Benny's program in the middle of the night!

WILLY I'm definitely going to get one. Because lots of times I'm on the road, and I think to myself, what I must be missing on the radio!

HOWARD Don't you have a radio in the car?

WILLY Well, yeah, but who ever thinks of turning it on?

HOWARD Say, aren't you supposed to be in Boston?

WILLY That's what I want to talk to you about, Howard. You got a minute? [He draws a chair in from the wing.]

HOWARD What happened? What're you doing here?

WILLY Well . . .

HOWARD You didn't crack up again, did you?

WILLY Oh, no. No . . .

HOWARD Geez, you had me worried there for a minute. What's the trouble?

WILLY Well, tell you the truth, Howard. I've come to the decision that I'd rather not travel any more.

HOWARD Not travel! Well, what'll you do?

WILLY Remember, Christmas time, when you had the party here? You said you'd try to think of some spot for me here in town.

HOWARD With us?

WILLY Well, sure.

HOWARD Oh, yeah, yeah. I remember. Well, I couldn't think of anything for you, Willy.

WILLY I tell ya, Howard. The kids are all grown up, y'know. I don't need much any more. If I could take home—well, sixty-five dollars a week, I could swing it.

HOWARD Yeah, but Willy, see I . . .

WILLY I tell ya why, Howard. Speaking frankly and between the two of us, y'know—I'm just a little tired.

HOWARD   Oh, I could understand that, Willy. But you're a road man, Willy, and we do a road business. We've only got a half-dozen salesmen on the floor here.

WILLY   God knows, Howard, I never asked a favor of any man. But I was with the firm when your father used to carry you in here in his arms.

HOWARD   I know that, Willy, but . . .

WILLY   Your father came to me the day you were born and asked me what I thought of the name of Howard, may he rest in peace.

HOWARD   I appreciate that, Willy, but there just is no spot here for you. If I had a spot I'd slam you right in, but I just don't have a single solitary spot.

[*He looks for his lighter.* WILLY *has picked it up and gives it to him. Pause.*]

WILLY   [*With increasing anger.*]   Howard, all I need to set my table is fifty dollars a week.

HOWARD   But where am I going to put you, kid?

WILLY   Look, it isn't a question of whether I can sell merchandise, is it?

HOWARD   No, but it's a business, kid, and everybody's gotta pull his own weight.

WILLY   [*Desperately.*]   Just let me tell you a story, Howard . . .

HOWARD   'Cause you gotta admit, business is business.

WILLY   [*Angrily.*]   Business is definitely business, but just listen for a minute. You don't understand this. When I was a boy— eighteen, nineteen—I was already on the road. And there was a question in my mind as to whether selling had a future for me. Because in those days I had a yearning to go to Alaska. See, there were three gold strikes in one month in Alaska, and I felt like going out. Just for the ride, you might say.

HOWARD   [*Barely interested.*]   Don't say.

WILLY   Oh, yeah, my father lived many years in Alaska. He was an adventurous man. We've got quite a little streak of self-reliance in our family. I thought I'd go out with my older brother and try to locate him, and maybe settle in the North with the old man. And I was almost decided to go, when I met a salesman in the Parker House. His name was Dave Singleman. And he was eighty-four years old, and he'd drummed merchandise in thirty-one states. And old Dave, he'd go up to his room, y'understand, put on his green velvet slippers—I'll never forget—and pick up his phone and call the buyers, and without ever leaving his room, at the age of eighty-four, he made his living. And when I saw that, I realized that selling was the greatest career a man could want. 'Cause what could be more satisfying than to be able to go, at the age of eighty-four, into twenty or thirty different cities, and pick up a phone, and be remembered and loved and helped by so many different people? Do you know? when he died—and by the way he died the death of a salesman, in his green velvet slippers in the smoker of the New York, New Haven and Hartford, going into Boston—when he died, hundreds of salesmen and buyers were at his funeral. Things were sad on a lotta trains for months after that. [*He stands up. Howard has not looked at him.*] In those days there was personality in it, Howard. There was respect, and comradeship, and gratitude in it. Today, it's all cut and dried, and there's no chance for bringing friendship to bear —or personality. You see what I mean? They don't know me any more.

HOWARD [*Moving away, to the right.*] That's just the thing, Willy.

WILLY If I had forty dollars a week—that's all I'd need. Forty dollars, Howard.

HOWARD Kid, I can't take blood from a stone, I . . .

WILLY [*Desperation is on him now.*] Howard, the year Al Smith was nominated, your father came to me and . . .

HOWARD [*Starting to go off.*] I've got to see some people, kid.

WILLY [*Stopping him.*] I'm talking about your father! There were promises made across this desk! You mustn't tell me you've got people to see—I put thirty-four years into this firm, Howard, and now I can't pay my insurance! You can't eat the orange and throw the peel away—a man is not a piece of fruit! [*After a pause.*] Now pay attention. Your father—in 1928 I had a big year. I averaged a hundred and seventy dollars a week in commissions.

HOWARD [*Impatiently.*]   Now, Willy, you never averaged . . .

WILLY [*Banging his hand on the desk.*]   I averaged a hundred and seventy dollars a week in the year of 1928! And your father came to me—or rather, I was in the office here—it was right over this desk—and he put his hand on my shoulder . . .

HOWARD [*Getting up.*]   You'll have to excuse me, Willy, I gotta see some people. Pull yourself together. [*Going out.*]   I'll be back in a little while.

[*On* HOWARD'S *exit, the light on his chair grows very bright and strange.*]

WILLY   Pull myself together! What the hell did I say to him? My God, I was yelling at him! How could I! [WILLY *breaks off, staring at the light, which occupies the chair, animating it. He approaches this chair, standing across the desk from it.*]   Frank, Frank, don't you remember what you told me that time? How you put your hand on my shoulder, and Frank . . . [*He leans on the desk and as he speaks the dead man's name he accidentally switches on the recorder, and instantly*]

HOWARD'S SON   ". . . of New York is Albany. The capital of Ohio is Cincinnati, the capital of Rhode Island is . . ." [*The recitation continues.*]

WILLY [*Leaping away with fright, shouting.*]   Ha! Howard! Howard! Howard!

HOWARD [*Rushing in.*]   What happened?

WILLY [*Pointing at the machine, which continues nasally, childishly, with the capital cities.*]   Shut it off! Shut it off!

HOWARD [*Pulling the plug out.*]   Look, Willy . . .

WILLY [*Pressing his hands to his eyes.*]   I gotta get myself some coffee. I'll get some coffee . . .

[WILLY *starts to walk out.* HOWARD *stops him.*]

HOWARD [*Rolling up the cord.*]   Willy, look . . .

WILLY   I'll go to Boston.

HOWARD   Willy, you can't go to Boston for us.

WILLY   Why can't I go?

HOWARD   I don't want you to represent us. I've been meaning to tell you for a long time now.

WILLY   Howard, are you firing me?

HOWARD   I think you need a good long rest, Willy.

WILLY   Howard . . .

HOWARD   And when you feel better, come back, and we'll see if we can work something out.

WILLY   But I gotta earn money, Howard. I'm in no position to . . .

HOWARD   Where are your sons? Why don't your sons give you a hand?

WILLY   They're working on a very big deal.

HOWARD   This is no time for false pride, Willy. You go to your sons and you tell them that you're tired. You've got two great boys, haven't you?

WILLY   Oh, no question, no question, but in the meantime . . .

HOWARD   Then that's that, heh?

WILLY   All right, I'll go to Boston tomorrow.

HOWARD   No, no.

WILLY   I can't throw myself on my sons. I'm not a cripple!

HOWARD   Look, kid, I'm busy this morning.

WILLY   [*Grasping* HOWARD's *arm*.]   Howard, you've got to let me go to Boston!

HOWARD   [*Hard, keeping himself under control*.]   I've got a line of people to see this morning. Sit down, take five minutes, and pull yourself together, and then go home, will ya? I need the office, Willy. [*He starts to go, turns, remembering the recorder, starts to push off the table holding the recorder*.]   Oh, yeah. Whenever you can this week, stop by and drop off the samples. You'll feel better, Willy, and then come back and we'll talk. Pull yourself together, kid, there's people outside.

[HOWARD *exits, pushing the table off left*. WILLY *stares into space, exhausted. Now the music is heard*—BEN's *music*—*first distantly, then closer, closer. As* WILLY *speaks,* BEN *enters from the right. He carries valise and umbrella.*]

WILLY   Oh, Ben, how did you do it? What is the answer? Did you wind up the Alaska deal already?

BEN   Doesn't take much time if you know what you're doing. Just a short business trip. Boarding ship in an hour. Wanted to say good-by.

WILLY   Ben, I've got to talk to you.

BEN   [*Glancing at his watch.*]   Haven't the time, William.

WILLY   [*Crossing the apron to* BEN.]   Ben, nothing's working out. I don't know what to do.

BEN   Now, look here, William. I've bought timberland in Alaska and I need a man to look after things for me.

WILLY   God, timberland! Me and my boys in those grand outdoors!

BEN   You've a new continent at your doorstep, William. Get out of these cities, they're full of talk and time payments and courts of law. Screw on your fists and you can fight for a fortune up there.

WILLY   Yes, yes! Linda, Linda!

[LINDA *enters as of old, with the wash.*]

LINDA   Oh, you're back?

BEN   I haven't much time.

WILLY   No, wait! Linda, he's got a proposition for me in Alaska.

LINDA   But you've got . . . [*To* BEN.]   He's got a beautiful job here.

WILLY   But in Alaska, kid, I could . . .

LINDA   You're doing well enough, Willy!

BEN   [*To* LINDA.]   Enough for what, my dear?

LINDA   [*Frightened of* BEN *and angry at him.*]   Don't say those things to him! Enough to be happy right here, right now. [*To* WILLY, *while* BEN *laughs.*]   Why must everybody conquer the world? You're well liked, and the boys love you, and someday— [*To* BEN]—why, old man Wagner told him just the other day that if he keeps it up he'll be a member of the firm, didn't he, Willy?

WILLY   Sure, sure. I am building something with this firm, Ben, and if a man is building something he must be on the right track, mustn't he?

BEN   What are you building? Lay your hand on it. Where is it?

WILLY   [*Hesitantly.*]   That's true, Linda, there's nothing.

LINDA Why? [*To* BEN.] There's a man eighty-four years old . . .

WILLY That's right, Ben, that's right. When I look at that man I say, what is there to worry about?

BEN Bah!

WILLY It's true, Ben. All he has to do is go into any city, pick up the phone, and he's making his living and you know why?

BEN [*Picking up his valise.*] I've got to go.

WILLY [*Holding* BEN *back.*] Look at this boy!

[BIFF, *in his high school sweater, enters carrying suitcase.* HAPPY *carries* BIFF's *shoulder guards, gold helmet, and football pants.*]

WILLY Without a penny to his name, three great universities are begging for him, and from there the sky's the limit, because it's not what you do, Ben. It's who you know and the smile on your face! It's contacts, Ben, contacts! The whole wealth of Alaska passes over the lunch table at the Commodore Hotel, and that's the wonder, the wonder of this country, that a man can end with diamonds here on the basis of being liked! [*He turns to* BIFF.] And that's why when you get out on that field today it's important. Because thousands of people will be rooting for you and loving you. [*To* BEN, *who has again begun to leave.*] And Ben! when he walks into a business office his name will sound out like a bell and all the doors will open to him! I've seen it, Ben, I've seen it a thousand times! You can't feel it with your hand like timber, but it's there!

BEN Good-by, William.

WILLY Ben, am I right? Don't you think I'm right? I value your advice.

BEN There's a new continent at your doorstep, William. You could talk out rich. Rich! [*He is gone.*]

WILLY We'll do it here, Ben! You hear me? We're gonna do it here!

[YOUNG BERNARD *rushes in. The gay music of the* BOYS *is heard.*]

BERNARD Oh, gee, I was afraid you left already!

WILLY Why? What time is it?

BERNARD It's half-past one!

WILLY Well, come on, everybody! Ebbets Field next stop! Where's the pennants? [*He rushes through the wall-line of the kitchen and out into the living room.*]

LINDA [*To* BIFF.] Did you pack fresh underwear?

BIFF [*Who has been limbering up.*] I want to go!

BERNARD Biff, I'm carrying your helmet, ain't I?

HAPPY No, I'm carrying the helmet.

BERNARD Oh, Biff, you promised me.

HAPPY I'm carrying the helmet.

BERNARD How am I going to get in the locker room?

LINDA Let him carry the shoulder guards. [*She puts her coat and hat on in the kitchen.*]

BERNARD Can I, Biff? 'Cause I told everybody I'm going to be in the locker room.

HAPPY In Ebbets Field it's the clubhouse.

BERNARD I meant the clubhouse. Biff!

HAPPY Biff!

BIFF [*Grandly, after a slight pause.*] Let him carry the shoulder guards.

HAPPY [*As he gives* BERNARD *the shoulder guards.*] Stay close to us now.

[WILLY *rushes in with the pennants.*]

WILLY [*Handing them out.*] Everybody wave when Biff comes out on the field. [HAPPY *and* BERNARD *run off.*] You set now, boy?

[*The music has died away.*]

BIFF Ready to go, Pop. Every muscle is ready.

WILLY [*At the edge of the apron.*] You realize what this means?

BIFF That's right, Pop.

WILLY [*Feeling* BIFF's *muscles.*] You're comin' home this afternoon captain of the All-Scholastic Championship Team of the City of New York.

BIFF I got it, Pop. And remember, pal, when I take off my helmet, that touchdown is for you.

WILLY Let's go! [*He is starting out, with his arm around* BIFF, *when* CHARLEY *enters, as of old, in knickers.*] I got no room for you, Charley.

CHARLEY Room? For what?

WILLY In the car.

CHARLEY You goin' for a ride? I wanted to shoot some casino.

WILLY [*Furiously.*] Casino! [*Incredulously.*] Don't you realize what today is?

LINDA Oh, he knows, Willy. He's just kidding you.

WILLY That's nothing to kid about!

CHARLEY No, Linda, what's goin' on?

LINDA He's playing in Ebbets Field.

CHARLEY Baseball in this weather?

WILLY Don't talk to him. Come on, come on! [*He is pushing them out.*]

CHARLEY Wait a minute, didn't you hear the news?

WILLY What?

CHARLEY Don't you listen to the radio? Ebbets Field just blew up.

WILLY You go to hell! [CHARLEY *laughs. Pushing them out.*] Come on, come on! We're late.

CHARLEY [*As they go.*] Knock a homer, Biff, knock a homer!

WILLY [*The last to leave, turning to* CHARLEY.] I don't think that was funny, Charley. This is the greatest day of his life.

CHARLEY Willy, when are you going to grow up?

WILLY Yeah, heh? When this game is over, Charley, you'll be laughing out of the other side of your face. They'll be calling him another Red Grange. Twenty-five thousand a year.

CHARLEY [*Kidding.*] Is that so?

WILLY Yeah, that's so.

CHARLEY Well, then, I'm sorry, Willy. But tell me something.

WILLY What?

CHARLEY Who is Red Grange?

WILLY Put up your hands. Goddam you, put up your hands!
[CHARLEY, *chuckling, shakes his head and walks away, around the left corner of the stage.* WILLY *follows him. The music rises to a mocking frenzy.*]

WILLY   Who the hell do you think you are, better than every-body else? You don't know everything, you big, ignorant, stupid . . . Put up your hands!

[*Light rises, on the right side of the forestage, on a small table in the reception room of* CHARLEY'S *office. Traffic sounds are heard.* BERNARD, *now mature, sits whistling to himself. A pair of tennis rackets and an overnight bag are on the floor beside him.*]

WILLY [*Offstage.*]   What are you walking away for? Don't walk away! If you're going to say something say it to my face! I know you laugh at me behind my back. You'll laugh out of the other side of your goddam face after this game. Touchdown! Touchdown! Eighty thousand people! Touchdown! Right between the goal posts.

[BERNARD *is a quiet, earnest, but self-assured young man.* WILLY'S *voice is coming from right upstage now.* BERNARD *lowers his feet off the table and listens.* JENNY, *his father's secretary, enters.*]

JENNY [*Distressed.*]   Say, Bernard, will you go out in the hall?

BERNARD   What is that noise? Who is it?

JENNY   Mr. Loman. He just got off the elevator.

BERNARD [*Getting up.*]   Who's he arguing with?

JENNY   Nobody. There's nobody with him. I can't deal with him any more, and your father gets all upset everytime he comes. I've got a lot of typing to do, and your father's waiting to sign it. Will you see him?

WILLY [*Entering.*]   Touchdown! Touch—[*He sees* JENNY.] Jenny, Jenny, good to see you. How're ya? Workin'? Or still honest?

JENNY   Fine. How've you been feeling?

WILLY   Not much any more, Jenny. Ha, ha! [*He is surprised to see the rackets.*]

BERNARD   Hello, Uncle Willy.

WILLY [*Almost shocked.*]   Bernard! Well, look who's here! [*He comes quickly, guiltily, to* BERNARD *and warmly shakes his hand.*]

BERNARD   How are you? Good to see you.

WILLY   What are you doing here?

BERNARD   Oh, just stopped by to see Pop. Get off my feet till my train leaves. I'm going to Washington in a few minutes.

WILLY   Is he in?

BERNARD   Yes, he's in his office with the accountant. Sit down.

WILLY   [Sitting down.]   What're you going to do in Washington?

BERNARD   Oh, just a case I've got there, Willy.

WILLY   That so? [Indicating the rackets.]   You going to play tennis there?

BERNARD   I'm staying with a friend who's got a court.

WILLY   Don't say. His own tennis court. Must be fine people, I bet.

BERNARD   They are, very nice. Dad tells me Biff's in town.

WILLY   [With a big smile.]   Yeah, Biff's in. Working on a very big deal, Bernard.

BERNARD   What's Biff doing?

WILLY   Well, he's been doing very big things in the West. But he decided to establish himself here. Very big. We're having dinner. Did I hear your wife had a boy?

BERNARD   That's right. Our second.

WILLY   Two boys! What do you know!

BERNARD   What kind of a deal has Biff got?

WILLY   Well, Bill Oliver—very big sporting-goods man—he wants Biff very badly. Called him in from the West. Long distance, carte blanche, special deliveries. Your friends have their own private tennis court?

BERNARD   You still with the old firm, Willy?

WILLY   [After a pause.]   I'm—I'm overjoyed to see how you made the grade, Bernard, overjoyed. It's an encouraging thing to see a young man really—really . . . Looks very good for Biff——very . . . [He breaks off, then.]   Bernard . . . [He is so full of emotion, he breaks off again.]

BERNARD   What is it, Willy?

WILLY   [Small and alone.]   What—what's the secret?

BERNARD   What secret?

WILLY   How—how did you? Why didn't he ever catch on?

BERNARD I wouldn't know that, Willy.

WILLY [*Confidentially, desperately.*] You were his friend, his boyhood friend. There's something I don't understand about it. His life ended after that Ebbets Field game. From the age of seventeen nothing good ever happened to him.

BERNARD He never trained himself for anything.

WILLY But he did, he did. After high school he took so many correspondence courses. Radio mechanics; television; God knows what, and never made the slightest mark.

BERNARD [*Taking off his glasses.*] Willy, do you want to talk candidly?

WILLY [*Rising, faces* BERNARD.] I regard you as a very brilliant man, Bernard. I value your advice.

BERNARD Oh, the hell with the advice, Willy. I couldn't advise you. There's just one thing I've always wanted to ask you. When he was supposed to graduate, and the math teacher flunked him . . .

WILLY Oh, that son-of-a-bitch ruined his life.

BERNARD Yeah, but, Willy, all he had to do was go to summer school and make up that subject.

WILLY That's right, that's right.

BERNARD Did you tell him not to go to summer school?

WILLY Me? I begged him to go. I ordered him to go!

BERNARD Then why wouldn't he go?

WILLY Why? Why! Bernard, that question has been trailing me like a ghost for the last fifteen years. He flunked the subject, and laid down and died like a hammer hit him!

BERNARD Take it easy, kid.

WILLY Let me talk to you—I got nobody to talk to. Bernard, Bernard, was it my fault? Y'see? It keeps going around in my mind, maybe I did something to him. I got nothing to give him.

BERNARD Don't take it so hard.

WILLY Why did he lay down? What is the story there? You were his friend!

BERNARD Willy, I remember, it was June, and our grades came out. And he'd flunked math.

WILLY That son-of-a-bitch!

BERNARD No, it wasn't right then. Biff just got very angry, I remember, and he was ready to enroll in summer school.

WILLY [*Surprised.*] He was?

BERNARD He wasn't beaten by it at all. But then, Willy, he disappeared from the block for almost a month. And I got the idea that he'd gone up to New England to see you. Did he have a talk with you then?

[WILLY *stares in silence.*]

BERNARD Willy?

WILLY [*With a strong edge of resentment in his voice.*] Yeah, he came to Boston. What about it?

BERNARD Well, just that when he came back—I'll never forget this, it always mystifies me. Because I'd thought so well of Biff, even though he'd always taken advantage of me. I loved him, Willy, y'know? And he came back after that month and took his sneakers—remember those sneakers with "University of Virginia" printed on them? He was so proud of those, wore them every day. And he took them down in the cellar, and burned them up in the furnace. We had a fist fight. It lasted at least half an hour. Just the two of us, punching each other down the cellar, and crying right through it. I've often thought of how strange it was that I knew he'd given up his life. What happened in Boston, Willy?

[WILLY *looks at him as at an intruder.*]

BERNARD I just bring it up because you asked me.

WILLY [*Angrily.*] Nothing. What do you mean, "What happened?" What's that got to do with anything?

BERNARD Well, don't get sore.

WILLY What are you trying to do, blame it on me? If a boy lays down is that my fault?

BERNARD Now, Willy, don't get . . .

WILLY Well, don't—don't talk to me that way! What does that mean, "What happened?"

[CHARLEY *enters. He is in his vest, and he carries a bottle of bourbon.*]

CHARLEY Hey, you're going to miss that train. [*He waves the bottle.*]

BERNARD   Yeah, I'm going. [*He takes the bottle.*]   Thanks, Pop. [*He picks up his rackets and bag.*]   Good-by, Willy, and don't worry about it. You know, "If at first you don't succeed . . ."

WILLY   Yes, I believe in that.

BERNARD   But sometimes, Willy, it's better for a man just to walk away.

WILLY   Walk away?

BERNARD   That's right.

WILLY   But if you can't walk away?

BERNARD   [*After a slight pause.*]   I guess that's when it's tough. [*Extending his hand.*]   Good-by, Willy.

WILLY   [*Shaking* BERNARD's *hand.*]   Good-by, boy.

CHARLEY   [*An arm on* BERNARD's *shoulder.*]   How do you like this kid? Gonna argue a case in front of the Supreme Court.

BERNARD   [*Protesting.*]   Pop!

WILLY   [*Genuinely shocked, pained, and happy.*]   No! The Supreme Court!

BERNARD   I gotta run. 'By, Dad!

CHARLEY   Knock 'em dead, Bernard!

[BERNARD *goes off.*]

WILLY   [*As* CHARLEY *takes out his wallet.*]   The Supreme Court! And he didn't even mention it!

CHARLEY   [*Counting out money on the desk.*]   He don't have to—he's gonna do it.

WILLY   And you never told him what to do, did you? You never took any interest in him.

CHARLEY   My salvation is that I never took any interest in anything. There's some money—fifty dollars. I got an accountant inside.

WILLY   Charley, look . . . [*With difficulty.*]   I got my insurance to pay. If you can manage it—I need a hundred and ten dollars.

[CHARLEY *doesn't reply for a moment; merely stops moving.*]

WILLY   I'd draw it from my bank but Linda would know, and I . . .

CHARLEY   Sit down, Willy.

WILLY   [*Moving toward the chair.*]   I'm keeping an account of everything, remember. I'll pay every penny back. [*He sits.*]

CHARLEY Now listen to me, Willy.

WILLY I want you to know I appreciate . . .

CHARLEY [*Sitting down on the table.*] Willy, what're you doin'? What the hell is goin' on in your head?

WILLY Why? I'm simply . . .

CHARLEY I offered you a job. You can make fifty dollars a week. And I won't send you on the road.

WILLY I've got a job.

CHARLEY Without pay? What kind of a job is a job without pay? [*He rises.*] Now, look, kid, enough is enough. I'm no genius but I know when I'm being insulted.

WILLY Insulted!

CHARLEY Why don't you want to work for me?

WILLY What's the matter with you? I've got a job.

CHARLEY Then what're you walkin' in here every week for?

WILLY [*Getting up.*] Well, if you don't want me to walk in here . . .

CHARLEY I'm offering you a job.

WILLY I don't want your goddam job!

CHARLEY When the hell are you going to grow up?

WILLY [*Furiously.*] You big ignoramus, if you say that to me again I'll rap you one! I don't care how big you are! [*He's ready to fight.*]

[*Pause.*]

CHARLEY [*Kindly, going to him.*] How much do you need, Willy?

WILLY Charley, I'm strapped. I'm strapped. I don't know what to do. I was just fired.

CHARLEY Howard fired you?

WILLY That snotnose. Imagine that? I named him. I named him Howard.

CHARLEY Willy, when're you gonna realize that them things don't mean anything? You named him Howard, but you can't sell that. The only thing you got in this world is what you can sell. And the funny thing is that you're a salesman, and you don't know that.

WILLY   I've always tried to think otherwise, I guess. I always felt that if a man was impressive, and well liked, that nothing . . .

CHARLEY   Why must everybody like you? Who liked J. P. Morgan? Was he impressive? In a Turkish bath he'd look like a butcher. But with his pockets on he was very well liked. Now listen, Willy, I know you don't like me, and nobody can say I'm in love with you, but I'll give you a job because—just for the hell of it, put it that way. Now what do you say?

WILLY   I—I just can't work for you, Charley.

CHARLEY   What're you, jealous of me?

WILLY   I can't work for you, that's all, don't ask me why.

CHARLEY   [Angered, takes out more bills.]   You been jealous of me all your life, you damned fool! Here, pay your insurance. [He puts the money in WILLY's hand.]

WILLY   I'm keeping strict accounts.

CHARLEY   I've got some work to do. Take care of yourself. And pay your insurance.

WILLY   [Moving to the right.]   Funny, y'know? After all the highways, and the trains, and the appointments, and the years, you end up worth more dead than alive.

CHARLEY   Willy, nobody's worth nothin' dead. [After a slight pause.]   Did you hear what I said?

[WILLY stands still, dreaming.]

CHARLEY   Willy!

WILLY   Apologize to Bernard for me when you see him. I didn't mean to argue with him. He's a fine boy. They're all fine boys, and they'll end up big—all of them. Someday they'll all play tennis together. Wish me luck, Charley. He saw Bill Oliver today.

CHARLEY   Good luck.

WILLY   [On the verge of tears.]   Charley, you're the only friend I got. Isn't that a remarkable thing? [He goes out.]

CHARLEY   Jesus!

[CHARLEY stares after him a moment and follows. All light blacks out. Suddenly raucous music is heard, and a red glow rises behind *the screen at right.* STANLEY, *a young waiter, appears, carrying a table, followed by* HAPPY, *who is carrying two chairs.*]

STANLEY [*Putting the table down.*] That's all right, Mr. Loman, I can handle it myself. [*He turns and takes the chairs from* HAPPY *and places them at the table.*]

HAPPY [*Glancing around.*] Oh, this is better.

STANLEY Sure, in the front there you're in the middle of all kinds a noise. Whenever you got a party, Mr. Loman, you just tell me and I'll put you back here. Y'know, there's a lotta people they don't like it private, because when they go out they like to see a lotta action around them because they're sick and tired to stay in the house by theirself. But I know you, you ain't from Hackensack. You know what I mean?

HAPPY [*Sitting down.*] So how's it coming, Stanley?

STANLEY Ah, it's a dog's life. I only wish during the war they'd a took me in the Army. I coulda been dead by now.

HAPPY My brother's back, Stanley.

STANLEY Oh, he come back, heh? From the Far West.

HAPPY Yeah, big cattle man, my brother, so treat him right. And my father's coming too.

STANLEY Oh, your father too!

HAPPY You got a couple of nice lobsters?

STANLEY Hundred per cent, big.

HAPPY I want them with the claws.

STANLEY Don't worry, I don't give you no mice. [HAPPY *laughs.*] How about some wine? It'll put a head on the meal.

HAPPY No. You remember, Stanley, that recipe I brought you from overseas? With the champagne in it?

STANLEY Oh, yeah, sure. I still got it tacked up yet in the kitchen. But that'll have to cost a buck apiece anyways.

HAPPY That's all right.

STANLEY What'd you, hit a number or somethin'?

HAPPY No, it's a little celebration. My brother is—I think he pulled off a big deal today. I think we're going into business together.

STANLEY Great! That's the best for you. Because a family business, you know what I mean?—that's the best.

HAPPY That's what I think.

STANLEY 'Cause what's the difference? Somebody steals? It's in the family. Know what I mean? [*Sotto voce.*] Like this bartender here. The boss is goin' crazy what kinda leak he's got in the cash register. You put it in but it don't come out.

HAPPY [*Raising his head.*] Sh!

STANLEY What?

HAPPY You notice I wasn't lookin' right or left, was I?

STANLEY No.

HAPPY And my eyes are closed.

STANLEY So what's the . . . ?

HAPPY Strudel's comin'.

STANLEY [*Catching on, looks around.*] Ah, no, there's no . . . [*He breaks off as a furred, lavishly dressed girl enters and sits at the next table. Both follow her with their eyes.*]

STANLEY Geez, how'd ya know?

HAPPY I got radar or something. [*Staring directly at her profile.*] Oooooooo . . . Stanley.

STANLEY I think that's for you, Mr. Loman.

HAPPY Look at that mouth. Oh, God. And the binoculars.

STANLEY Geez, you got a life, Mr. Loman.

HAPPY Wait on her.

STANLEY [*Going to the girl's table.*] Would you like a menu, ma'am?

GIRL I'm expecting someone, but I'd like a . . .

HAPPY Why don't you bring her—excuse me, miss, do you mind? I sell champagne, and I'd like you to try my brand. Bring her a champagne, Stanley.

GIRL That's awfully nice of you.

HAPPY Don't mention it. It's all company money. [*He laughs.*]

GIRL That's a charming product to be selling, isn't it?

HAPPY Oh, gets to be like everything else. Selling is selling, y'know.

GIRL I suppose.

HAPPY You don't happen to sell, do you?

GIRL   No, I don't sell.

HAPPY   Would you object to a compliment from a stranger? You ought to be on a magazine cover.

GIRL   [*Looking at him a little archly.*]   I have been.

[STANLEY *comes in with a glass of champagne.*]

HAPPY   What'd I say before, Stanley? You see? She's a cover girl.

STANLEY   Oh, I could see, I could see.

HAPPY   [*To the Girl.*]   What magazine?

GIRL   Oh, a lot of them. [*She takes the drink.*]   Thank you.

HAPPY   You know what they say in France, don't you? "Champagne is the drink of the complexion"—Hya, Biff!

[BIFF *has entered and sits with* HAPPY.]

BIFF   Hello, kid. Sorry I'm late.

HAPPY   I just got here. Uh, Miss . . . ?

GIRL   Forsythe.

HAPPY   Miss Forsythe, this is my brother.

BIFF   Is Dad here?

HAPPY   His name is Biff. You might've heard of him. Great football player.

GIRL   Really? What team?

HAPPY   Are you familiar with football?

GIRL   No, I'm afraid I'm not.

HAPPY   Biff is quarterback with the New York Giants.

GIRL   Well, that is nice, isn't it? [*She drinks.*]

HAPPY   Good health.

GIRL   I'm happy to meet you.

HAPPY   That's my name. Hap. It's really Harold, but at West Point they called me Happy.

GIRL   [*Now really impressed.*]   Oh, I see. How do you do? [*She turns her profile.*]

BIFF   Isn't Dad coming?

HAPPY   You want her?

BIFF   Oh, I could never make that.

HAPPY   I remember the time that idea would never come into your head. Where's the old confidence, Biff?

BIFF   I just saw Oliver . . .

HAPPY   Wait a minute. I've got to see that old confidence again. Do you want her? She's on call.

BIFF   Oh, no. [*He turns to look at the* GIRL.]

HAPPY   I'm telling you. Watch this. [*Turning to the* GIRL.] Honey? [*She turns to him.*] Are you busy?

GIRL   Well, I am . . . but I could make a phone call.

HAPPY   Do that, will you, honey? And see if you can get a friend. We'll be here for a while. Biff is one of the greatest football players in the country.

GIRL   [*Standing up.*] Well, I'm certainly happy to meet you.

HAPPY   Come back soon.

GIRL   I'll try.

HAPPY   Don't try, honey, try hard.

[*The* GIRL *exits.* STANLEY *follows, shaking his head in bewildered admiration.*]

HAPPY   Isn't that a shame now? A beautiful girl like that? That's why I can't get married. There's not a good woman in a thousand. New York is loaded with them, kid!

BIFF   Hap, look . . .

HAPPY   I told you she was on call!

BIFF   [*Strangely unnerved.*] Cut it out, will ya? I want to say something to you.

HAPPY   Did you see Oliver?

BIFF   I saw him all right. Now look, I want to tell Dad a couple of things and I want you to help me.

HAPPY   What? Is he going to back you?

BIFF   Are you crazy? You're out of your goddam head, you know that?

HAPPY   Why? What happened?

BIFF   [*Breathlessly.*] I did a terrible thing today, Hap. It's been the strangest day I ever went through. I'm all numb, I swear.

HAPPY   You mean he wouldn't see you?

BIFF   Well, I waited six hours for him, see? All day. Kept sending my name in. Even tried to date his secretary so she'd get me to him, but no soap.

HAPPY   Because you're not showin' the old confidence, Biff. He remembered you, didn't he?

BIFF [*Stopping* HAPPY *with a gesture.*] Finally, about five o'clock, he comes out. Didn't remember who I was or anything. I felt like such an idiot, Hap.

HAPPY   Did you tell him my Florida idea?

BIFF   He walked away. I saw him for one minute. I got so mad I could've torn the walls down! How the hell did I ever get the idea I was a salesman there? I even believed myself that I'd been a salesman for him! And then he gave me one look and—I realized what a ridiculous lie my whole life has been! We've been talking in a dream for fifteen years. I was a shipping clerk.

HAPPY   What'd you do?

BIFF [*With great tension and wonder.*] Well, he left, see. And the secretary went out. I was all alone in the waiting room. I don't know what came over me, Hap. The next thing I know I'm in his office—paneled walls, everything. I can't explain it. I— Hap, I took his fountain pen.

HAPPY   Geez, did he catch you?

BIFF   I ran out. I ran down all eleven flights. I ran and ran and ran.

HAPPY   That was an awful dumb—what'd you do that for?

BIFF [*Agonized.*] I don't know, I just—wanted to take something, I don't know. You gotta help me, Hap, I'm gonna tell Pop.

HAPPY   You crazy? What for?

BIFF   Hap, he's got to understand that I'm not the man somebody lends that kind of money to. He thinks I've been spiting him all these years and it's eating him up.

HAPPY   That's just it. You tell him something nice.

BIFF   I can't.

HAPPY   Say you got a lunch date with Oliver tomorrow.

BIFF   So what do I do tomorrow?

HAPPY   You leave the house tomorrow and come back at night and say Oliver is thinking it over. And he thinks it over for a couple of weeks, and gradually it fades away and nobody's the worse.

BIFF   But it'll go on forever!

HAPPY   Dad is never so happy as when he's looking forward to something!

[WILLY *enters.*]

HAPPY   Hello, scout!

WILLY   Gee, I haven't been here in years!

[STANLEY *has followed* WILLY *in and sets a chair for him.* STANLEY *starts off but* HAPPY *stops him.*]

HAPPY   Stanley!

[STANLEY *stands by, waiting for an order.*]

BIFF [*Going to* WILLY *with guilt, as to an invalid.*]   Sit down, Pop. You want a drink?

WILLY   Sure, I don't mind.

BIFF   Let's get a load on.

WILLY   You look worried.

BIFF   N-no. [*To* STANLEY.]   Scotch all around. Make it doubles.

STANLEY   Doubles, right. [*He goes.*]

WILLY   You had a couple already, didn't you?

BIFF   Just a couple, yeah.

WILLY   Well, what happened, boy? [*Nodding affirmatively, with a smile.*]   Everything go all right?

BIFF [*Takes a breath, then reaches out and grasps* WILLY'S *hand.*]   Pal . . . [*He is smiling bravely, and* WILLY *is smiling too.*]   I had an experience today.

HAPPY   Terrific, Pop.

WILLY   That so? What happened?

BIFF [*High, slightly alcoholic, above the earth.*]   I'm going to tell you everything from first to last. It's been a strange day. [*Silence. He looks around, composes himself as best he can, but his breath keeps breaking the rhythm of his voice.*]   I had to wait quite a while for him, and . . .

WILLY   Oliver?

BIFF   Yeah, Oliver. All day, as a matter of cold fact. And a lot of—instances—facts, Pop, facts about my life came back to me. Who was it, Pop? Who ever said I was a salesman with Oliver?

WILLY   Well, you were.

BIFF   No, Dad, I was a shipping clerk.

WILLY   But you were practically . . .

BIFF [*With determination.*] Dad, I don't know who said it first, but I was never a salesman for Bill Oliver.

WILLY What're you talking about?

BIFF Let's hold on to the facts tonight, Pop. We're not going to get anywhere bullin' around. I was a shipping clerk.

WILLY [*Angrily.*] All right, now listen to me . . .

BIFF Why don't you let me finish?

WILLY I'm not interested in stories about the past or any crap of that kind because the woods are burning, boys, you understand? There's a big blaze going on all around. I was fired today.

BIFF [*Shocked.*] How could you be?

WILLY I was fired, and I'm looking for a little good news to tell your mother, because the woman has waited and the woman has suffered. The gist of it is that I haven't got a story left in my head, Biff. So don't give me a lecture about facts and aspects. I am not interested. Now what've you got to say to me?

[STANLEY *enters with three drinks. They wait until he leaves.*]

WILLY Did you see Oliver?

BIFF Jesus, Dad!

WILLY You mean you didn't go up there?

HAPPY Sure he went up there.

BIFF I did. I—saw him. How could they fire you?

WILLY [*On the edge of his chair.*] What kind of a welcome did he give you?

BIFF He won't even let you work on commission?

WILLY I'm out! [*Driving.*] So tell me, he gave you a warm welcome?

HAPPY Sure, Pop, sure!

BIFF [*Driven.*] Well, it was kind of . . .

WILLY I was wondering if he'd remember you. [*To* HAPPY.] Imagine, man doesn't see him for ten, twelve years and gives him that kind of a welcome!

HAPPY Damn right!

BIFF [*Trying to return to the offensive.*] Pop, look . . .

WILLY You know why he remembered you, don't you? Because you impressed him in those days.

BIFF Let's talk quietly and get this down to the facts, huh?

WILLY [*As though* BIFF *had been interrupting.*] Well, what happened? It's great news, Biff. Did he take you into his office or'd you talk in the waiting room?

BIFF Well, he came in, see, and . . .

WILLY [*With a big smile.*] What'd he say? Betcha he threw his arm around you.

BIFF Well, he kinda . . .

WILLY He's a fine man. [*To* HAPPY.] Very hard man to see, y'know.

HAPPY [*Agreeing.*] Oh, I know.

WILLY [*To* BIFF.] Is that where you had the drinks?

BIFF Yeah, he gave me a couple of—no, no!

HAPPY [*Cutting in.*] He told him my Florida idea.

WILLY Don't interrupt. [*To* BIFF.] How'd he react to the Florida idea?

BIFF Dad, will you give me a minute to explain?

WILLY I've been waiting for you to explain since I sat down here! What happened? He took you into his office and what?

BIFF Well—I talked. And—and he listened, see.

WILLY Famous for the way he listens, y'know. What was his answer?

BIFF His answer was—[*He breaks off, suddenly angry.*] Dad, you're not letting me tell you what I want to tell you!

WILLY [*Accusing, angered.*] You didn't see him, did you?

BIFF I did see him!

WILLY What'd you insult him or something? You insulted him, didn't you?

BIFF Listen, will you let me out of it, will you just let me out of it!

HAPPY What the hell!

WILLY Tell me what happened!

BIFF [*To* HAPPY.] I can't talk to him!

[*A single trumpet note jars the ear. The light of green leaves stains the house, which holds the air of night and a dream.* YOUNG BERNARD *enters and knocks on the door of the house.*]

YOUNG BERNARD [*Frantically.*]   Mrs. Loman, Mrs. Loman!

HAPPY   Tell him what happened!

BIFF [*To* HAPPY.]   Shut up and leave me alone!

WILLY   No, no! You had to go and flunk math!

BIFF   What math? What're you talking about?

YOUNG BERNARD   Mrs. Loman, Mrs. Loman!

[LINDA *appears in the house, as of old.*]

WILLY [*Wildly.*]   Math, math, math!

BIFF   Take it easy, Pop!

YOUNG BERNARD   Mrs. Loman!

WILLY [*Furiously.*]   If you hadn't flunked you'd've been set by now!

BIFF   Now, look, I'm gonna tell you what happened, and you're going to listen to me.

YOUNG BERNARD   Mrs. Loman!

BIFF   I waited six hours . . .

HAPPY   What the hell are you saying?

BIFF   I kept sending in my name but he wouldn't see me. So finally he . . . [*He continues unheard as light fades low on the restaurant.*]

YOUNG BERNARD   Biff flunked math!

LINDA   No!

YOUNG BERNARD   Birnbaum flunked him! They won't graduate him!

LINDA   But they have to. He's gotta go to the university. Where is he? Biff! Biff!

YOUNG BERNARD   No, he left. He went to Grand Central.

LINDA   Grand—You mean he went to Boston!

YOUNG BERNARD   Is Uncle Willy in Boston?

LINDA   Oh, maybe Willy can talk to the teacher. Oh, the poor, poor boy!

[*Light on house area snaps out.*]

BIFF [*At the table, now audible, holding up a gold fountain pen.*] . . . so I'm washed up with Oliver, you understand? Are you listening to me?

WILLY [*At a loss.*] Yeah, sure. If you hadn't flunked . . .

BIFF Flunked what? What're you talking about?

WILLY Don't blame everything on me! I didn't flunk math—you did! What pen?

HAPPY That was awful dumb, Biff, a pen like that is worth—

WILLY [*Seeing the pen for the first time.*] You took Oliver's pen?

BIFF [*Weakening.*] Dad, I just explained it to you.

WILLY You stole Bill Oliver's fountain pen!

BIFF I didn't exactly steal it! That's just what I've been explaining to you!

HAPPY He had it in his hand and just then Oliver walked in, so he got nervous and stuck it in his pocket!

WILLY My God, Biff!

BIFF I never intended to do it, Dad!

OPERATOR'S VOICE Standish Arms, good evening!

WILLY [*Shouting.*] I'm not in my room!

BIFF [*Frightened.*] Dad, what's the matter? [*He and* HAPPY *stand up.*]

OPERATOR Ringing Mr. Loman for you!

WILLY I'm not there, stop it!

BIFF [*Horrified, gets down on one knee before* WILLY.] Dad, I'll make good, I'll make good. [WILLY *tries to get to his feet.* BIFF *holds him down.*] Sit down now.

WILLY No, you're no good, you're no good for anything.

BIFF I am, Dad, I'll find something else, you understand? Now don't worry about anything. [*He holds up* WILLY's *face.*] Talk to me, Dad.

OPERATOR Mr. Loman does not answer. Shall I page him?

WILLY [*Attempting to stand, as though to rush and silence the* OPERATOR.] No, no, no!

HAPPY He'll strike something, Pop.

WILLY No, no . . .

BIFF [*Desperately, standing over* WILLY.] Pop, listen! Listen to me! I'm telling you something good. Oliver talked to his partner about the Florida idea. You listening? He—he talked to his partner, and he came to me . . . I'm going to be all right, you hear? Dad, listen to me, he said it was just a question of the amount!

WILLY Then you . . . got it?

HAPPY He's gonna be terrific, Pop!

WILLY [*Trying to stand.*] Then you got it, haven't you? You got it! You got it!

BIFF [*Agonized, holds* WILLY *down.*] No, no. Look, Pop. I'm supposed to have lunch with them tomorrow. I'm just telling you this so you'll know that I can still make an impression, Pop. And I'll make good somewhere, but I can't go tomorrow, see?

WILLY Why not? You simply . . .

BIFF But the pen, Pop!

WILLY You give it to him and tell him it was an oversight!

HAPPY Sure, have lunch tomorrow!

BIFF I can't say that . . .

WILLY You were doing a crossword puzzle and accidentally used his pen!

BIFF Listen, kid, I took those balls years ago, now I walk in with his fountain pen? That clinches it, don't you see? I can't face him like that! I'll try elsewhere.

PAGE'S VOICE Paging Mr. Loman!

WILLY Don't you want to be anything?

BIFF Pop, how can I go back?

WILLY You don't want to be anything, is that what's behind it?

BIFF [*Now angry at* WILLY *for not crediting his sympathy.*] Don't take it that way! You think it was easy walking into that office after what I'd done to him? A team of horses couldn't have dragged me back to Bill Oliver!

WILLY Then why'd you go?

BIFF Why did I go? Why did I go! Look at you! Look at what's become of you!

[*Off left,* THE WOMAN *laughs.*]

WILLY Biff, you're going to go to that lunch tomorrow, or . . .

BIFF I can't go. I've got no appointment!

HAPPY Biff, for . . . !

WILLY Are you spiting me?

BIFF Don't take it that way! Goddammit!

WILLY [Strikes BIFF and falters away from the table.] You rotten little louse! Are you spiting me?

THE WOMAN Someone's at the door, Willy!

BIFF I'm no good, can't you see what I am?

HAPPY [Separating them.] Hey, you're in a restaurant! Now cut it out, both of you! [The girls enter.] Hello, girls, sit down.

[THE WOMAN laughs, off left.]

MISS FORSYTHE I guess we might as well. This is Letta.

THE WOMAN Willy, are you going to wake up?

BIFF [Ignoring WILLY.] How're ya, miss, sit down. What do you drink?

MISS FORSYTHE Letta might not be able to stay long.

LETTA I gotta get up very early tomorrow. I got jury duty. I'm so excited! Were you fellows ever on a jury?

BIFF No, but I been in front of them! [The girls laugh.] This is my father.

LETTA Isn't he cute? Sit down with us, Pop.

HAPPY Sit him down, Biff!

BIFF [Going to him.] Come on, slugger, drink us under the table. To hell with it! Come on, sit down, pal.

[On BIFF's last insistence, WILLY is about to sit.]

THE WOMAN [Now urgently.] Willy, are you going to answer the door!

[THE WOMAN's call pulls WILLY back. He starts right, befuddled.]

BIFF Hey, where are you going?

WILLY Open the door.

BIFF The door?

WILLY The washroom . . . the door . . . where's the door?

BIFF [Leading WILLY to the left.] Just go straight down.

[WILLY moves left.]

THE WOMAN Willy, Willy, are you going to get up, get up, get up, get up?

[WILLY exits left.]

LETTA I think it's sweet you bring your daddy along.

MISS FORSYTHE   Oh, he isn't really your father!

BIFF [*At left, turning to her resentfully.*]   Miss Forsythe, you've just seen a prince walk by. A fine, troubled prince. A hard-working, unappreciated prince. A pal, you understand? A good companion. Always for his boys.

LETTA   That's so sweet.

HAPPY   Well, girls, what's the program? We're wasting time. Come on, Biff. Gather round. Where would you like to go?

BIFF   Why don't you do something for him?

HAPPY   Me!

BIFF   Don't you give a damn for him, Hap?

HAPPY   What're you talking about? I'm the one who . . .

BIFF   I sense it, you don't give a good goddam about him. [*He takes the rolled-up hose from his pocket and puts it on the table in front of* HAPPY.]   Look what I found in the cellar, for Christ's sake. How can you bear to let it go on?

HAPPY   Me? Who goes away? Who runs off and . . .

BIFF   Yeah, but he doesn't mean anything to you. You could help him—I can't! Don't you understand what I'm talking about? He's going to kill himself, don't you know that?

HAPPY   Don't I know it! Me!

BIFF   Hap, help him! Jesus . . . help him . . . Help me, help me, I can't bear to look at his face! [*Ready to weep, he hurries out, up right.*]

HAPPY [*Starting after him.*]   Where are you going?

MISS FORSYTHE   What's he so mad about?

HAPPY   Come on, girls, we'll catch up with him.

MISS FORSYTHE [*As* HAPPY *pushes her out.*]   Say, I don't like that temper of his!

HAPPY   He's just a little overstrung, he'll be all right!

WILLY [*Off left, as* THE WOMAN *laughs.*]   Don't answer! Don't answer!

LETTA   Don't you want to tell your father . . .

HAPPY   No, that's not my father. He's just a guy. Come on, we'll catch Biff, and, honey, we're going to paint this town! Stanley, where's the check! Hey, Stanley!

[*They exit.* STANLEY *looks toward left.*]

STANLEY [*Calling to* HAPPY *indignantly.*] Mr. Loman! Mr. Loman!

[STANLEY *picks up a chair and follows them off. Knocking is heard off left.* THE WOMAN *enters, laughing.* WILLY *follows her. She is in a black slip; he is buttoning his shirt. Raw, sensuous music accompanies their speech.*]

WILLY Will you stop laughing? Will you stop?

THE WOMAN Aren't you going to answer the door? He'll wake the whole hotel.

WILLY I'm not expecting anybody.

THE WOMAN Whyn't you have another drink, honey, and stop being so damn self-centered?

WILLY I'm so lonely.

THE WOMAN You know you ruined me, Willy? From now on, whenever you come to the office, I'll see that you go right through to the buyers. No waiting at my desk anymore, Willy. You ruined me.

WILLY That's nice of you to say that.

THE WOMAN Gee, you are self-centered! Why so sad? You are the saddest, self-centeredest soul I ever did see-saw. [*She laughs. He kisses her.*] Come on inside, drummer boy. It's silly to be dressing in the middle of the night. [*As knocking is heard.*] Aren't you going to answer the door?

WILLY They're knocking on the wrong door.

THE WOMAN But I felt the knocking. And he heard us talking in here. Maybe the hotel's on fire!

WILLY [*His terror rising.*] It's a mistake.

THE WOMAN Then tell him to go away!

WILLY There's nobody there.

THE WOMAN It's getting on my nerves, Willy. There's somebody standing out there and it's getting on my nerves!

WILLY [*Pushing her away from him.*] All right, stay in the bathroom here, and don't come out. I think there's a law in Massachusetts about it, so don't come out. It may be that new room clerk. He looked very mean. So don't come out. It's a mistake, there's no fire.

[*The knocking is heard again. He takes a few steps away from her, and she vanishes into the wing. The light follows him, and now he is facing* YOUNG BIFF, *who carries a suitcase.* BIFF *steps toward him. The music is gone.*]

BIFF   Why didn't you answer?

WILLY   Biff! What are you doing in Boston?

BIFF   Why didn't you answer? I've been knocking for five minutes, I called you on the phone . . .

WILLY   I just heard you. I was in the bathroom and had the door shut. Did anything happen home?

BIFF   Dad—I let you down.

WILLY   What do you mean?

BIFF   Dad . . .

WILLY   Biffo, what's this about? [*Putting his arm around* BIFF.] Come on, let's go downstairs and get you a malted.

BIFF   Dad, I flunked math.

WILLY   Not for the term?

BIFF   The term. I haven't got enough credits to graduate.

WILLY   You mean to say Bernard wouldn't give you the answers?

BIFF   He did, he tried, but I only got a sixty-one.

WILLY   And they wouldn't give you four points?

BIFF   Birnbaum refused absolutely. I begged him, Pop, but he won't give me those points. You gotta talk to him before they close the school. Because if he saw the kind of man you are, and you just talked to him in your way, I'm sure he'd come through for me. The class came right before practice, see, and I didn't go enough. Would you talk to him? He'd like you, Pop. You know the way you could talk.

WILLY   You're on. We'll drive right back.

BIFF   Oh, Dad, good work! I'm sure he'll change it for you!

WILLY   Go downstairs and tell the clerk I'm checkin' out. Go right down.

BIFF   Yes, sir! See, the reason he hates me, Pop—one day he was late for class so I got up at the blackboard and imitated him. I crossed my eyes and talked with a lithp.

WILLY [*Laughing.*]   You did? The kids like it?

BIFF They nearly died laughing!

WILLY Yeah? What'd you do?

BIFF The thquare root of thixthy twee is . . . [WILLY *bursts out laughing;* BIFF *joins him.*] And in the middle of it he walked in!

[WILLY *laughs and* THE WOMAN *joins in offstage.*]

WILLY [*Without hesitation.*] Hurry downstairs and . . .

BIFF Somebody in there?

WILLY No, that was next door.

[THE WOMAN *laughs offstage.*]

BIFF Somebody got in your bathroom!

WILLY No, it's the next room, there's a party . . .

THE WOMAN [*Enters, laughing. She lisps this.*] Can I come in? There's something in the bathtub, Willy, and it's moving!

[WILLY *looks at* BIFF, *who is staring open-mouthed and horrified at* THE WOMAN.]

WILLY Ah—you better go back to your room. They must be finished painting by now. They're painting her room so I let her take a shower here. Go back, go back . . . [*He pushes her.*]

THE WOMAN [*Resisting.*] But I've got to get dressed, Willy, I can't . . .

WILLY Get out of here! Go back, go back . . . [*Suddenly striving for the ordinary.*] This is Miss Francis, Biff, she's a buyer. They're painting her room. Go back, Miss Francis, go back . . .

THE WOMAN But my clothes, I can't go out naked in the hall!

WILLY [*Pushing her offstage.*] Get outa here! Go back, go back!

[BIFF *slowly sits down on his suitcase as the argument continues offstage.*]

THE WOMAN Where's my stockings? You promised me stockings, Willy!

WILLY I have no stockings here!

THE WOMAN You had two boxes of size nine sheers for me, and I want them!

WILLY Here, for God's sake, will you get outa here!

THE WOMAN [*Enters holding a box of stockings.*] I just hope there's nobody in the hall. That's all I hope. [*To* BIFF.]   Are you football or baseball?

BIFF   Football.

THE WOMAN [*Angry, humiliated.*]   That's me too. G'night. [*She snatches her clothes from* WILLY, *and walks out.*]

WILLY [*After a pause.*]   Well, better get going. I want to get to the school first thing in the morning. Get my suits out of the closet. I'll get my valise. [BIFF *doesn't move.*]   What's the matter? [BIFF *remains motionless, tears falling.*]   She's a buyer. Buys for J. H. Simmons. She lives down the hall—they're painting. You don't imagine—[*He breaks off. After a pause.*]   Now listen, pal, she's just a buyer. She sees merchandise in her room and they have to keep it looking just so . . . [*Pause. Assuming command.*] All right, get my suits. [BIFF *doesn't move.*]   Now stop crying and do as I say. I gave you an order. Biff, I gave you an order! Is that what you do when I give you an order? How dare you cry! [*Putting his arm around* BIFF.]   Now look, Biff, when you grow up you'll understand about these things. You mustn't—you mustn't overemphasize a thing like this. I'll see Birnbaum first thing in the morning.

BIFF   Never mind.

WILLY [*Getting down beside* BIFF.]   Never mind! He's going to give you those points. I'll see to it.

BIFF   He wouldn't listen to you.

WILLY   He certainly will listen to me. You need those points for the U. of Virginia.

BIFF   I'm not going there.

WILLY   Heh? If I can't get him to change that mark you'll make it up in summer school. You've got all summer to . . .

BIFF [*His weeping breaking from him.*]   Dad . . .

WILLY [*Infected by it.*]   Oh, my boy . . .

BIFF   Dad . . .

WILLY   She's nothing to me, Biff. I was lonely, I was terribly lonely.

BIFF   You—you gave her Mama's stockings! [*His tears break through and he rises to go.*]

WILLY [*Grabbing for* BIFF.]   I gave you an order!

BIFF Don't touch me, you—liar!

WILLY Apologize for that!

BIFF You fake! You phony little fake! You fake! [*Overcome, he turns quickly and weeping fully goes out with his suitcase.* WILLY *is left on the floor on his knees.*]

WILLY I gave you an order! Biff, come back here or I'll beat you! Come back here! I'll whip you!

[STANLEY *comes quickly in from the right and stands in front of* WILLY.]

WILLY [*Shouts at* STANLEY.] I gave you an order . . .

STANLEY Hey, let's pick it up, pick it up, Mr. Loman. [*He helps* WILLY *to his feet.*] Your boys left with the chippies. They said they'll see you home.

[*A second waiter watches some distance away.*]

WILLY But we were supposed to have dinner together.

[*Music is heard,* WILLY'S *theme.*]

STANLEY Can you make it?

WILLY I'll—sure, I can make it. [*Suddenly concerned about his clothes.*] Do I—I look all right?

STANLEY Sure, you look all right. [*He flicks a speck off* WILLY'S *lapel.*]

WILLY Here—here's a dollar.

STANLEY Oh, your son paid me. It's all right.

WILLY [*Putting it in* STANLEY'S *hand.*] No, take it. You're a good boy.

STANLEY Oh, no, you don't have to . . .

WILLY Here—here's some more, I don't need it any more. [*After a slight pause.*] Tell me—is there a seed store in the neighborhood?

STANLEY Seeds? You mean like to plant?

[*As* WILLY *turns,* STANLEY *slips the money back into his jacket pocket.*]

WILLY Yes. Carrots, peas . . .

STANLEY Well, there's hardware stores on Sixth Avenue, but it may be too late now.

WILLY [*Anxiously.*] Oh, I'd better hurry. I've got to get some seeds. [*He starts off to the right.*] I've got to get some seeds, right away. Nothing's planted. I don't have a thing in the ground.

[WILLY *hurries out as the light goes down.* STANLEY *moves over to the right after him, watches him off. The other waiter has been staring at* WILLY.]

STANLEY [*To the waiter.*]   Well, whatta you looking at?

[*The waiter picks up the chairs and moves off right.* STANLEY *takes the table and follows him. The light fades on this area. There is a long pause, the sound of the flute coming over. The light gradually rises on the kitchen, which is empty.* HAPPY *appears at the door of the house, followed by* BIFF. HAPPY *is carrying a large bunch of long-stemmed roses. He enters the kitchen, looks around for* LINDA. *Not seeing her, he turns to* BIFF, *who is just outside the house door, and makes a gesture with his hands, indicating "Not here, I guess." He looks into the living room and freezes. Inside,* LINDA, *unseen, is seated,* WILLY's *coat on her lap. She rises ominously and quietly and moves toward* HAPPY, *who backs up into the kitchen, afraid.*]

HAPPY   Hey, what're you doing up? [LINDA *says nothing but moves toward him implacably.*]   Where's Pop? [*He keeps backing to the right, and now* LINDA *is in full view in the doorway to the living room.*]   Is he sleeping?

LINDA   Where were you?

HAPPY [*Trying to laugh it off.*]   We met two girls, Mom, very fine types. Here, we brought you some flowers. [*Offering them to her.*]   Put them in your room, Ma.

[*She knocks them to the floor at* BIFF's *feet. He has now come inside and closed the door behind him. She stares at* BIFF, *silent.*]

HAPPY   Now what'd you do that for? Mom, I want you to have some flowers . . .

LINDA [*Cutting* HAPPY *off, violently to* BIFF.]   Don't you care whether he lives or dies?

HAPPY [*Going to the stairs.*]   Come upstairs, Biff.

BIFF [*With a flare of disgust, to* HAPPY.]   Go away from me! [*To* LINDA.]   What do you mean, lives or dies? Nobody's dying around here, pal.

LINDA   Get out of my sight! Get out of here!

BIFF   I wanna see the boss.

LINDA   You're not going near him!

BIFF   Where is he? [*He moves into the living room and* LINDA *follows.*]

LINDA [*Shouting after* BIFF.]   You invite him for dinner. He looks forward to it all day—[BIFF *appears in his parents' bedroom, looks around, and exits*]—and then you desert him there. There's no stranger you'd do that to!

HAPPY   Why? He had a swell time with us. Listen, when I—[LINDA *comes back into the kitchen*]—desert him I hope I don't outlive the day!

LINDA   Get out of here!

HAPPY   Now look, Mom . . .

LINDA   Did you have to go to women tonight? You and your lousy rotten whores!

[BIFF *re-enters the kitchen.*]

HAPPY   Mom, all we did was follow Biff around trying to cheer him up! [*To* BIFF.]   Boy, what a night you gave me!

LINDA   Get out of here, both of you, and don't come back! I don't want you tormenting him any more. Go on now, get your things together! [*To* BIFF.]   You can sleep in his apartment. [*She starts to pick up the flowers and stops herself.*]   Pick up this stuff, I'm not your maid any more. Pick it up, you bum, you!

[HAPPY *turns his back to her in refusal.* BIFF *slowly moves over and gets down on his knees, picking up the flowers.*]

LINDA   You're a pair of animals! Not one, not another living soul would have had the cruelty to walk out on that man in a restaurant!

BIFF [*Not looking at her.*]   Is that what he said?

LINDA   He didn't have to say anything. He was so humiliated he nearly limped when he came in.

HAPPY   But, Mom, he had a great time with us . . .

BIFF [*Cutting him off violently.*]   Shut up!

[*Without another word,* HAPPY *goes upstairs.*]

LINDA   You! You didn't even go in to see if he was all right!

BIFF [*Still on the floor in front of* LINDA, *the flowers in his hand; with self-loathing.*]   No. Didn't. Didn't do a damned thing. How do you like that, heh? Left him babbling in a toilet.

LINDA   You louse. You . . .

BIFF   Now you hit it on the nose! [*He gets up, throws the flowers in the wastebasket.*]   The scum of the earth, and you're looking at him!

LINDA   Get out of here!

BIFF   I gotta talk to the boss, Mom. Where is he?

LINDA   You're not going near him. Get out of this house!

BIFF [*With absolute assurance, determination.*]   No. We're gonna have an abrupt conversation, him and me.

LINDA   You're not talking to him!

[*Hammering is heard from outside the house, off right.* BIFF *turns toward the noise.*]

LINDA [*Suddenly pleading.*]   Will you please leave him alone?

BIFF   What's he doing out there?

LINDA   He's planting the garden!

BIFF [*Quietly.*]   Now? Oh, my God!

[BIFF *moves outside,* LINDA *following. The light dies down on them and comes up on the center of the apron as* WILLY *walks into it. He is carrying a flashlight, a hoe, and a handful of seed packets. He raps the top of the hoe sharply to fix it firmly, and then moves to the left, measuring off the distance with his foot. He holds the flashlight to look at the seed packets, reading off the instructions. He is in the blue of night.*]

WILLY   Carrots . . . quarter-inch apart. Rows . . . one-foot rows. [*He measures it off.*]   One foot. [*He puts down a package and measures off.*]   Beets. [*He puts down another package and measures again.*]   Lettuce. [*He reads the package, puts it down.*] One foot—[*He breaks off as* BEN *appears at the right and moves slowly down to him.*]   What a proposition, ts,ts. Terrific, terrific. 'Cause she's suffered, Ben, the woman has suffered. You understand me? A man can't go out the way he came in, Ben, a man has got to add up to something. You can't, you can't—[BEN *moves toward him as though to interrupt.*]   You gotta consider, now.

Don't answer so quick. Remember, it's a guaranteed twenty-thousand-dollar proposition. Now look, Ben, I want you to go through the ins and outs of this thing with me. I've got nobody to talk to, Ben, and the woman has suffered, you hear me?

BEN [*Standing still, considering.*] What's the proposition?

WILLY It's twenty thousand dollars on the barrelhead. Guaranteed, gilt-edged, you understand?

BEN You don't want to make a fool of yourself. They might not honor the policy.

WILLY How can they dare refuse? Didn't I work like a coolie to meet every premium on the nose? And now they don't pay off? Impossible!

BEN It's called a cowardly thing, William.

WILLY Why? Does it take more guts to stand here the rest of my life ringing up a zero?

BEN [*Yielding.*] That's a point, William. [*He moves, thinking, turns*] And twenty thousand—that *is* something one can feel with the hand, it is there.

WILLY [*Now assured, with rising power.*] Oh, Ben, that's the whole beauty of it! I see it like a diamond, shining in the dark, hard and rough, that I can pick up and touch in my hand. Not like—like an appointment! This would not be another damned-fool appointment, Ben, and it changes all the aspects. Because he thinks I'm nothing, see, and so he spites me. But the funeral . . . [*Straightening up.*] Ben, that funeral will be massive! They'll come from Maine, Massachusetts, Vermont, New Hampshire! All the old-timers with the strange license plates—that boy will be thunderstruck, Ben, because he never realized—I am known! Rhode Island, New York, New Jersey—I am known, Ben, and he'll see it with his eyes once and for all. He'll see what I am, Ben! He's in for a shock, that boy!

BEN [*Coming down to the edge of the garden.*] He'll call you a coward.

WILLY [*Suddenly fearful.*] No, that would be terrible.

BEN Yes. And a damned fool.

WILLY No, no, he mustn't, I won't have that! [*He is broken and desperate.*]

BEN   He'll hate you, William.

[*The gay music of the* BOYS *is heard.*]

WILLY   Oh, Ben, how do we get back to all the great times? Used to be so full of light, and comradeship, the sleigh-riding in winter, and the ruddiness on his cheeks. And always some kind of good news coming up, always something nice coming up ahead. And never even let me carry the valises in the house, and simonizing, simonizing that little red car! Why, why can't I give him something and not have him hate me?

BEN   Let me think about it. [*He glances at his watch.*]   I still have a little time. Remarkable proposition, but you've got to be sure you're not making a fool of yourself.

[BEN *drifts off upstage and goes out of sight.* BIFF *comes down from the left.*]

WILLY   [*Suddenly conscious of* BIFF, *turns and looks up at him, then begins picking up the packages of seeds in confusion.*] Where the hell is that seed? [*Indignantly.*]   You can't see noth-ing out here! They boxed in the whole goddam neighborhood!

BIFF   There are people all around here. Don't you realize that?

WILLY   I'm busy. Don't bother me.

BIFF   [*Taking the hoe from* WILLY.]   I'm saying good-by to you, Pop. [WILLY *looks at him, silent, unable to move.*]   I'm not com-ing back any more.

WILLY   You're not going to see Oliver tomorrow?

BIFF   I've got no appointment, Dad.

WILLY   He put his arm around you, and you've got no ap-pointment?

BIFF   Pop, get this now, will you? Everytime I've left it's been a fight that sent me out of here. Today I realized something about myself and I tried to explain it to you and I—I think I'm just not smart enough to make any sense out of it for you. To hell with whose fault it is or anything like that. [*He takes* WILLY'S *arm.*]   Let's just wrap it up, heh? Come on in, we'll tell Mom. [*He gently tries to pull* WILLY *to left.*]

WILLY   [*Frozen, immobile, with guilt in his voice.*]   No, I don't want to see her.

BIFF   Come on! [*He pulls again, and* WILLY *tries to pull away.*]

WILLY [*Highly nervous.*]   No, no, I don't want to see her.

BIFF [*Tries to look into* WILLY's *face, as if to find the answer there.*]   Why don't you want to see her?

WILLY [*More harshly now.*]   Don't bother me, will you?

BIFF   What do you mean, you don't want to see her? You don't want them calling you yellow, do you? This isn't your fault; it's me, I'm a bum. Now come inside! [WILLY *strains to get away.*] Did you hear what I said to you?

[WILLY *pulls away and quickly goes by himself into the house.* BIFF *follows.*]

LINDA [*To* WILLY.]   Did you plant, dear?

BIFF [*At the door, to* LINDA.]   All right, we had it out. I'm going and I'm not writing any more.

LINDA [*Going to* WILLY *in the kitchen.*]   I think that's the best way, dear. 'Cause there's no use drawing it out, you'll just never get along.

[WILLY *doesn't respond.*]

BIFF   People ask where I am and what I'm doing, you don't know, and you don't care. That way it'll be off your mind and you can start brightening up again. All right? That clears it, doesn't it? [WILLY *is silent, and* BIFF *goes to him.*]   You gonna wish me luck, scout? [*He extends his hand.*]   What do you say?

LINDA   Shake his hand, Willy.

WILLY [*Turning to her, seething with hurt.*]   There's no necessity to mention the pen at all, y'know.

BIFF [*Gently.*]   I've got no appointment, Dad.

WILLY [*Erupting fiercely.*]   He put his arm around . . . ?

BIFF   Dad, you're never going to see what I am, so what's the use of arguing? If I strike oil I'll send you a check. Meantime forget I'm alive.

WILLY [*To* LINDA.]   Spite, see?

BIFF   Shake hands, Dad.

WILLY   Not my hand.

BIFF   I was hoping not to go this way.

WILLY   Well, this is the way you're going. Good-by.

[BIFF *looks at him a moment, then turns sharply and goes to the stairs.*]

WILLY [*Stops him with.*]   May you rot in hell if you leave this house!

BIFF [*Turning.*]   Exactly what is it that you want from me?

WILLY   I want you to know, on the train, in the mountains, in the valleys, wherever you go, that you cut down your life for spite!

BIFF   No, no.

WILLY   Spite, spite, is the word of your undoing! And when you're down and out, remember what did it. When you're rotting somewhere beside the railroad tracks, remember, and don't you dare blame it on me!

BIFF   I'm not blaming it on you!

WILLY   I won't take the rap for this, you hear?

[HAPPY *comes down the stairs and stands on the bottom step, watching.*]

BIFF   That's just what I'm telling you!

WILLY [*Sinking into a chair at the table, with full accusation.*] You're trying to put a knife in me—don't think I don't know what you're doing!

BIFF   All right, phony! Then let's lay it on the line. [*He whips the rubber tube out of his pocket and puts it on the table.*]

HAPPY   You crazy . . .

LINDA   Biff! [*She moves to grab the hose, but* BIFF *holds it down with his hand.*]

BIFF   Leave it there! Don't move it!

WILLY [*Not looking at it.*]   What is that?

BIFF   You know goddam well what that is.

WILLY [*Caged, wanting to escape.*]   I never saw that.

BIFF   You saw it. The mice didn't bring it into the cellar! What is this supposed to do, make a hero out of you? This supposed to make me sorry for you?

WILLY   Never heard of it.

BIFF   There'll be no pity for you, you hear it? No pity!

WILLY [*To* LINDA.]   You hear the spite!

BIFF   No, you're going to hear the truth—what you are and what I am!

LINDA   Stop it!

WILLY   Spite!

HAPPY [*Coming down toward* BIFF.]   You cut it now!

BIFF [*To* HAPPY.]   The man don't know who we are! The man is gonna know! [*To* WILLY.]   We never told the truth for ten minutes in this house!

HAPPY   We always told the truth!

BIFF [*Turning on him.*]   You big blow, are you the assistant buyer? You're one of the two assistants to the assistant, aren't you?

HAPPY   Well, I'm practically . . .

BIFF   You're practically full of it! We all are! And I'm through with it. [*To* WILLY.]   Now hear this, Willy, this is me.

WILLY   I know you!

BIFF   You know why I had no address for three months? I stole a suit in Kansas City and I was in jail. [*To* LINDA, *who is sobbing.*]   Stop crying. I'm through with it.

[LINDA *turns away from them, her hands covering her face.*]

WILLY   I suppose that's my fault!

BIFF   I stole myself out of every good job since high school!

WILLY   And whose fault is that?

BIFF   And I never got anywhere because you blew me so full of hot air I could never stand taking orders from anybody! That's whose fault it is!

WILLY   I hear that!

LINDA   Don't, Biff!

BIFF   It's goddam time you heard that! I had to be boss big shot in two weeks, and I'm through with it!

WILLY   Then hang yourself! For spite, hang yourself!

BIFF   No! Nobody's hanging himself, Willy! I ran down eleven flights with a pen in my hand today. And suddenly I stopped, you hear me? And in the middle of that office building, do you hear this? I stopped in the middle of that building and I saw—the sky. I saw the things that I love in this world. The work and the food and time to sit and smoke. And I looked at the pen and said to myself, what the hell am I grabbing this for? Why am I trying to become what I don't want to be? What am I doing in an office, making a contemptuous, begging fool of myself, when all I want

is out there, waiting for me the minute I say I know who I am!
Why can't I say that, Willy? [*He tries to make* WILLY *face him,
but* WILLY *pulls away and moves to the left.*]

WILLY [*With hatred, threateningly.*]   The door of your life is
wide open!

BIFF   Pop! I'm a dime a dozen, and so are you!

WILLY [*Turning on him now in an uncontrolled outburst.*]   I
am not a dime a dozen! I am Willy Loman, and you are Biff
Loman!

[BIFF *starts for* WILLY, *but is blocked by* HAPPY. *In his fury,*
BIFF *seems on the verge of attacking his father.*]

BIFF   I am not a leader of men, Willy, and neither are you.
You were never anything but a hard-working drummer who
landed in the ash can like all the rest of them! I'm one dollar
an hour, Willy! I tried seven states and couldn't raise it. A buck
an hour! Do you gather my meaning? I'm not bringing home any
prizes any more, and you're going to stop waiting for me to bring
them home!

WILLY [*Directly to* BIFF.]   You vengeful, spiteful mut!

[BIFF *breaks from* HAPPY. WILLY, *in fright, starts up the stairs.*
BIFF *grabs him.*]

BIFF [*At the peak of his fury.*]   Pop, I'm nothing! I'm nothing,
Pop. Can't you understand that? There's no spite in it any more.
I'm just what I am, that's all.

[BIFF's *fury has spent itself, and he breaks down, sobbing, holding on to* WILLY, *who dumbly fumbles for* BIFF's *face.*]

WILLY [*Astonished.*]   What're you doing? What're you doing?
[*To* LINDA.]   Why is he crying?

BIFF [*Crying, broken.*]   Will you let me go, for Christ's sake?
Will you take that phony dream and burn it before something
happens? [*Struggling to contain himself, he pulls away and moves
to the stairs.*]   I'll go in the morning. Put him—put him to bed.
[*Exhausted,* BIFF *moves up the stairs to his room.*]

WILLY [*After a long pause, astonished, elevated.*]   Isn't that—
isn't that remarkable? Biff—he likes me!

LINDA   He loves you, Willy!

HAPPY [*Deeply moved.*]   Always did, Pop.

WILLY   Oh, Biff! [*Staring wildly.*]   He cried! Cried to me. [*He is choking with his love, and now cries out his promise.*] That boy—that boy is going to be magnificent!

[BEN *appears in the light just outside the kitchen.*]

BEN   Yes, outstanding, with twenty thousand behind him.

LINDA [*Sensing the racing of his mind, fearfully, carefully.*] Now come to bed, Willy. It's all settled now.

WILLY [*Finding it difficult not to rush out of the house.*]   Yes, we'll sleep. Come on. Go to sleep, Hap.

BEN   And it does take a great kind of a man to crack the jungle.

[*In accents of dread,* BEN'S *idyllic music starts up.*]

HAPPY [*His arm around* LINDA.]   I'm getting married, Pop, don't forget it. I'm changing everything. I'm gonna run that department before the year is up. You'll see, Mom. [*He kisses her.*]

BEN   The jungle is dark but full of diamonds, Willy.

[WILLY *turns, moves, listening to* BEN.]

LINDA   Be good. You're both good boys, just act that way, that's all.

HAPPY   'Night, Pop. [*He goes upstairs.*]

LINDA [*To* WILLY.]   Come, dear.

BEN [*With greater force.*]   One must go in to fetch a diamond out.

WILLY [*To* LINDA, *as he moves slowly along the edge of the kitchen, toward the door.*]   I just want to get settled down, Linda. Let me sit alone for a little.

LINDA [*Almost uttering her fear.*]   I want you upstairs.

WILLY [*Taking her in his arms.*]   In a few minutes, Linda. I couldn't sleep right now. Go on, you look awful tired. [*He kisses her.*]

BEN   Not like an appointment at all. A diamond is rough and hard to the touch.

WILLY   Go on now. I'll be right up.

LINDA   I think this is the only way, Willy.

WILLY   Sure, it's the best thing.

BEN   Best thing!

WILLY The only way. Everything is gonna be—go on, kid, get to bed. You look so tired.

LINDA Come right up.

WILLY Two minutes.

[LINDA *goes into the living room, then reappears in her bedroom.* WILLY *moves just outside the kitchen door.*]

WILLY Loves me. [*Wonderingly.*] Always loved me. Isn't that a remarkable thing? Ben, he'll worship me for it!

BEN [*With promise.*] It's dark there, but full of diamonds.

WILLY Can you imagine that magnificence with twenty thousand dollars in his pocket?

LINDA [*Calling from her room.*] Willy! Come up!

WILLY [*Calling into the kitchen.*] Yes! yes. Coming! It's very smart, you realize that, don't you, sweetheart? Even Ben sees it. I gotta go, baby. 'By! 'By! [*Going over to* BEN, *almost dancing.*] Imagine? When the mail comes he'll be ahead of Bernard again!

BEN A perfect proposition all around.

WILLY Did you see how he cried to me? Oh, if I could kiss him, Ben!

BEN Time, William, time!

WILLY Oh, Ben, I always knew one way or another we were gonna make it, Biff and I!

BEN [*Looking at his watch.*] The boat. We'll be late. [*He moves slowly off into the darkness.*]

WILLY [*Elegiacally, turning to the house.*] Now when you kick off, boy, I want a seventy-yard boot, and get right down the field under the ball, and when you hit, hit low and hit hard, because it's important, boy. [*He swings around and faces the audience.*] There's all kinds of important people in the stands, and the first thing you know . . . [*Suddenly realizing he is alone.*] Ben! Ben, where do I . . . ? [*He makes a sudden movement of search.*] Ben, how do I . . . ?

LINDA [*Calling.*] Willy, you coming up?

WILLY [*Uttering a gasp of fear, whirling about as if to quiet her.*] Sh! [*He turns around as if to find his way; sounds, faces, voices, seem to be swarming in upon him and he flicks at them,* crying.] Sh! Sh! [*Suddenly music, faint and high, stops him. It rises in intensity, almost to an unbearable scream. He goes up and down on his toes, and rushes off around the house.*] Shhh!

LINDA Willy?

[*There is no answer.* LINDA *waits.* BIFF *gets up off his bed. He is still in his clothes.* HAPPY *sits up.* BIFF *stands listening.*]

LINDA [*With real fear.*] Willy, answer me! Willy!

[*There is the sound of a car starting and moving away at full speed.*]

LINDA No!

BIFF [*Rushing down the stairs.*] Pop!

[*As the car speeds off, the music crashes down in a frenzy of sound, which becomes the soft pulsation of a single cello string.* BIFF *slowly returns to his bedroom. He and* HAPPY *gravely don their jackets.* LINDA *slowly walks out of her room. The music has developed into a dead march. The leaves of day are appearing over everything.* CHARLEY *and* BERNARD, *somberly dressed, appear and knock on the kitchen door.* BIFF *and* HAPPY *slowly descend the stairs to the kitchen as* CHARLEY *and* BERNARD *enter. All stop a moment when* LINDA, *in clothes of mourning, bearing a little bunch of roses, comes through the draped doorway into the kitchen. She goes to* CHARLEY *and takes his arm. Now all move toward the audience, through the wall-line of the kitchen. At the limit of the apron,* LINDA *lays down the flowers, kneels, and sits back on her heels. All stare down at the grave.*]

REQUIEM

CHARLEY It's getting dark, Linda.

[LINDA *doesn't react. She stares at the grave.*]

BIFF How about it, Mom? Better get some rest, heh? They'll be closing the gate soon.

[LINDA *makes no move. Pause.*]

HAPPY [*Deeply angered.*] He had no right to do that. There was no necessity for it. We would've helped him.

CHARLEY [*Grunting.*] Hmmm.

BIFF Come along, Mom.

LINDA Why didn't anybody come?

CHARLEY It was a very nice funeral.

LINDA But where are all the people he knew? Maybe they blame him.

CHARLEY Naa. It's a rough world, Linda. They wouldn't blame him.

LINDA I can't understand it. At this time especially. First time in thirty-five years we were just about free and clear. He only needed a little salary. He was even finished with the dentist.

CHARLEY No man only needs a little salary.

LINDA I can't understand it.

BIFF There were a lot of nice days. When he'd come home from a trip; or on Sundays, making the stoop; finishing the cellar; putting on the new porch; when he built the extra bathroom; and put up the garage. You know something, Charley, there's more of him in that front stoop than in all the sales he ever made.

CHARLEY Yeah. He was a happy man with a batch of cement.

LINDA He was so wonderful with his hands.

BIFF He had the wrong dreams. All, all, wrong.

HAPPY [*Almost ready to fight* BIFF.] Don't say that!

BIFF He never knew who he was.

CHARLEY [*Stopping* HAPPY's *movement and reply. To* BIFF.] Nobody dast blame this man. You don't understand: Willy was a salesman. And for a salesman, there is no rock bottom to the life. He don't put a bolt to a nut, he don't tell you the law or give you medicine. He's a man way out there in the blue, riding on a smile and a shoeshine. And when they start not smiling back— that's an earthquake. And then you get yourself a couple of spots on your hat, and you're finished. Nobody dast blame this man. A salesman is got to dream, boy. It comes with the territory.

BIFF Charley, the man didn't know who he was.

HAPPY [*Infuriated.*] Don't say that!

BIFF Why don't you come with me, Happy?

HAPPY   I'm not licked that easily. I'm staying right in this city, and I'm gonna beat this racket! [*He looks at* BIFF, *his chin set.*] The Loman Brothers!

BIFF   I know who I am, kid.

HAPPY   All right, boy. I'm gonna show you and everybody else that Willy Loman did not die in vain. He had a good dream. It's the only dream you can have—to come out number-one man. He fought it out here, and this is where I'm gonna win it for him.

BIFF   [*With a hopeless glance at* HAPPY, *bends toward his mother.*]   Let's go, Mom.

LINDA   I'll be with you in a minute. Go on, Charley. [*He hesitates.*]   I want to, just for a minute. I never had a chance to say good-by.

[CHARLEY *moves away, followed by* HAPPY. BIFF *remains a slight distance up and left of* LINDA. *She sits there, summoning herself. The flute begins, not far away, playing behind her speech.*]

LINDA   Forgive me, dear. I can't cry. I don't know what it is, but I can't cry. I don't understand it. Why did you ever do that? Help me, Willy, I can't cry. It seems to me that you're just on another trip. I keep expecting you. Willy, dear, I can't cry. Why did you do it? I search and search and I search, and I can't understand it, Willy. I made the last payment on the house today. To-day, dear. And there'll be nobody home. [*A sob rises in her throat.*]   We're free and clear. [*Sobbing more fully, released.*] We're free. [BIFF *comes slowly toward her.*]   We're free . . . We're free . . .

[BIFF *lifts her to her feet and moves out up right with her in his arms.* LINDA *sobs quietly.* BERNARD *and* CHARLEY *come together and follow them, followed by* HAPPY. *Only the music of the flute is left on the darkening stage as over the house the hard towers of the apartment buildings rise into sharp focus, and the curtain falls.*]

Rinehart Editions